KINDERCULTURE

KINDERCULTURE

The Corporate Construction of Childhood

THIRD EDITION

Edited by

Shirley R. Steinberg

**WESTVIEW
PRESS**
A Member of the Perseus Books Group

Westview Press was founded in 1975 in Boulder, Colorado, by notable publisher and intellectual Fred Praeger. Westview Press continues to publish scholarly titles and high-quality undergraduate- and graduate-level textbooks in core social science disciplines. With books developed, written, and edited with the needs of serious nonfiction readers, professors, and students in mind, Westview Press honors its long history of publishing books that matter.

Published by Westview Press,
A Member of the Perseus Books Group

Find us on the World Wide Web at www.westviewpress.com.

Westview Press books are available at special discounts for bulk purchases in the United States by corporations, institutions, and other organizations. For more information, please contact the Special Markets Department at the Perseus Books Group, 2300 Chestnut Street, Suite 200, Philadelphia, PA 19103, or call (800) 810-4145, ext. 5000, or e-mail special.markets@perseusbooks.com.

Library of Congress Cataloging-in-Publication Data
  Kinderculture : the corporate construction of childhood / edited by Shirley R. Steinberg.
     p.   cm.
  Includes bibliographical references and index.
  ISBN 978-0-8133-4489-8 (alk. paper)
  1. Early childhood education—Social aspects—United States.
2. Popular culture—United States.   3. Critical pedagogy—United States.
4. Curriculum planning—United States.   5. Child development—United States.   6. Educational anthropology—United States.   I. Steinberg, Shirley R., 1952-
  LB1139.25.K55 2011
  372.21—dc22
                                              2010041436

10 9 8 7 6 5 4 3 2 1

2/28/12

To our girls:

Hava, Luna, and Maci

Bronwyn, Christine, Marissa, and Meghann

CONTENTS

Chapter 1

KINDERCULTURE: MEDIATING, SIMULACRALIZING, AND PATHOLOGIZING THE NEW CHILDHOOD

Shirley R. Steinberg

On June 30, 2010, *La Vanguardia* noted a poll listing the top one hundred most influential newsmakers in the world. Among the group ranked were Taylor Swift (twelve), Miley Cyrus (thirteen), and the Jonas Brothers (forty). In the six years since the publication of the second edition of *Kinderculture,* the world has changed. Along with a sweeping tsunami of politics, religious influences, struggles, and advancing web 2.0 globalization comes an incredible phenomenon, kinderculture: Children and youth have become infantilized by popular culture, schools, and adults, and while being considered "too" young for almost anything, at the same time, they are being marketed to as seasoned adults. The result is a consumer public of little girls, for example, who wear chastity rings and hip-clinging jogging pants with "Kiss My Booty" in glitter on the backside. With one voice, adults tell kids to stay clean, avoid sex and drugs, go to Disneyland, and make vows of celibacy . . . with another other voice, the corporate side markets booty clothing, faux bling, and sexualized images of twelve-year-olds. This edition of *Kinderculture* adds to the other editions by claiming that new times have created a new childhood. However, these new times are conservative and liberal, sexual and celibate, and innocent and seasoned. Evidence of this dramatic cultural change surrounds each of us, but many individuals have not yet noticed it. When Joe Kincheloe and I wrote the first edition of *Kinderculture* in 1997, many people who made their living studying or caring for children had not yet recognized this phenomenon. By the middle of the first decade of the twenty-first century, more and more people had begun to understand this historic change, however many child professionals remained oblivious to these social and cultural alterations. Now, in the second decade of the twenty-first century, the notions of childhood and youth are more complex, more pathologized, and more alien to adults who educate and parent.

In the domains of psychology, education, and to a lesser degree sociology, few observers have seriously studied the ways that the information explosion so characteristic of our contemporary era has operated to undermine traditional notions of childhood. Those who have shaped, directed, and used contemporary information technology have played an exaggerated role in the reformulation of childhood. *Kinderculture* analyzes these changes in childhood, especially the role that information technology has played in this process. Of course, information technology alone has not produced a new era of childhood. Numerous social, political, and economic factors have operated to produce such changes. Our focus here is not to cover all of these issues but to question the ways media in particular have helped construct what I am calling "the new childhood."

Childhood is a social and historical artifact—not simply a biological entity. Many argue that childhood is a natural phase of growing up, of becoming an adult. The cardinal concept here involves the format of this human phase that has been produced by social, cultural, political, and economic forces operating upon it. Indeed, what is labeled as "traditional childhood" is only about 150 years old. In the Middle Ages, for example, children participated daily in the adult world, gaining knowledge of vocational and life skills as part of such engagement. The concept of children as a particular classification of human beings demanding special treatment differing from adults had not yet developed in the Middle Ages.

SOCIALLY CONSTRUCTED CHILDHOOD

Childhood is a creation of society that is subject to change whenever major social transformations take place. The zenith of the traditional childhood lasted from about 1850 to 1950. Protected from the dangers of the adult world, many children (up until the twentieth century, boys) during this period were removed from factories and placed into schools. As the prototype of the modern family developed in the late nineteenth century, "proper" parental behavior toward children coalesced around notions of tenderness and adult accountability for children's welfare. By 1900 many believed that childhood was a birthright—a perspective that eventuated in a biological, not a cultural, definition of childhood. Emerging in this era of the protected child, modern child psychology was inadvertently constructed by the tacit assumptions of the period. The great child psychologists, from Erik Erikson to Arnold Gesell to Jean Piaget, viewed child development as shaped by biological forces.

Piaget's brilliance was constrained by his nonhistorical, socially de-contextualized scientific approach. What he observed as the genetic expression of child behavior in the early twentieth century he generalized to all cultures and historical eras—an error that holds serious consequences for those concerned with children. Considering biological stages of child development fixed and unchangeable, teachers, psychologists, parents, welfare workers, and the community at large view and judge children along a fictional taxonomy of development. Those children who don't "measure up" will be relegated to the land of low and self-fulfilling expectations. Those who "make the grade" will find that their racial and economic privilege will be confused with ability (Polakow, 1992; Postman, 1994). *Kinderculture* joins the emerging body of literature that questions the biological assumptions of "classical" child psychology (Kincheloe, 2008).

Living in a historical period of great change and social upheaval, critical observers are just beginning to notice changing social and cultural conditions in relation to this view of childhood. Categories of child development appropriated from modernist psychology may hold little relevance for raising and educating contemporary children. In the 1950s, 80 percent of all children lived in homes where their two biological parents were married to each other (Lipsky and Abrams, 1994). No one has to be told that families have changed in the past fifty years. Volumes have been written specifying the scope and causes of the social transformation. Before the 1980s ended, children who lived with their two biological parents had fallen to merely 12 percent. Children of divorced parents—a group made up of more than half of the North American population—are almost three times as likely as children raised in two-parent homes to suffer emotional and behavioral difficulties—maybe more the result of parental conflict than the actual divorce (Mason and Steadman, 1997). Despite such understandings, social institutions have been slow to recognize different, nontraditional family configurations and the special needs they encounter. Without support, the contemporary "postmodern" family, with its plethora of working and single mothers, is beset with problems emanating from the feminization of poverty and the vulnerable position of women in both the public and private spaces (Polakow, 1992).

PARADIGMS FOR STUDYING CHILDHOOD: THE POSITIVIST VIEW OF CHILDREN

It is important to place *Kinderculture* in paradigmatic context, to understand what I am promoting here in relation to other scholarship on childhood studies and childhood education. To begin with, we are directly challenging the positivist view of children promoted in mainstream articulations of psychology, sociology, education, and anthropology. Positivism is an epistemological position maintaining that all knowledge of worth is produced by the traditional scientific method. All scientific knowledge constructed in this context is thus proclaimed neutral and objective. Critics of positivism (see Kincheloe, 1993, 2001, 2003, 2004, 2008) argue that because of the narrow nature of what positivist research studies (what it *can* study given its rules of analysis), it often overlooks powerful normative and ideological assumptions built into its research design. In this naïve realistic context it often seeks empirical proof of what are normative or political assertions—for example, that adults always know better when it comes to issues involving children.

A key goal of critics of positivism involves bringing these normative and ideological assumptions to the surface so observers can gain a much more textured perspective of what research involves and indicates. Indeed, critics of positivism insist that one dimension of research involves the researcher's analysis of his or her own assumptions, ideologies, and values, and how they shape the knowledge produced. In such a spirit, the editors and authors of *Kinderculture* openly admit their antipositivist, hermeneutic epistemological orientations. Concurrently, we admit our critical democratic values, our vision of race, class, gender, and sexual equality, and the necessity of exposing the effects of power in shaping individual identity and political/educational purpose. This is not an act of politicization of research; research has always been politicized. Instead, we are attempting to understand and act ethically in light of such politicization.

In the positivist perspective, children are assumed to be subservient and dependent on adults as part of the order of the cosmos. In this context adults are seen as having a "natural" prerogative to hold power over children. Positivists turn to biology to justify such assumptions, contending that the physical immaturity of children is manifested in other domains as inferiority, an absence of development, incompleteness, and weakness. One does not have to probe deeply into these biological assumptions to discern similarities between the positivist hierarchy of adults and children and the one subordinating "emotional" women to "rational" men. In our challenge to the positivist view of children, we focus on age and generation to depict children as different from adults but not inferior to them. Children are not merely entities on their way to adulthood; they are individuals intrinsically valuable for who they presently are. When positivists view children as lesser than adults, they consistently ignore the way power operates to oppress children around the axes of race, class, gender, sexuality, ability, etc. The positivist construction of the "vulnerable" child in this context actually becomes more vulnerable as real and specific threats are overlooked because childhood is viewed as a naturally vulnerable state. The threats of different social, economic, political, and cultural "childhoods" are erased (Mason and Steadman, 1997).

The positivist view of childhood has been firmly grounded on developmental psychology's universal rules of child development. Regardless of historical or social context, these rules lay out the proper development of "normal" children. This mythos of the universal innocent and developing child transforms cultural dimensions of childhood into something produced by nature. By the second decade of the twentieth century, this universal norm for the developing child had been established on the basis of "scientific authority," based almost exclusively on North American white, middle-class norms and experiences. Schools fell into line, developing a white, middle-class, patriarchal curriculum that reflected the norms of proper development. Reformers, blessed with the imprimatur of science, based their efforts to regulate play on the principles of developmental psychology. Advocates of municipal playgrounds, the Boy Scouts and Girl Scouts worked to make sure that children made appropriate use of leisure time (Spigel, 1998).

The decontextualized aspect of the positivist view of childhood shapes numerous problems for those who don't fit into the dominant cultural bases of the proper development of normal children. In failing to understand the impact of race, class, gender, linguistics, national origin, etc., positivism fails to understand the nature of and the reasons for differences between children. Too often—especially in twenty-first-century education, with its obsession with standards, standardization, and testing—such differences are viewed as deficiencies. In this positivist regime of truth, children from lower socioeconomic, nonwhite, or immigrant backgrounds are relegated to the lower rungs of the developmental ladder. The idea that life experiences and contextual factors might affect development is not considered in the positivist paradigm because it does not account for such social and cultural dynamics (Mason and Steadman, 1997).

In addition, as positivism came to delineate the scientific dimensions of child development, male psychologists replaced mothers as child-rearing experts. In the early part of the twentieth century, the psychologist took on a socially important role. Many people believed that if scientific principles were not followed, innocent, malleable children would be led en masse into immorality and weakness. A significant feature of these scientific principles involved exposing children only to developmentally appropriate adult knowledge. The secret knowledge of adulthood, the positivist psychologists believed, should only be delivered to children at appropriate times in their development. With these ideas in mind, one can better understand the impact TV made on a nation that bought into major dimensions of the positivist mythos. TV was the fly in the ointment, the window to adult knowledge that could undermine the nation's strength and moral fiber.

The positivist view of childhood could be maintained only through constant social regulation and surveillance of the young. Since childhood is vulnerable and socially unstable, the control of knowledge becomes especially important in the maintenance of its innocent format. Indeed, in the positivist view childhood no longer exists if the young gain access to certain forms of adult knowledge. No wonder the last half of the twentieth century witnessed so many claims that after TV and other electronic media, childhood was dead. The positivist position has been deemed by many as an elitist perspective, as adults are deemed the trolls of the bridge of childhood. It is adults who decide what children should know and how they should be socialized. The idea that children should be participants in making decisions about their own lives is irrelevant here. Simply put, in the positivist paradigm children are passive entities who must be made to submit to adult decisions about their lives (Spigel, 1998).

FINDING A NEW PARADIGM FOR A NEW CHILDHOOD

With the advent of a plethora of socioeconomic changes, technological developments, globalization, and the perceived inadequacy of the old paradigm, which helps produce profoundly diverse actions and reactions, Western societies and increasingly other parts of the world have entered into a transitional phase of childhood. This transitional phase has been accompanied by a paradigm shift in the way many scholars study childhood and situate it in social, cultural, political, and economic relations. This scholarly shift takes direct exception to the positivist view of childhood and its expression of a universal, uniformly developmentalist conception of the normal child. This conception of the child as a passive receiver of adult input and socialization strategies has been replaced by a view of the child as an active agent capable of contributing to the construction of his or her own subjectivity. For those operating in the parameters of the new paradigm, the purpose of studying and working with children is not to remove the boundary between childhood and adulthood but to gain a thicker, more compelling picture of the complexity of the culture, politics, and psychology of childhood. With its penchant for decontextualization and inability to account for contemporary social, cultural, political, economic, and epistemological changes, the positivist paradigm is not adequate for this task (Cannella, 1997; Hengst, 2001; Cannella and Kincheloe, 2002; Cannella, 2002; Cook, 2004; Steinberg, 2010).

Insisting that children existed outside society and could be brought in from the cold only by adult socialization that led to development, the positivist view constructed research and childhood professional practices that routinely excluded children's voices. Advocates of the new paradigm have maintained time and again that such positivist silencing and general disempowerment is not in the best interests of children. In the name of child protection, advocates of the new paradigm have argued, children are often rendered powerless and vulnerable in their everyday lives. As they construct their view of children as active constructors of their own worlds, proponents of the new paradigm work hard to emphasize the personhood of children. The children of the new paradigm both construct their worlds and are constructed by them. Thus, in ethnographic and other forms of new paradigm childhood study, children, like adults, are positioned as co-participants in research—not as mere objects to be observed and categorized. Advocates of the new paradigm operating in the domain of social and educational policy-making for children contend that such activity must always take into account the perspectives of children to inform their understanding of particular situations (Mason and Steadman, 1997; Seaton, 2002; Cook, 2004; Steinberg, 2010).

Thus, central to the new paradigm is the effort to make sure children are intimately involved in shaping their social, psychological, and educational lives. In many ways accomplishing such a task is much easier said than done. In contemporary U.S. society in particular, to attempt it is to expose oneself to ridicule and dismissal by conservative child advocates in diverse social, political, cultural, and educational arenas. Such child-empowerment advocacy is represented by right-wing commentators as a permissive relinquishing of adult power over impudent and disrespectful children (Mason and Steadman, 1997; Ottosen, 2003). Undoubtedly, it will be a difficult struggle to reposition the child in twenty-first-century social relationships. In this context Henry Jenkins argues, as an advocate of the new paradigm, that his work seeks to provide children with tools that facilitate children's efforts to achieve their own political goals and help them construct their own culture.

In rejecting the positivist paradigm of childhood passivity and innocence, advocates of the new empowerment paradigm are not contending that there is no time when children need adult protection—that would be a silly assertion. Children, like human beings in general, too often find themselves victimized by abuse, neglect, racism, class bias, and sexism. The salient point is that instead of further infantilizing children and rendering them more passive, the new paradigm attempts to employ their perspectives in solving their problems (Mason and Steadman, 1997). In addition, such transformative researchers and child professionals work to help children develop a critical political consciousness as they protect their access to diverse knowledge and technologies. As is the nature of developing a critical consciousness in any context, we are arguing that children in social, cultural, psychological, and pedagogical contexts need help in developing the ability to analyze, critique, and improve their position in the world. This task is a central objective of *Kinderculture*.

Another dimension of the new paradigm of child study involves the explicit rejection of positivism's universalist conception of childhood and child development. When advocates of the new paradigm enter diverse class and racial/ethnic cultures, they find childhoods that look quite different from the white, middle- and upper-middle-class, English-speaking one presented by positivism. In these particularistic childhoods researchers find great complexity and diversity within these categories. For example, the social, cultural, and political structures that shape these childhoods and the children who inhabit them are engaged in profoundly different ways by particular children in specific circumstances. Thus, such structures never determine who children are no matter how much consistency in macrostructures may exist. The particular and the general, the micro and the macro, agency and structure always interact in unpredictable ways to shape the everyday life of children. A central theme of the new paradigm re-emerges—children shape and are shaped by the world around them.

The editors and authors of *Kinderculture* maintain that the delicate and complex balance between these constructive forces must be carefully studied and maintained. If we move too far in our emphasis of structure over agency, we lapse into a structural determinism that undermines the prerogative of individual social actors—thus, there is nothing a child can do to escape the ravages of poverty. If we move too far in our emphasis of agency, we often lose sight of the way dominant power operates to undermine children's role in shaping their own lives and constructing their own subjectivities. Indeed, the overemphasis of particularism and agency will often obscure just how powerless children can be. Thus, to develop our thicker and more complex view of childhood, we must constantly work to integrate the micro and the macro, to discern new cultural and political economic contexts in which to view and make sense of child behavior (Garey and Arendell, 1999; Ottosen, 2003). In this context new paradigmatic researchers must not only nurture these macro (social, political economic), meso (institutional, e.g., school, media, religious institution, welfare agency), and micro (individuals) interactions but attend to the ways such levels connect to one another. For example, what is the proximity of the individual child to particular social and institutional structures?

These are complex questions, and different students of childhood will answer them in divergent ways. Indeed, some scholars of childhood make distinctions between proponents of the new paradigm who emphasize structural issues and those who stress the agency of individual children. In this dichotomy scholars who emphasize the importance of commercial relations and corporate marketing in shaping children's culture have been relegated to the "structuralist" camp—the authors and editors of *Kinderculture* included. Structuralists are represented in this configuration as emphasizing the corporate invasion of childhood and its resulting exploitation. In this context structuralists are said to view such exploitation as similar in nature to the exploitation of women. The agential perspective often focuses not on the exploitative but the "empowering" dimensions of children's participation in commercial culture.

By arguing that children construct their own lives, such agential schol-ars maintain that children are capable of avoiding the manipulations of corporate advertising and making positive use of the consumptive act and consumer products. For example, advocates of agency maintain that children appropriate toys and media productions in creative ways that make meanings of them totally unanticipated by the producer.

Illustrating the divergence of the agential and structuralist positions, those labeled structuralists contend that while such creative appropria-tion certainly does take place, it often does nothing to subvert the ide-ological meanings inscribed on corporate constructions. When children appropriate toys and media productions, they sometimes make mean-ings that subvert ideological inscriptions while at other times their ap-propriations operate to validate the status quo. Such appropriations are complex and must be studied on a case-by-case basis. Our notion of kinderculture is dedicated to the notion that often the separation of structural and agential interpretations creates a false binarism. Indeed, in every situation we study (see Joe Kincheloe's *Sign of the Burger: Mc-Donald's and the Culture of Power* for an expansion of these ideas) we discern both structural and agential dimensions at work. A child, like an adult, can concurrently be exploited and possess agency. Whenever individuals deal with hegemonic and ideological productions, they deal with these competing dynamics (Mason and Steadman, 1997; Ottosen, 2003; Cook, 2004).

As in any sociopolitical situation with the potential for hegemonic and ideological exploitation, children (or adults) can learn to be more sensitive to the ways exploitation takes place while developing strategies for avoiding it. And, as in any pedagogical situation, children (and adults) can develop these strategies on their own or, in a Vygotskian sense, in cooperation with teachers who provide a new zone of proximal development that allows for a deeper understanding of the way power operates. This, of course, is the basis of *Kinderculture's* critical media lit-eracy for children (Steinberg, 2007).

David Buckingham (2003) dismisses the value of structuralist con-cerns with exploitation and argues that pedagogies of empowerment such as the one advocated here have "increasingly been seen to amount to lit-tle more than rhetoric." By denying the possibility of a media literacy of power, Buckingham lapses into a pedagogy of nihilism that provides no raison d'être for scholarly activity in the area of children's culture. Power and exploitation are erased in Buckingham's articulation, as any effort to alert children to the ways the social, cultural, political, and economic domains operate to harm both them and other individuals is represented as a misguided form of "salvationism." Buckingham then equates this so-called salvationism with right-wing attempts to protect childhood innocence via forms of censorship and moralistic regulation. Most discussions between the agential and structuralist positions in the new paradigm of child studies are not—nor should be—this contentious. It is important to specify *Kinderculture*'s location in this conceptual matrix.

Kinderculture represents the critical new paradigm in childhood studies and childhood education. The use of "critical" in this context signals the "critical" in critical theory (Kincheloe, 2004, 2008) and its concern with power structures and their influence in everyday life. In the case of contemporary children, the sociopolitical and economic structures shaped by corporate power buoyed by the logic of capital as well as patriarchal structures, with their oppressive positioning of women and children, are central concerns of the critical paradigm (Garey and Arendell, 1999; Scott, 2002). Using the production of pleasure as its ultimate weapon, the corporate children's consumer culture we are labeling "kinderculture" commodifies cultural objects and turns them into things to purchase rather than objects to contemplate. Kinderculture, thus, is subversive but in a way that challenges authority in an effort to maintain rather than transform the status quo. It appeals to the agential child and agential child advocates as it offers children identities that Jane Kenway and Elizabeth Bullen (2001) label as autonomous, rational, and hedonistic. Thus, kinderculture is produced by ingenious marketers who possess profound insights into the lives, desires, and cultural context of contemporary children. Such marketers know how to cultivate intense affect among children and use such emotion to elicit particular consumptive and, in turn, ideological reactions.

A key dimension of this consumptive-ideological dimension of *Kinderculture* involves the marketers' understanding that children, particularly middle-class children, are especially interested in TV, movies,

Internet, toys, and even foods (see Kincheloe's chapter on McDonald's and Kincheloe, 2002) that transgress parental norms of "good taste," social status, and educational development. Indeed, this ideology of opposition is central in many cases to what separates contemporary children from their parents and other adults. Such oppositionality operates to subvert the bourgeois educational project of modernity—rational child development based on the achievement of universal stages of reason reflecting adult behavior and ways of being. As it commodifies and lures children into this oppositional conspiracy, it meshes consumption, education, information, knowledge, cultural capital, emotional bonding, entertainment, and advertising (Kenway and Bullen, 2001; Hengst, 2001; Steinberg, 2007). Advocates of the critical new paradigm of childhood studies argue that kinderculture can no longer be ignored in the effort to understand the social, psychological, and educational dimensions of children. In the late twentieth and early twenty-first centuries, corporate children's culture has replaced schooling as the producer of the central curriculum of childhood.

IS THERE A CRISIS OF CHILDHOOD?

Changing economic realities coupled with children's access to information about the adult world have drastically changed childhood. The traditional childhood genie is out of the bottle and is unable to return. Recent writing about childhood in both the popular and scholarly presses speaks of "childhood lost," "children growing up too fast," and "child terror in the isolation of the fragmented home and community." Images of mothers drowning children, baby-sitters torturing infants, kids pushing kids out of fourteen-story windows, and trick-or-treat razor blades in apples saturate the contemporary conversation about children. Popular culture provides haunting images of this crisis of childhood that terrify and engage our worst fears. The film *Halloween*, for example, is at one level a story of the postmodern childhood—fear in isolation. The isolation referenced here involves separation from both absent parents and a nonexistent community. No one is there to help; even on the once-festive Halloween night, children are not present.

Even in "safe" suburbia, the community has fragmented to the point that the safety of children trick-or-treating cannot be guaranteed (Ferguson, 1994; Paul, 1994). The crisis of contemporary childhood can be signified in many ways, all of which involve at some level the horror of danger faced in solitude.

This crisis of childhood is part imagination, part reality. While children, like all people, are vulnerable to social ills and the manipulations of unscrupulous adults and power wielders, there is a degree of moral panic and general hyperbole in the view that children are facing threats from predators unlike anything they have experienced in the historical past. While certainly not dismissing everyday threats to childhood in the twenty-first century, we should be careful not to let hysterics from diverse ideological perspectives paint a fear-driven portrait of the social landscape. A balanced view would demand that we position the crisis of childhood within the twenty-first-century social, cultural, and economic context. There is no doubt that childhood in Western societies is affected by the decline of industrialized economic arrangements.

In such industrialized societies labor was the most important social force for social integration. In a postindustrial condition people make life meanings outside the boundaries of their work lives. The labor process in this new context plays less and less of a role in shaping identity and constructing life experiences. As industrial jobs that lasted a lifetime with pensions and social benefits decline, more women have entered the workforce. Buoyed by the women's movement, more and more mothers have sought work outside the home, subsequently placing more pressure on fathers to participate in child-rearing activities. In such contexts children learn to cope with busy and often preoccupied parents. Consequently, they become more self-reliant than middle- and upper-middle-class children from previous generations earlier in the twentieth century.

The changing role of women profoundly changes the role of children in contemporary Western societies. Even though more and more women work outside the home, this does not lead to an equal sharing of domestic work—women still do more than men (du Bois-Reymond, Suenker, and Kruger, 2001). Increasing numbers of single poor women combine both paid labor and child care without the help of a spouse or partner and with little assistance from the state. Without economic or social support women and children in these categories have experienced harsher and harsher conditions and less and less hope for upward mobility. For middle- and upper-middle-class children, these social, economic, and cultural trends have sometimes provided them more independence and influence in the family. In lower socioeconomic circumstances, such trends exacerbate the effects of poverty and sometimes lead to more neglect and alienation.

In many middle- and lower-class homes, these larger socioeconomic trends operate to make children "more useful" than they had been throughout much of the twentieth century. As women become more and more embedded in the workplace, traditional role expectations continue to erode. In order to adjust to these modified familial relationships, children and youth from the ages of six to nineteen have taken on more responsibilities for caring not only for themselves but for their parents as well. Studies (Hengst, 2001) illustrate that children increasingly are the family members who buy the food. Indeed, the home appliance industry—understanding this trend—is directing more and more of its advertising budget toward children and youth magazines. Industry demographics tell them that a key and growing segment of those who buy food, microwaves, and other kitchen appliances are from this six-to-nineteen age bracket (du Bois-Reymond, Suenker, and Kruger, 2001). This represents a profound change in the way children are positioned in the social order.

This change of the social positioning of children holds dramatic implications for the education of children. As age boundaries blur and age becomes less important in shaping human abilities and role expectations, the crisis of childhood becomes the crisis of education. Children emerging in the new social conditions no longer reflect the expectations for childhood embedded in the structures and organization of schools. "New children" who experience more adultlike roles in other phases of their lives may not react positively to being treated like "children" in the classroom. Teachers who infantilize their elementary students may be shocked by the resentment independent children direct back toward them. Indeed, such dynamics already occur as teachers voice complaints about "children who talk like adults and have little or no respect for their demands." What teachers sometimes perceive as impudence and a lack of respect may be as much a reflection of independent, self-sufficient children reacting to forms of regulation that they experience in no other aspect of their lives. We see this redirection of anger to teachers and adults in media representations of children and youth. A savvy kid is often in complete control of not only her or his own destiny but that of a family or possibly the school or entire community. The knowing kindercultured youth of the new millennium walks a balance beam of complexity as the naïve being promoted by caregivers and teachers and as the in-control leader of the covert ops of being a kid in today's society.

In this changing social context many scholars (Casas, 1998; Hengst, 2001) are making the argument that children are far more cognitively capable than traditionally maintained by developmental psychology. The world of electronic media, along with these changing notions of the social role of the child, has expanded what Lev Vygotsky referred to as the ZPD (zone of proximal development)—the context that facilitates the learning process—of contemporary children. In the ZPD individuals learn to take part in social and cultural activities that catalyze their intellectual development. In the media-created electronic ZPD, with its videos, TV, computers, video games, Internet, popular music, and virtual realities, children learn to use the tools of culture, e.g., language, mathematics, reasoning, etc. (Fu, 2003). The skills learned may or may not be abilities valued by the school. They are valuable abilities nonetheless.

When sociologists, psychologists, and cultural scholars examine what children are able to construct employing the symbols and tools of mediated culture, they realize how sophisticated and intellectually advanced children's abilities can become in this new ZPD. This electronic kinderculture has quickly become a new culture of childhood learning. Indeed, the space within which many contemporary children play is the same domain in which their parents work. Children access these national and international information networks using the same tools as their parents. In this new domain of learning many children free themselves from the educational project of modern Western societies. Many children in Western societies are no longer learning along a preplanned program of selected exposure to the adult world by adults. Instead, they are accessing previously considered "adult" information via electronic media. As this takes place, such children are freed from particular parental norms and parental regulations common to bourgeois culture. A cultural aesthetic develops that eschews cultural products provided for the purposes of education and refinement. Kinderculture thus emerges and is produced around the new childhood desire for independence and resistance to things adult. Traditional forms of school learning become less and less important and less applicable to the needs of these new children (Hengst, 2001). Thus, childhood is perceived in crisis because it resembles nothing most people have ever seen before.

CORPORATE EDUCATORS

The corporate production of popular kinderculture and its impact on children is a central concern of this book. Such an effort falls under the umbrella term "cultural pedagogy," which refers to the idea that education takes place in a variety of social sites including but not limited to schooling. Pedagogical sites are those places where power is organized and deployed including libraries, TV, movies, newspapers, magazines, toys, advertisements, video games, books, sports, etc. Our work as education scholars, we believe, demands that we examine both school and cultural pedagogy if we are to make sense of the educational process (Giroux, 1994). Operating on the assumption that profound learning changes one's identity, we see the pedagogical process as one that engages our desire (our yearning for something beyond ourselves shaped by the social context in which we operate, our affective investment in that which surrounds us), captures our imagination, and constructs our consciousness. The emergence of cultural studies (Grossberg, 1995) has facilitated our effort to examine the cultural practices through which individuals come to understand themselves and the world that surrounds them (Steinberg, 2007). Supported by the insights of cultural studies, we are better equipped to examine the effects of cultural pedagogy, with its identity formation and its production and legitimation of knowledge, i.e., the cultural curriculum (Kasturi, 2002).

The organizations that create this cultural curriculum are not educational agencies but rather commercial concerns that operate not for the social good but for individual gain. Cultural pedagogy is structured by commercial dynamics, forces that impose themselves into all aspects of our own and our children's private lives (Giroux, 1994). Patterns of consumption shaped by corporate advertising empower commercial institutions as the teachers of the contemporary era. Corporate cultural pedagogy has "done its homework"—it has produced educational forms that are wildly successful when judged on the basis of their capitalist intent. Replacing traditional classroom lectures and seatwork with magic kingdoms, animated fantasies, interactive videos, virtual realities, kickboxing TV heroes, dolls (complete with their own recorded "history"), and an entire array of entertainment forms produced ostensibly for adults but eagerly consumed by children, corporate America has helped revolutionize childhood.

Such a revolution has not taken place in some crass manner with Stalinesque corporate wizards checking off a list of institutions they have captured. Instead, the revolution (contrary to the '60s idiom) has been televised, brought to you and your children in HD and digital color. Using fantasy and desire, corporate functionaries have created a perspective on the world that melds with business ideologies and free-market values. The worldviews produced by corporate advertisers to some degree always let children know that the most exciting things life can provide are produced by their friends in corporate America. The economics lesson is powerful when it is repeated hundreds of thousands of times.

While researching schools, education, and corporate childhood, we have become seasoned in the corporate interventions by brands like Pizza Hut (reading program), McDonald's (A students), and Nike (most school sports teams). It is also a time when publishing companies create curriculum for students, with little or no educational or academic input. Certainly, No Child Left Behind was a reflection of the agenda created by McGraw-Hill in the 1990s. Pearson Publishing has been retained to redesign the New York State primary curriculum, without one academic or schoolteacher on the design team. Up until this point, Disney has always had a hegemonic hold on children's culture through the participation of both families and teachers. It has never been unusual to walk into a primary school, really anywhere in the world, and spy bulletin boards, reading charts, and classroom assignment ledgers thematically displayed by Mickey, Donald, or a princess. In schools that claim a diverse and multicultural view, one will see representations of Mulan, Pocahontas, and Aladdin proclaiming that "It's a small world after all." Disney has recently taken the grandiose step of creating "Disney English." Disney claims an expertise in English, as it has been writing children's books for more than three-quarters of a century. These "qualifications" opened a market in Asia for English-language teaching. Disney English is a multimillion-dollar enterprise that has blurred the boundaries of education and corporate book-making.

One of the most profound events of the last century in world history in general and certainly in the history of childhood involves the successful commodification of childhood. Not only did corporate marketers open a new market but they helped generate a body of meanings, cultural practices, and ideological understandings that continues to shape our world and children around the planet (Cook, 2004). By gaining access to children, advertisers found out early in the twentieth century not only that they could induce children to buy more but that they could get children to nag their parents to consume more (Spigel, 1998). Though many argue to the contrary, it seems increasingly obvious that a large percentage of children and young people in the twenty-first century are enthusiastic participants in consumer society. In recent polls they express the belief that having more money would most improve their lives. Concurrently, they express great faith in the American economic system. Increasing numbers of children and young people own more than one credit card, and many own stocks. Corporate power wielders have worked hard to win such perspectives and orientations among the young. Indeed, consumer capitalism has succeeded in ways unimagined by previous advocates, as more and more children and young people come to hold the values and ideological dispositions that serve the best interests of corporate leaders (Spigel, 1998; Allen, 2003).

In an interesting and insidious way, the marketers and children enter into an unspoken alliance that helps children escape both the control and the educational-developmental agenda of middle- and upper-middle-class parents. Video games, Internet, texting, TV, MP3 players, and DVDs help create a personal, secluded domain for children free from direct parental regulation. Of course, many parents find such independence frightening, and many understandably worry about children becoming targets for advertising and marketing. While many concerned individuals have expressed anxiety over what they thought was corporate advertising's violation of the social contract protecting the sanctity of childhood, others such as David Buckingham have argued that such fears are overblown. Children, Buckingham maintains, possess the ability to discern advertising strategies early in their lives and can thus protect themselves from corporate exploitation. Moreover, Buckingham posits, there is no evidence that indicates that advertising makes children more materialistic than they would have been otherwise. In an empirical research context Buckingham's assertion is a safe one. Since no one knows how children would have been otherwise, it is empirically impossible to prove such an assertion either true or false. We could not disagree more.

The argument made in this volume maintains that it is our parental, civic, and professional responsibility to study the corporate curriculum and its social and political effects. Indeed, we maintain that as parents, citizens, and teachers we must hold corporations accountable for the pedagogical features of their activities, for the kinderculture they produce. We must intervene in the cozy relationship between popular culture and pedagogy that shapes our identities. In the interest of both our children and the larger society, we must exercise our personal and collective power to transform the variety of ways corporate power (gained via its access to media) oppresses and dominates us. We must cultivate an awareness of the ways cultural pedagogy operates so that we can scold when appropriate and rewrite popular texts when the opportunity presents itself. Kinderculture is primarily a pedagogy of pleasure, and as such it cannot be countered merely by ostracizing ourselves and our children from it. Strategies of resistance must be formulated that understand the relationship between pedagogy, knowledge production, identity formation, and desire. This book attempts to open a public conversation about the effect of kinderculture as the central curriculum of contemporary childhood.

THE CULTURAL STUDIES OF KINDERCULTURE

Questions concerning kinderculture and its relationship to cultural pedagogy can be clarified and discussed within the academic field of cultural studies. This book resides at the intersection of educational/ childhood studies and cultural studies. Attempts to define cultural studies are delicate operations in that the field has consciously operated in a manner that avoids traditional academic disciplinary definitions. Nevertheless, cultural studies has something to do with the effort to produce an interdisciplinary (or counterdisciplinary) way of studying, interpreting, and often evaluating cultural practices in historical, social, and theoretical contexts. Refusing to equate "culture" with high culture, cultural studies attempts to examine the diversity of a society's artistic, institutional, and communicative expressions and practices. Because it examines cultural expressions ignored by the traditional social sciences, cultural studies is often equated with the study of popular culture. Such an equation is misleading; while popular culture is addressed by cultural studies, it is not the exclusive concern. Indeed, the interests of cultural studies are much broader, including the "rules" of academic study itself—i.e., the discursive practices (tacit regulations that define what can and cannot be said, who speaks and who must listen, and whose constructions of reality are valid and whose are unlearned and unimportant) that guide scholarly endeavor.

Thus, cultural studies holds exciting possibilities for new ways of studying education—specifically childhood education, with its attention to the discursive dynamics of the field. How do children embody kinderculture? How do the power dynamics embedded in kinderculture produce pleasure and pain in the daily lives of children? How do critically grounded parents, teachers, child psychologists, and childhood professionals in general gain a view of children that accounts for the effects of popular culture in their self-images and worldviews? Such questions open new domains of analysis in childhood studies, as they seek out previously marginalized voices and the vantage points they bring to both the scholarly and practitioner-based conversation (Grossberg, 1995; Nelson, Treichler, and Grossberg, 1992). While we are enthused by the benefits of cultural studies of childhood, we are simultaneously critical of expressions of elitism within the discourse of cultural studies itself—a recognition made more disturbing by cultural studies' claim to the moral high ground of a politics of inclusivity. Unfortunately, the study of children has traditionally been regarded as a low-status exercise in the culture of academia. So far, at least, the field of cultural studies has reproduced this power/status dynamic in its neglect of childhood study. Indeed, few students of cultural studies have targeted children as the subjects of their scholarship. *Kinderculture* attempts to address this absence and promote new literature in the area.

TO STUDY POPULAR CULTURE

The study of traditional forms of kinderculture—fairy tales, for example— has granted scholars insights into hard-to-reach domains of child consciousness. Moreover, the more disturbing and violent the fairy tale, some would argue, the more insight into the "primitive" feelings that arise and shape us in early childhood and, in turn, in adulthood. The connection between kinderculture and childhood desires and feelings blows the rational cultural fuse, thus connecting adults to the *Lebenswelt* (life world) of children and granting them better access to childhood perceptions (Paul, 1994). Not only does the study of children's popular culture grant insights into childhood consciousness; it also provides new pictures of culture in general. Kinderculture, in this context, inadvertently reveals at a very basic level what is disturbing us in our everyday lives, what irritants reside at the level of our individual and collective subconsciousness.

THE POWER AND PLEASURE OF KINDERCULTURE

Our objective in this book is to promote understandings of kinderculture that lead to smart and democratic pedagogies for childhood at the cultural, familial, and school levels. Cultural studies connected to a democratic pedagogy for children involves investigations of how children's consciousness is produced around issues of cultural expectations for children, social justice, and egalitarian power relations. Thus, our analyses focus on exposing the footprints of power left by the corporate producers of kinderculture and their effects on the psyches of our children. Appreciating the ambiguity and complexity of power, our democratic pedagogy for children is committed to challenging ideologically manipulative and racist, sexist, and class-biased entertainment for children. It is equally opposed to other manifestations of kinderculture that promote violence and social and psychological pathologies. Children's entertainment, like other social spheres, is a contested public space where different social, economic, and political interests compete for control. Unfortunately, North Americans are uncomfortable with overt discussions of power. Such unease allows power wielders to hide in the recesses of the cultural and political landscape all the while shaping cultural expression and public policy in their own interests—interests that may conflict with those of less powerful social groups such as children.

We are not good students of power. All too often references to power are vague to the point of meaninglessness in the worst literature produced by critical scholars. For the purpose of clarification, when we refer to power wielders we are not merely referencing a social class or a category of human beings. Picking up on John Fiske's (1993) use of the term "power bloc," we are referring to particular social formations designated by race, class, gender, and ethnicity that hold special access to various resources (e.g., money, information, cultural capital, media, etc.) that can be used for economic or political gain. Power, as we use the term, involves a panoply of operations that work to maintain the status quo and keep it running with as little friction (social conflict) as possible. Therefore, it is beneficial to those individuals and groups that profit most from existing power relations to protect them from pests like us. When studying this power bloc, we employ Fiske's notion that it can be better understood by "what it does than what it is" (p. 11). Importantly, our use of the concept of the power bloc in the production of kinderculture is not meant to imply some conspiracy of diabolical corporate and political kingpins churning out material to harm our children. Rather, our notion of the power bloc revolves around alliances of interests that may never involve individual relationships between representatives of the interests or organizations in question. Power bloc alliances, we believe, are often temporary, coming together around particular issues but falling apart when the issue is no longer pertinent.

Those who perceive power to be a complex issue will encounter little disagreement from us. Power and power bloc alliances are nothing if not complex and ambiguous. But because of the power bloc's contradictions and ephemerality, it is never able to dominate in some incontestable manner. Along the lines of its contradictions may exist points of contestation that open possibilities of democratic change. Larry Grossberg (1995) contends that since power never gets all it wants, there are always opportunities to challenge its authority. In this context we begin our study of the corporate production of kinderculture, analyzing the ways power represses the production of democratic artifacts and produces pleasure for children. If power was always expressed by "just saying no" to children's desires, it would gain little authority in their eyes. The power of Disney, Microsoft, Apple, Dreamworks, Pixar, and McDonald's is never greater than when it produces pleasure among consumers. Recent cultural studies of consumption link it to the identity formation of the consumer (Warde, 1994; Kincheloe, 2002), meaning that to some degree we are what we consume. Status in one's subculture, individual creations of style, knowledge of cultural texts, role in the community of consumers, emulation of fictional characters, internalization of values promoted by popular cultural expressions—all contribute to our personal identities. Popular culture provides children with intense emotional experiences often unmatched in any other phase of their lives. It is not surprising that such energy and intensity exert powerful influences on self-definition, on the ways children choose to organize their lives.

Obviously, power mixed with desire produces an explosive cocktail; the colonization of desire, however, is not the end of the story. Power enfolds into consciousness and unconsciousness in a way that evokes desire, no doubt, but also guilt and anxiety. The intensity of the guilt and anxiety a child may experience as a result of her brush with power is inseparable from the cultural context in which she lives. Desire in many cases may take a back seat to the repression of desire in the construction of child consciousness/unconsciousness and the production of identity (Donald, 1993). The cocktail's effects may be longer-lasting than first assumed, as expression of the repression may reveal itself in bizarre and unpredictable ways. To make this observation about the relationship among power, desire, and the way that the repression of desire expresses itself at the psychological level is not to deny human agency (self-direction). While the power bloc has successfully commodified kinderculture, both adults and children can successfully deflect its repressive elements. The role of the critical childhood professional involves helping children develop what Fiske (1993) calls the affective moments of power evasion. Using their abilities to re-read Disney films along fault lines of gender or to re-encode Barbie and Ken in a satirical mode, children take their first steps toward self-assertion and power resistance. Such affective moments of power evasion certainly do not constitute the ultimate expression of resistance, but they do provide a space around which more significant forms of critical consciousness and civic action can be developed (Steinberg, 2007).

NEEDED: MEDIA AND POPULAR CULTURAL LITERACY

The information explosion—the media saturation of contemporary Western societies, with its access to private realms of human consciousness—has created a social vertigo. This social condition, labeled by Baudrillard as hyperreality, exaggerates the importance of power wielders in all phases of human experience. Hyperreality's flood of signifiers in everything from megabytes to TV advertising diminishes our ability to either find meaning or engender passion for commitment. With so much power-generated information bombarding our senses, adults and children lose the faith that we can make sense of anything (for an expansion of these themes see Kincheloe, 1995). Thus, the existence of hyperreality forces us to rethink our conversation about literacy. Children, who have been educated by popular culture, approach literacy from a very different angle. Media literacy becomes not some rarefied add-on to a traditional curriculum but a basic skill necessary to negotiating one's identity, values, and well-being in power-soaked hyperreality. In many schools such ideas have never been considered, not to mention seriously discussed. Media literacy, like power, is not viewed in mainstream circles as a topic for children (or even adults). The same educators who reject the study of media literacy or kinderculture are the ones who have to cope with its effects.

As Donaldo Macedo and Shirley R. Steinberg contend in *Media Literacy: A Reader* (2007), a critical understanding of media culture requires students not simply to develop the ability to interpret media meanings but to understand the ways they consume and affectively invest in media. Such an attempt encourages both critical thinking and self-analysis, as students begin to realize that everyday decisions are not necessarily made freely and rationally. Rather, they are encoded and inscribed by emotional and bodily commitments relating to the production of desire and mood, all of which leads, in Noam Chomsky's famous phrase, to the "manufacture of consent." These are complex pedagogical and ideological issues, and they demand rigorous skills of questioning, analyzing, interpreting, and meaning making. Contrary to the decontextualized pronouncements of developmental psychology, relatively young children are capable of engaging in these cognitive activities (Nations, 2001). Of course, in the contemporary right-wing, test-driven educational context, such abilities are not emphasized, as memorization for standards tests becomes more and more the order of the school day.

The political dimension of our critical pedagogy of childhood requires developing and teaching this media literacy. Such a literacy respects children's intellectual ability to deal with the complexities of power, oppression, and exploitation, as it refuses to position them as innocent, passive, and helpless victims. In an era when children can instantaneously access diverse types of information, they need the ability to traverse this knowledge terrain in savvy and well-informed ways. A critical pedagogy of childhood finds this approach much more helpful than pietistic right-wing efforts to censor potentially offensive data from innocent childhood eyes. In their effort to perpetuate the discourse of childhood innocence, right-wing child advocates maintain a positivist developmentalist view that media literacy is irrelevant because children do not have the intellectual and emotional maturity to understand TV advertising or subtle marketing appeals (Cassell and Jenkins, 2002). As much as the advocates of childhood innocence might wish for it, children in the twenty-first century are not going to return to the mythical secret garden of innocence. For better and worse children now live in a wider, information-saturated adult world. The authors of *Kinderculture* believe that the best thing we can do in this circumstance is to prepare children to cope with it, make sense of it, and participate in it in ways that benefit everyone (Vieira, 2001).

In this context our critical politics of kinderculture re-emerges. Childhood has always been shaped by a potpourri of adult desires and childhood fantasies. The difference between childhood in hyperreality and in other places and times is that in the electronic, mediated world of the present era these desires and fantasies have been commodified and play themselves out in the corporate-produced children's culture central to this book. A critical politics of childhood recognizes these unique and complex dimensions of kinderculture and in this understanding develops new and exciting ways for families, educators, and the society at large to care for and nurture children. Understanding that the positivist developmentalist paradigm always underestimated the abilities of children, advocates of a critical politics of childhood help children develop the strategies and skills necessary for social reform and the pursuit of justice (Cannella and Viruru, 2002). In this context educators, psychologists, sociologists, parents, and other citizens can reflect on children's activities represented by many as "misbehavior." Can we empathize with children who are positioned as self-directed agents in one social domain and incompetent adults in need of constant surveillance and punitive regulation in another? Can we understand the difficulty of dealing with such contradictions in one's everyday pursuits? A critical politics of childhood urges us to take such questions seriously. Indeed, the authors and editors of *Kinderculture* maintain that a politics of childhood involves far more than just protecting children. As we reconsider the notion of competence, advocates of a critical politics of childhood work to ensure that children can use their abilities in a way that improves their quality of life (Casas, 1998).

TELEVISION AD COMPLEXITY

Commercial TV in America has always been structured by conflicting demands of commerce and democracy. Any study of kinderculture will find these competing dynamics at work at various levels of the texts examined. When analysts and consumers begin to understand the cultural authority mustered by children's TV and other entertainment forms, the bifurcated imperatives for the medium begin to take on unprecedented significance. The democratic moments of TV are profound but far too rare. The exposure of the insanity of Joseph McCarthy, the evils of racial segregation, the perils of pollution, the most obvious abuses of patriarchy, the inhumane excesses of Vietnam, and the criminality of Watergate undoubtedly represented the zenith of TV's democratic impulse. The unfortunate consequence of such successes has been corporate constraint and governmental regulation of attempts to replicate such achievements. When such media management is combined with TV's tendency to fragment and decontextualize issues, events are often stripped of their meaning. Children (and adults) who depend heavily on TV for their entertainment and thus their worldviews are cognitively impaired by this dynamic (Kellner, 1990; Hammer and Kellner, 2009). Make no mistake, TV's curriculum for children is not crafted by media moguls' fidelity to the principles of democracy. Commercial concerns dictate media kinderculture—profit margins are too important to dicker around with concerns for the well-being of kids.

Society's most important teachers don't ply their trade in schools, just as the nation's "official" children's policy is not constructed by elected officials in Washington, D.C. America's corporate producers of kinderculture are the most influential pedagogues and children's policy makers. In this book, Henry Giroux writes of the blurring boundaries between entertainment, education, and commerce, as Disney Imagineers inject their teachings into the dream world of children. There is nothing transparent about children's TV or movies—clear messages are being delivered to our children with the intent of eliciting particular beliefs and actions that are in the best interests of those who produce them. Bifurcated as TV's imperatives may be, democracy takes a backseat to the logic of capital. Compared with the nonstop promotion of the multiple "products" of kinderculture, child advocates have limited access to the airwaves. Those corporations that advertise children's consumer paraphernalia promote a "consumption theology" that, in effect, promises redemption and happiness via the consumptive act (ritual). Such advertising and pleasure production grant a direct line to the imaginative landscape of our children—a mindscape that children use to define their view of society and self.

Thus, child professionals and parents must understand that humans are the historical products of the mechanisms of power—an appreciation often missed in the everyday world. This paradox of human consciousness confounds observers with its Zen master double-talk—folks make culture, yet culture makes folks. Meaning emerges from this maze at the level of the social, and individual consciousness is shaped by this interaction and the ways of seeing (ideologies) it produces. As a social and ideological phenomenon, consciousness is constructed not simply by its contact with culture but by an interaction with a view of culture— a view "edited" by ideological refraction. Refraction involves the manner in which the direction of light is changed when it passes through one medium to another—for example, from a crystal to a wall.

The refracted light we see on the wall is different from the light that originally encountered the crystal—one aspect of the light's "reality" has been displaced. Ideology is like the crystal in that it refracts perceptions of the lived world. This is not to say that the light (world perceptions), prior to its encounter with the crystal (ideology), is God-like or pristine. Our view of ideology understands that no transcendental, totalizing view of the light (reality) exists—we always perceive it from some position in the web of reality. Leaving our metaphor behind, the salient point here is that kinderculture serves as a mechanism of ideological refraction—a social force that produces particular meanings that induce children (and adults) to interpret events within a specific range of possibilities (Thiele, 1986; Donald, 1993; Mumby, 1989).

Kinderculture, like all social texts, speaks with an authorial voice that is either up-front or covert about its ideological inscription (Lincoln, 1995). Not surprisingly, corporate-produced kinderculture chooses *The Price Is Right*'s covert ideological Door Number Three. In this way kinderculture colonizes consciousness in a manner that represses conflict and differences. Thus, the critical childhood professional understands ideology, its refraction, and its effect on consciousness construction as the conceptual basis for his or her effort to expose kinderculture as a politically pristine, uncontested sphere of social activity. Just as classroom teaching and the school curriculum are never simply neutral, disinterested messengers or data transmitters, corporate kinderculture harbors an agenda. Our recognition of, say, McDonald's family values–promoting ad campaigns of the early Reagan years and the company's financial ties to the right wing of the Republican Party is important to our understanding of the way politics works and the context within which kinderculture is conceived and displayed.

Such a recognition does not necessarily mean that we deprive our five-year-olds of their Happy Meals or their fascination with the Hamburglar. Our understanding of the patriarchal depiction of Kevin's (Macaulay Culkin) mother as failed caretaker of children in the *Home Alone* movies while excusing his equally culpable father of blame for his part in the abandonment grants insight into the way misogyny is transmitted across generations. It doesn't mean that we have to, as gender police, bar our eight-year-olds from renting the movies. Maybe an explanation of what is happening along gender lines and a mutual celebration of Kevin's self-sufficiency would turn *Home Alone* into a positive experience of (as our daughter puts it) "family bondation."

Childhood professionals have not traditionally been students of power—but given the power of kinderculture, they now have to be. As students of the power dynamics of children's popular culture, parents and professionals begin to understand the actions of children from a new perspective. Given their power to sink their kinderculture deep into the private lives of children, the corporate producers of kinderculture constantly destabilize the identity of children. At the same time, however, new products—toys, movies, TV, video games, fashion, texts—attempt to restabilize new identities through the consumptive act. The study of power vis-à-vis children and contemporary kinderculture provides a conceptual tool for criticizing social, economic, and political practices and explaining the ways young people's life choices are restricted. Artifacts of culture, whether they are toys or automobiles, have always helped us create our sense of self and our social affiliations.

Our task as kinderculturalists is to expose these invisible yet influential forces, the micropractices that shape our children's lives. Our task is complicated by the fact that those practices that are the most visible and unquestionable in commonsense observations of children at play are those most fully saturated by the humidity of power. The ability to appreciate these realities provides us the wisdom to distinguish between just and unjust kindertexts, manipulative and liberatory corporate activities. Thus empowered, we can begin to piece together the complex and often ambiguous ways corporate actions modify children's behavior, the ways advertising and its promotion of childhood hedonism produce an ethic of pleasure and a redefinition of authority. Such issues reside at the core of who we are as a people and who we want to become (Kellner, 1992; Wartenberg, 1992; Seiter, 1993; Ball, 1992; Grossberg, 1995; Abercrombie, 1994; Steinberg and Kincheloe, 2004; Steinberg, 2007).

KINDERCULTURE AND CORPORATE POWER

The study of power and kinderculture reveals insights into North American politics that may at first glance seem only incidental to parents and child professionals—especially those of the positivist paradigm. When one begins to explore child activist avenues, he or she is immediately confronted with the concentration of power into fewer and increasingly corporate hands. Such a reality cannot be ignored by child advocates and concerned parents, since the corporate-dominated power bloc is unafraid to retaliate against those who would question the impact of its products. In light of the failure of oppositional institutions to challenge corporate hegemony, corporations to a large extent have free rein to produce almost any kinderculture that is profitable. Of the 7,000 interest organizations that are active in Washington, D.C., most are business- or corporate-sponsored. Public-interest organizations are typically outnumbered ten to one in formal congressional proceedings on regulatory issues. The antidemocratic implications of the system, with its corporate curriculum designed to adjust public opinion to support business agendas, are chilling (Greider, 1992).

This expansion of corporate power has occurred over the past couple of decades. When pollsters in the 1970s uncovered a decline in public confidence in businesses and corporations, corporate leaders jumped into action. To counter public perceptions of themselves as greedy and uninterested in the public good, corporations dropped hundreds of millions of dollars into public-relations advertising designed to promote positive corporate images and ideological dispositions. Designed to engineer consent, these legitimation ads focused on treasured common experiences in our lives, family, childhood, and parental events in particular. Among many others, the Ethan Allen furniture company latched on to the family, childhood, and parental triad, attaching its corporate identity to a right-wing notion of traditional family values. The Ethan Allen legitimation ads talked about the rise of juvenile delinquency and its threat to those of "us" who care about "our" children. Our treasured ways of raising our children, the ads asserted, are under threat by an unidentified group who just don't care about traditional family values and the sanctity of old-fashioned ideals.

Joe Kincheloe's chapter on McDonald's family values–oriented legitimation ads in this volume documents one of the highest expressions of the corporate colonization of family values and parental and child consciousness. In one ad a young boy and a younger girl stroll along a tree-lined trail in a park. The camera watches them walk away from the TV viewer. The small girl runs to catch up with her big brother. Both are wearing oversize baseball uniforms with "Tigers" spelled across their backs. With baseball caps worn backward, they are obviously "adorable" American children. The little sister loves her older brother, who waits for her when she gets too far behind and allows her to grab his baseball shirttail for her support on the way home. The music-over sings, "You, you're the one / You're moms and dads and brothers, sisters and sons / We're stronger for each other." The attempt here, of course, is to connect the company's image with the best interests of children and to legitimate McDonald's as a company with a heart, an organization that would never do anything counter to the best interests of the family. Viewers don't have to remember the specifics of the ad for it to work as McDonald's intended—the emotional valence it imprints, the positive connection between treasured childhood memories and the golden arches, is all that matters.

Corporations and the free-enterprise system that protects their right to operate in the best way they see fit make possible the commodification of these warm, familial moments of our lives. Maybe "we" should protect these moments from those meddlers who want to regulate them and interfere with all the good that they do. Of course, the truth is obviously irrelevant in these legitimation ads. Indeed, General Motors was audacious enough in the early 1980s to run a multimillion-dollar ad campaign demonstrating the extraordinary amount of input line workers had in the automobile production decision-making process. As far as the veracity of the McDonald's ad, Kincheloe reveals founder Ray Kroc's demands that employees keep concern for their families far down on their list of priorities if they hope to climb Kroc's corporate ladder. McDonald's corporate culture is by no means unique in the pantheon of American corporations. Indeed, the decline of particular forms of traditional family life and the safe climate for children is a casualty of corporate development (Goldman, 1992). After the end of World War II corporate America pursued a variety of policies jeopardizing traditional family arrangements, including raising its expectations of employees, promoting hedonistic and individualized life courses, opposing government aid to families fragmented by economic need, and promoting childhood consumption designed to pit children versus parents and parents versus children in a battle for consumer satisfaction. Despite all of this, the legitimation ads have worked well enough to protect companies from calls for some authentic form of social responsibility.

CHANGED: CHILDHOOD AND YOUTH

There is no doubt that childhood has changed, often as a result of its contact with kinderculture and other, more adult, manifestations of media culture. While all consumers of popular culture play an important role in making their own meanings of its texts, kinderculture and adult popular culture exert specific affective influences, mattering maps that emerge in the social contexts in which children encounter them. Since parents are no longer in control of their children's cultural experiences, they have lost the role that parents once played in shaping their children's values and worldviews. In the 1920s, for example, when the protected childhood was firmly established, middle- and upper-middle-class children had few experiences that fell outside either parental supervision or child-produced activities shared with other children. Since the 1950s, more and more of our children's experiences have been produced by corporations—not as much by parents or even children themselves. TV shows, movies (now on cable TV), Internet, video games, and music (with earphones that allow seclusion from adults) are now the private domain of children. The key theme of this book rests here: Traditional conceptions of childhood as a time of innocence and adult dependency have been undermined in part by children's access to popular culture.

Children no longer live in the so-called secret garden of childhood. This is very disturbing to the elements of the culture that constructed the mythology of such a garden. In this new social space children possess an open door to the adult world. Through this door they see images and hear messages constantly delivered about a variety of topics (Vieira, 2001; Hengst, 2001). While some scholars argue that such mediated access is not real access, such observations imply a positivist epistemological notion that there is only one true understanding of the adult world. David Allen (2003) writes:

> I have often observed that the fascination children experience in watching TV is connected to the promise that many of the mysteries of adult life are bound to be revealed by simply watching more. But just how many? The contrived stories on television that children see so often take back with one hand what they offer with the other. Kids may enjoy the feeling they have access but in reality they don't.

When children participate in "real-life" adult activities, do they have access to the adult world? Are their constructions of such events the "correct" ones? What exactly counts as a real revelation of adult life? The most profound experiences human beings encounter are all "mediated" in some manner. Of course, actual media experiences involving TV, computers, videos, video games, etc., continue to increase in number and show no sign of abating in the future (Spigel, 1998). All people's access to the world, not just children's, is affected by these media. Instead of denying the reality of such experiences, it is better to understand how they filter and construct our view of the world and ourselves and whose interests they serve. Unfortunately, this is not a form of literacy deemed to be very important by political and educational leaders, in the United States in particular, in the contemporary era.

THE POST-POSTMODERN CHILDHOOD DILEMMA

Such a new reality presents adults (parents and teachers in particular) with a complex problem that we once called "the dilemma of the post-modern childhood." Contemporary children's access to commercial kinderculture and popular culture not only motivates them to become hedonistic consumers but changes the nature of their relationship to adults. Advocates of traditional family values and severe discipline for children understand that something has changed, that for some reason their authority has broken down. Such advocates often attribute the breakdown of authority to feminism and its encouragement of mothers to pursue careers outside the home, and to permissive liberals who oppose corporal punishment and other harsh forms of child control—but they are wrong. Adult authority over children, no doubt, has broken down but not because of feminist mothers or wimpy liberals. Children's access to the adult world via the electronic media of hyperreality has subverted contemporary children's consciousness of themselves as incompetent and dependent entities. Such a self-perception does not mix well with institutions such as the traditional family or the authoritarian school, institutions grounded on a view of children as incapable of making decisions for themselves.

Why do children often seem to many adults so defiant, so hard to control, in the first decade of the twenty-first century? The answer involves the fact that they don't see themselves in the same way that adults in these institutions view them. Postmodern children are not accustomed to thinking and operating as little tykes who need adult permission to operate. We understand that not all children react to kinderculture and their access to popular culture in this way, for diverse groups of children will respond differently. The reality remains, however, that adults have lost the authority they used to have because they knew things that sheltered kids didn't. Adult information is uncontainable; children now see the world as it is—or at least how it is mediated by corporate information producers. Daily examples of the effects of children's information access and the new view of themselves it produces are ubiquitous. In the *Home Alone* movies Macaulay Culkin's Kevin character is constantly embarrassed and bothered by adult assumptions that a ten-year-old is a child. In the *Problem Child* movies, the problem child performs "knowing looks" for the camera (and his fellow kids-with-adult-knowledge), indicating his adult take on an unfolding situation. In the *Spy Kids* trilogy of the early twenty-first century, the spy kids are the ones with the greatest abilities to perform dangerous and ingenious acts of espionage. Movie depictions of this real-life change in the social role of children dominate kids' movies from the early 1970s to the present.

This change in children's access to adult knowledge about the world and the changes in the nature of childhood that it produces have undermined the conceptual/curricular/managerial bases on which schooling has been organized. We do not believe it is hyperbolic to argue that in light of these cultural changes, schools must be reconceived from the bottom up. Presently, the school curriculum is organized as a continuum of experience developmentally sequenced as if children learned about the world in school in progressive increments. Right-wing efforts to protect outmoded school organizations and the traditional notions of childhood that come with them are ultimately doomed to failure. Bush's No Child Left Behind reforms of the first decade of the twenty-first century and Obama's Race to the Top competitions, with their standardized and fragmented knowledge and promotion of low-level cognition, attempt to protect an innocent and disempowered childhood with a positivistic vengeance.

We cannot protect our children from the knowledge of the world that hyperreality has made available to them. Such a task would demand a form of sequestration tantamount to incarceration. The task that faces us is intimidating but essential. Advocates of a critical politics of childhood must develop education curricula, parenting skills, and social institutions that will address this cultural revolution in a way that teaches our children to make sense of the chaos of information in hyperreality. In this context school becomes not as much an institution of information delivery as a hermeneutical site—that is, a place where meaning is made, where understanding and interpretation are engendered. The task is difficult, but road maps to negotiate it are already being produced (for a detailed picture of what this meaning-making education might look like, see Kincheloe, 1995, 2001, 2003).

There is no doubt that children are at the center of an information revolution—they understand it better than anyone else, they are connected to one another by it, and their self-images and view of their social role are altered by it. Educators, psychologists, sociologists, parents, and citizens in general must come to terms with these realities. Presently, many political and educational leaders are resisting such changes at every opportunity. Of course, advocates of a critical politics of childhood must be careful not to overstate the impact of technology on the nature of childhood. Technology, like any other structural force, does not determine everyday life. Instead, it interacts with a variety of social and cultural contexts and diverse individual agents to produce an interactive social process. We can see this interactive process in twenty-first-century kinderculture with the diverse and idiosyncratic responses to children's interaction with technology. Nevertheless, this interaction of children and technology has produced profound—but not uniform—social changes. It is the responsibility of those concerned with the welfare of children to understand the impact of these changes and what it means for young people to construct social spaces (cyber- and other knowledge-locales) outside traditional forms of adult control (Jenkins, 1998; Vieira, 2001; Steinberg, 2010).

In a marketing report titled *Power to the Children,* advertising experts argue that children have never had more social, political, and economic power than in the present. Because of their computer and Internet skills, many children are obtaining power from parents who are still uncomfortable with cyber-technologies. Because of these realities, the advertisers contend, marketing strategies to both adults and children must change immediately—children must be viewed and approached in a more empowered, adultlike manner (Vieira, 2001). Hyperreality has helped construct this new childhood. Operating in addition to TV, radio, video, and CDs as yet another site of knowledge and social access, the Internet creates the possibility for children to move farther outside the orbit of adult regulation. Children using the Internet can not only access even more adult secrets but produce secrets of their own as they create virtual children's cultures via websites and webspaces inaccessible to technologically challenged adults.

In cyberspace we find the ultimate contemporary expression of the dilemma of the postmodern childhood. Cyberspace offers unlimited possibilities for changing children's relationship with adults. By way of Internet usage—for example, in chat rooms—children can impersonate adults (and adults can impersonate children), creating in the process an often disconcerting type of child-adult interaction. Thus, in this social space children can assume adult powers in not only chat rooms but in economic transactions and other situations. While there is a playful dimension of Internet usage that promotes the blurring of age distinctions between adults and children by promoting "juvenation," the "adultification" dimension of children's Internet activity is certainly very important (Vieira, 2001; Kasturi, 2002; Cannella, 2002). Whatever process dominates an Internet interaction, it certainly creates a new relationship between children and adults and new dilemmas in the postmodern childhood. Whatever direction these social dynamics ultimately take, a new day for childhood has arrived.

GROWN-UPS JUST HATE KIDS

The post-postmodern child is worldly, often presented in popular culture as a "smart-ass." As know-it-all wise guys, such children are often easy for adults to hate—a theme Joe Kincheloe discusses in Chapter 13 in his consideration of movies portraying children over the past several decades. Children with power are especially threatening to adults—a fear that manifests itself particularly in horror films since the early 1970s. *The Exorcist,* which presented the evil child, Regan, as a monster in need of punishment, encouraged an entire school of evil-children movies including *The Omen, It's Alive, It Lives Again, Firestarter, Children of the Corn, Halloween, The Brood,* etc. The precocious child is a threat to what Valerie Polakow (1992) calls "the order paradigm," a way of seeing that demands pedagogical adherence to the established positivist developmental sequence and reward for the docile and obedient student. Indeed, there is something frightening to the established order about the child-savant who learns about life "out of sequence" from TV, the Internet, and other electronic media. Independent and self-sufficient youths with an "inappropriate" insight into the adult world constitute the monsters in the evil-children movies. This fear and sometimes hatred of the worldly child creates yet another dimension of adult-child relationships in the new childhood.

Rhoda, the precocious child murderer in *The Bad Seed*, is simply "too adult" in her frequent manifestations of self-control and self-discipline. A conversation between Rhoda's mother and Miss Fern, the headmistress of Rhoda's private school, is revealing:

> MOTHER: I don't know how to say it, but there's a mature quality about her [Rhoda] that's disturbing in a child, and my husband and I thought that a school like yours where you believe in discipline and the old-fashioned virtues might, well, perhaps teach her to be more of a child.
>
> MISS FERN: Yes, yes, I know what you mean.

It is interesting that Miss Fern, a stickler for strong discipline, is agreeing with the mother that Rhoda needs to be less mature. Concurring with the mother without equivocation, Miss Fern tacitly shares the mother's recognition that Rhoda's evil revolves around her maturity, her precociousness. Rhoda's mother and Miss Fern see their roles as re-establishing control of Rhoda in an adult-child power hierarchy. The recent film history of demonization of such children is impressive: The six-year-old in *Halloween* is a murderer; in *Firestarter* the power of the young female protagonist, Charley, is best used in the destruction of those around her; in *The Other* the evil child kills his father and carries around his severed finger; the rebellious students portrayed in *The Exorcist* are objects of revulsion who must be controlled at any cost (Paul, 1994).

The list could continue—obviously, something involving fear of knowledgeable children is being expressed in these films, these cultural artifacts. An important theme in the recent history of childhood thus emerges: parents becoming fearful of the latent monster in all children, a parental fear of what their children may become. The middle-class and positivist concern with order and equilibrium is reasserted in light of these repressed parental fears. The precocious child must be rendered obedient, the body must be regulated in the it's-for-your-own-good discourse of justification. Parental fears find legal expression in new laws defining new classes of juvenile crime, making public juvenile records, establishing boot camps for young criminals, outlawing the scale of spray paint to curb graffiti, and eliminating age guidelines in the treatment of youth offenders (Vogel, 1994). Recently published children's books attempt to frighten precocious children who become "too big for their britches" into not only obedience but a new form of dependency. Written to counteract too much child identification with Macaulay Culkin's precocious, independent, and successful Kevin character in *Home Alone*, Francine Pascal, Molly Mia Stewart, and Ying-Hwa Hu's *Ellen Is Home Alone* (1993) paints a gruesome picture for children who want to stay home alone. Her message is simple and straightforward: Staying home alone is scary; as a child you are incompetent; if you try to act like an adult you will be severely punished; if you resist parental control you may *die*. Stewart's infantiphobia and the "hellfire pedagogy" she uses to enforce discipline is not unlike Jonathan Edwards's imagery of children in the hands of an angry God or the conclusion of *The Bad Seed*, when the precocious Rhoda is killed by a lightning bolt. Disney's *Hannah Montana* represents the new breed of brat in the knowing machinations of a tweenish girl: While undercover as a sweet kid, she gossips and manipulates her way through life, and this time comes out on top. Balancing the collective consciousness of the *Home Alone*'s generational mistakes of being repressed as smart-asses, today's new kid is a sweet smart-ass, and much more sneaky.

ANTI-KID AGENDA

The double-speak of the right-wing call for family values is in actuality a misleading code for an antifamily and antichildren agenda. It is an expression of fear of the empowered, agential child and the new childhood discussed here. The antifamily reality of family values establishes discouraging obstacles for working-class families—working single mothers in particular—and great suffering in the everyday lives of their children. In the Reagan/Bush revolution of the 1980s, the Gingrich/Dole insurrection of the mid-1990s, and the George W. Bush right-wing agenda of the first decade of the twenty-first century, family values were used as a cover for greed and excess and mean-spirited punishment of the poor. With the Obama years, the discourse of family values has been quieted, and the conversation has taken hold at the grassroots kid level. Chastity circles and Hard as Nails groups have circled the right-wing wagons of children and youth. Taking the notions of fundamentalist Christianity in hand, kids are policing themselves in creating a new morality—one that claims abstinence and innocence but contradicts itself through corporate-inspired "booty" clothing, sexual innuendo and language, and "sexting." As a smoke screen for more malevolent goals, the discourse of family values has served the right-wing agenda gloriously. Providing the facade of concern, conservatives are able to convince millions of Americans that new monies for education, antipoverty programs, and child care are pointless when the real problem is the absence of family values. A central but often unasked question involves how many families struggling in poverty would be saved if they embraced traditional family values. The answer: very few. To understand the economic problems that plague an alarming proportion of America's children, one must explore a panoply of structural changes in the global economy in the 1970s, '80s, '90s, and the first decades of the twenty-first century. Traditional family values and structures characterized by working fathers and home-making, child-caring mothers are inconsistent with changed economic realities. Stay-at-home fathers and double and triple job–holding mothers may often replace the notion of who makes up a family.

The family, Norman Denzin (1987) reminds us, has been a locale of political and ideological struggle since the late eighteenth century. In the second half of the twentieth century, such struggles revealed to many observers that the all-American nuclear family was no longer the social norm. Such a structure is not now and may never have been the familial model experienced by most Americans. In the present era the nuclear family is a site of submerged hostilities as precocious, empowered children wrestle with their parents for adult privileges and material goods. The *Home Alone* and *Spy Kids* movies, for example, work diligently to cover up the familial fault lines introduced by the plots. As a result, screenwriters and directors must walk a political tightrope over a canyon of family- and children-related issues. The seismic waves emanating from these family battles, from the fear of precocious, empowered children, are clearly reflected by the right-wing family-values rhetoric. Precocious behavioral problems, the conservative argument goes, are the direct product of a liberal age of permissiveness. Such problems of undisciplined youth, the right maintains, are especially prevalent among the poor and the nonwhite, and the only way to deal with these "sociopaths" is to get tough (Griffin, 1993). With the help of feminists in particular, the story continues, family values and traditional family structures continue to erode to the point that jailing youth is our only alternative to utter chaos. Thus, a juveniphobia is deployed for political capital. In this juveniphobic context the rhetoric of family values does not connote a loving, supportive approach to child advocacy.

As a collective group, children and youth are feared, and not trusted. Incarceration for criminal children is virtually antithetical to crime prevention, rehabilitation, or the reduction of repeat offenses. Juveniles in adult institutions are five times more likely to be sexually assaulted, twice as likely to be battered by institutional staff, and 50 percent more likely to be beaten with a weapon than young people in juvenile facilities. The likelihood of repeat offenses by juveniles in adult institutions is significantly higher (Vogel, 1994). Equally depressing is the discourse of many liberal child-advocacy groups premised on a positivist instrumental view of children that demands public investments in children must eventuate in quantitative cost-benefit outcomes. In this context childhood intervention programs are invaded by unending tests for academic progress, social appropriateness, crime reduction, and decreased welfare dependency. Such a positivist mind-set is often indifferent to the need for a quality child-care system in a nation where more than half of children under six years old have working mothers. Funds for such a service are withheld on the family-values belief that mothers, not child-care workers (or husbands), should care for their children at home. Thus, right-wing pro-family policies continue to throw up obstacles for working families, single mothers in particular, that cause children to suffer unnecessarily (Polakow, 1992; Books, 2002).

JUSTICE AND KINDERCULTURE

Any analysis of childhood must attend to questions of race, class, and gender-related injustice that plague segments of kinderculture's child audiences and shape the format of the media, print, and interactive dimensions of kinderculture. From the perspective of many poor, minority, and immigrant children, the world they have been encouraged to trust no longer works. Poor children have seen their dreams stolen from them, replaced by a hopelessness that narrows their choices and undermines their sense that their actions can make a difference. Youth suicide was not even a category before 1960; by the 1980s it was second to "accidents" as the leading cause of death among young people. By the 1990s suicide among kids was described as an epidemic. What kind of hopelessness must a child feel to take his or her own life? By the time many children enter middle school, they are world-weary, drained of a sense of possibility. Many have heard it all, the charlatans with their manipulative pseudo-hope grounded on everything from televangelism to drugs to schooling (Ferguson, 1994). Kinderculture must often provide a welcome escape from such harsh realities—no wonder TV viewing time is so high among poor and dispossessed children.

These sobering descriptions of marginalized children's experiences are not to be found in corporate-produced kinderculture. Too often kinderculture refuses to challenge patriarchal power structures or provide alternative vantage points on the world. The "good guys" of kinderculture are too often white males who fight the good fight for neo-imperialist causes. The advertising of children's consumer products that supports TV programming for kids is uncritical of the gross economic inequalities that characterize it (Seiter, 1993). In the name of a common culture, kinderculture ignores experiences of economic inequality and lived understandings of oppression endured by too many children. Here questions of children's differences in opportunity and privilege are erased. An important distinction here involves the fact that cultural racial differences may be represented by TV, movie, or print producers, but they are dehistoricized and stripped of any depiction of the power differences that cause suffering among marginalized children and their parents.

The TV heroes of kinderculture are typically inscribed with dominant and mainstream cultural values. As white, male, classless (read: middle-class) protagonists, they carry WASP values to violent villains who remarkably often are nonwhite or non-American. White heroes are frequently provided with a nonwhite or female sidekick to overtly signify the value of diversity—a strategy that covertly registers the need for white male control of a diverse society (Fiske, 1993). Thus, the presence of difference can be noted in kinderculture; indeed, advertisers and marketers have enthusiastically embraced difference, from exoticized Jamaican Barbies to ethnic snack foods. Mattel's multicultural Barbies and American Girl's Addy doll constitute a corporate "containment policy," not this time of communism but of creeping multiculturalism. A post-Fordist niche marketing strategy is at work here that uses diversity as a method of reaching beyond standardized mass production's economies of scale. It is, however, a safe, common-culture type of diversity that sanitizes and depoliticizes any challenge to the harmony of the status quo.

RACIALIZED KINDERCULTURE

Analysis of commercials on cable TV for children and Saturday morning network programs reveals advertising set in a WASP-oriented middle-class reality. The homes that serve as backdrops for toys are spacious, with kid-dominated play areas—suburban utopias. Casts for the ads are reported by talent agents to be chosen around the "all-American" standard of appearance (read: white). When nonwhites are cast they frequently are placed in the periphery (the left third of the TV screen), leaving leading and instigating roles to white boys. Black characters in children's commercials often dance and play basketball and often display vivacious and loose characteristics—they are not the scholars, the kids with a secure vocational future. McDonald's, more than most children's corporations, employs African American children in its ads. Often nonwhite children in McDonald's commercials are shown on the edges of the TV picture slightly out of focus. Outside the conscious realization of their viewers, children's commercials that use nonwhite actors reproduce racial hierarchies that privilege whites. In one McDonald's ad connecting the corporation to traditional family values, the song's lyrics "families like . . ." are visually accompanied by a picture of an early twentieth-century immigrant family arriving in America. By the time the lyrics get to " . . . yours" the scene has shifted to a WASP upper-middle-class family. While the browning and blacking of commercials and toys has begun to emerge, the inclusion of cultural difference is silenced. The immigration diaspora brings children who have left a familiar culture to a new children's culture to which they clearly do not belong. While referencing the great American melting pot, the commercial covertly labels "your" family, the normalized all-American family, as white and upper-middle-class (Seiter, 1993; Goldman, 1992; Steinberg, 2001, 2008).

GENDERED KINDERCULTURE

With all the gender analysis and reconceptualization that has taken place over the past several decades, it is amazing that kinderculture has remained so gender-differentiated. While the gender analysis of popular culture advances and grants important insights into media constructions of gender, kinderculture continues to promote delineated gender roles. Advertising for girls' toys has changed little since the 1950s—missing are the allusions to how well the toy stoves provide training for home economics and the demands of motherhood. Similarly, toy ads for boys have witnessed only minor alterations in the past forty years. The adult male voice-over is gone, but close-ups of the toys and boys' voices making engine and weapon sound effects continue uninterrupted. Boys still become one with their toys, while girls take care of theirs—ever the adoring spectators of their dolls in girl commercials. In Disney animated films, as Henry Giroux points out in his chapter, girls and women are depicted within constrictive gender roles. In *The Little Mermaid* and *The Lion King,* women characters are subordinate to men: Ariel, the mermaid, appears to be on a liberatory journey against parental domination, but in the end she gives up her voice in a deal to trade her fin for legs so she can pursue her fair prince; in *The Lion King* all leaders are male, recipients of patriarchal entitlement. After King Mufasa dies, the duplicitous Scar becomes the new monarch. The lionesses are powerless, granting Scar the same deference as they had Mufasa. The female lions have no agency, no moral sense—they are merely backdrops to the action that the males initiate and in which they take part. Similar gender dynamics are present in *Aladdin* and *Beauty and the Beast*.

At work in these films and other manifestations of kinderculture is a hegemonic masculinity. Such a patriarchal form obviously holds serious implications for women, but it distorts male development as well. Boys are encouraged by various forms of the kinderculture curriculum to assume patriarchal roles that allegedly entitle them by birthright to define reality and enjoy the rewards of privilege through their domination of subordinates. Such an identity, unfortunately, is often formed through the young boy's denial of his connections with other people. Conservative-oriented American patriarchal culture defines manhood in terms of separation and self-sufficiency—the Clint Eastwood character comes to mind in his man-with-no-name, *High Plains Drifter* movies. Here was a man who was such a loner he had no use for a name. Setting the standard for male disconnection, Eastwood's characters in this genre repressed their hurt feelings and learned to hide and disguise them from the world. Indeed, in hegemonic masculinity the only approved techniques for dealing with one's emotions involve evasiveness, bravado, boasting, bluster, lying, and various forms of aggression—the "how long" and "how many" motif. In the attempt to master such techniques, young boys in our culture begin to cultivate a "cool and detached male pose" around the time they enter the fifth or sixth grade. In its fullest manifestations, such a pose negates public emotional display—obviously crying is forbidden and even smiling and displays of enthusiasm are restricted (Nightingale, 1993).

The emotional repression and lack of interpersonal connection that this hegemonic masculinity breeds among boys creates severe social dysfunctionality. Boys who are unable to deal with emotional conflict and the interpersonal dynamics of family and peer relationships grow up to be men who have difficulty loving. They often become the types of men who leave and/or abuse their wives and families—an ever-growing trend in the last third of the twentieth century and the first part of the twenty-first. Such social psychological issues push the kinderculture gender curriculum to the front burner. A home or school curriculum that takes kinderculture seriously involves children in the recognition and analysis of such gender issues and their effects on the pedagogical formation of their own and others' self-concepts.

UNDERSTANDING KINDERCULTURE

What often inhibits understanding of the pedagogical power of popular culture in general and kinderculture in particular involves this society's failure to recognize that dominant power plays an exaggerated role in the shaping of personal experiences. This relationship is so apparent that it is often lost in its obviousness (Grossberg, 1995). Power produces images of the world and the people who inhabit it that help make meaning for those who receive the images. The films, books, video games, and TV shows of kinderculture shape the way white children, for example, understand the poor and racially marginalized—and, in turn, how they come to recognize and act on their own privilege. Language patterns connect with this production of images to reinforce power's influence, its ability to provide the context in which children encounter the world. The advent of electronic hyperreality has revolutionized the ways knowledge is produced in this culture and the ways children come to learn about the world. Parents and educators need to appreciate the nature of this revolution, children's relationship to it, and its role in identity formation. Simple condemnation of kinderculture à la right-wing politicians accompanied by calls for censorship is insufficient; equally ineffective is a policy of benign neglect. Concerned individuals should begin with an attempt to understand these dynamics in all their complexity and ambiguity, followed by an effort to involve themselves in the public conversation about them. In this context adults may come to appreciate the fact that postmodern children's confusion and identity-disorientation may be a reasonable reaction to the incongruity between kinderculture's and schooling's positioning of children.

RETHINKING EDUCATION

As we begin to understand these issues, the need for a reconceptualization of childhood education presents itself. At the foundation of this rethinking is the rejection of a child psychology predicated on the adjustment of children to the existing social order. Valerie Polakow (1992) argues that this adjustment psychology demands an "order ideology of schooling" that is structured around the removal of the child from any experience of conflict. Inherent in this psychological model is an infantilization impulse that denies children the autonomy to make decisions about issues that affect their lives and to negotiate their relationships to conflicting imperatives. Rejection of the order ideology does not mean that we embrace anarchy but instead understand and learn even to appreciate the desire, the libidinal impulse that begins to bubble in childhood, reaching full expression in adolescence.

Kinderculture in this context does not incite rebellion or violence; it pokes and irritates the beast of desire—an affective force that is present in romantic love, the bond between parent and child, advertising, fast food, Internet chat rooms, movies, TV shows, and video games (Ventura, 1994). A critical pedagogy of childhood is aware and unafraid of childhood desire, often connecting it to children's efforts to understand the world and themselves. As Paulo Freire maintained years ago, a critical childhood education is interested in the knowledge and intuitions children bring to school. In hyperreality such a pedagogical principle means that educators are obligated to study kinderculture, its effect on its consumers, and its relationship to desire. If we are interested in knowing our children, such a pedagogy provides a direct line into their consciousness as well as their perceptions of themselves, the world, and even us (adults). What happens when children nurtured by kinderculture encounter the certified knowledge of the school? The answer to such a question leads us to new forms of learning, new insights into the construction of contemporary childhood around which we can restructure schools and rethink the role of parenting in hyperreality.

Jane Kenway and Elizabeth Bullen (2001) convincingly maintain that education systems have not been very concerned with the new paradigm of childhood studies, especially its analysis of the impact of globalized hegemonic culture on the formation of children's identity. Schools have ignored the implications of this and other dimensions of the new childhood for thinking about the purpose of schools in the first decade of the twenty-first century. Instead, Kenway and Bullen conclude that many school systems around the world have moved in the opposite direction, retreating to a form of hyper-positivism that abstracts children from the world in the name of teaching to high standards and basic knowledge. In this process they accomplish neither the former nor the latter. It is important to reiterate that contemporary schooling, especially in the United States, has sought to use the classroom as the bulwark of the old positivist order. In this configuration the child is positioned as an incompetent, dependent, and passive entity who is regulated and socialized as she passes through determined developmental stages.

There is evidence (du Bois-Reymond, Suenker, and Kruger, 2001) that while many parenting styles have evolved in relation to the agential child, education in its mainstream articulation has resisted such changes. Thus, the gulf between childhood schooling and children's lives out of school grows wider in hyperreality. As more and more of their learning takes place in out-of-school leisure activities, in edutainment in particular, children perceive schools as more and more anachronistic and quaint. Schools and too many educational experts seem all too disinterested in the ways children use technology for recreation, communication, and relationship and community building. Educational and political leaders often seem more threatened than amazed by children's accomplishments in computer technology and forms of techno-literacy and knowledge production. Traditional conceptions of intergenerational divisions of intellectual labor in this context have been shaken like a monkey on a fuzzy tree. Indeed, a central tenet of kinderculture and its critical pedagogy of childhood involves, first, the reassessment of the everyday activities, cognitive processes, social and cultural experiences, and political positioning of contemporary children. Second, such a pedagogy demands the serious analysis of the relationship between these dynamics and the assumptions of childhood education.

Of course, kinderculture's critical pedagogy of childhood is not reticent about providing its "take" on this relationship. Our pedagogy for the new childhood moves away from the unproblematized transmission of dominant cultural norms and knowledges toward the development of cognitive skills and abilities that empower students to

- teach themselves to become rigorous scholars
- make sense of the mass of information with which they are confronted in hyperreality
- understand regardless of their social location questions of power and justice
- gain social mobility from marginalized and disempowered locales
- become good citizens, agents of democracy in an antidemocratic era
- make sense of complex real-life situations from which advocates of childhood innocence might try to protect them
- communicate their insights as children unabashedly to a variety of audiences

Kinderculture's depiction of these disjunctions between the policy drift of school pedagogy vis-à-vis out-of-school learning raises questions about the efficacy of schooling and the benefits of deschooling. The critical pedagogy of childhood is dedicated to the notion of universal public schooling that is intimately connected to informal, out-of-school learning. While we are harshly critical of the contemporary right-wing co-optation of public schooling, we have not given up on the possibilities offered by public education. Most teachers care deeply about what is best for children but are pushed and pulled by myriad forces working for disparate goals and political agendas. Central to any reasonable reform of schooling is the understanding of the social, cultural, and psychological dimensions of the new childhood and the ways right-wing reforms attempt to "recover" an older notion of childhood. In this context the issues raised by *Kinderculture* are central not only to the state of childhood in the twenty-first century but also to the future of public education itself.

References

Abercrombie, N. (1994). Authority and Consumer Society. In R. Keat, N. Whiteley, & N. Abercrombie (Eds.), *The Authority of the Consumer.* New York: Routledge.

Allen, D. (2003). Is Childhood Disappearing? International Social Theory Consortium Second Annual Conference at Sussex University. Paper presentation.

Ball, T. (1992). New Faces of Power. In T. Wartenberg (Ed.), *Rethinking Power.* Albany, New York: State University of New York Press.

Books, S. (2002). Making Poverty Pay: Children and the 1996 Welfare Law. In G. Cannella and J. Kincheloe (Eds.), *Kidworld: Childhood Studies, Global Perspectives, and Education.* New York: Peter Lang.

Buckingham, D. (2003). *Media Education, Literacy Learning, and Contemporary Culture.* London: Polity Press.

Cannella, G. (1997). *Deconstructing Early Childhood Education: Social Justice and Revolution.* New York: Peter Lang.

————. (2002). Global Perspectives, Cultural Studies, and the Construction of a Postmodern Childhood Studies. In G. Cannella & J. Kincheloe (Eds.), *Kidworld: Childhood Studies, Global Perspectives, and Education.* New York: Peter Lang.

Cannella, G. & J. Kincheloe (Eds.) (2002). *Kidworld: Childhood Studies, Global Perspectives, and Education.* New York: Peter Lang.

Cannella, G. & R. Viruru (2002). (Euro-American Constructions of) Education of Children (and Adults) Around the World: A Postcolonial Critique. In G. Cannella & J. Kincheloe (Eds.), *Kidworld: Childhood Studies, Global Perspectives, and Education.* New York: Peter Lang.

Casas, F. (1998). Children, Media, and the Relational Planet: Some Reflections from the European Context. http://webcache.googleusercontent.com/search?q=cache:QM 2zf1gj6UQJ:www.childwatch.uio.no/projects/thematic-groups/the-influence-of -information-and-communication-audio-visual-technologies/+Casas+Children,+ Media,+and+the+Relational+Planet&cd=1&hl=en&ct=clnk&client=firefox-a.

Cassell, J. & H. Jenkins (2002). Proper Playthings: The Politics of Play in Children, http://www.web.media.mit.edu/~andrew_s/andrew_sempere_2002_politics_of _play.pdf.

Cook, D. (2004). *The Commodification of Childhood: The Children's Clothing Industry and the Rise of the Child Consumer.* Durham: Duke University Press.

Denzin, N. (1987). Postmodern Children. Caring for Children. *Society.* Dordrecht: Springer Publishing. March/April, pp. 22–25.

Donald, J. (1993). The Natural Man and the Virtuous Woman: Reproducing Citizens. In C. Jenks (Ed.), *Cultural Reproduction.* New York: Routledge.

Dorfman, A. (1971). *How to Read Donald Duck: Imperialist Ideology in the Disney Comic.* Paris: International General.

du Bois-Reymond, M., H. Suenker, & H. Kruger (Eds.) (2001). *Childhood in Europe.* New York: Peter Lang.

Ferguson, S. (1994). The Comfort of Being Sad. *Utne Reader*, 64. July/August, pp. 60–61.

Fiske, J. (1993). *Power Plays, Power Works.* New York: Verso.

Fu, V. (2003). Multiculturalism in Early Childhood Programs: Culture, Schooling, and Education in a Democracy. http://ericeece.org/pubs/books/ multicul/fu.html.

Garey, A. & T. Arendell (1999). Children, Work, and Family: Some Thoughts on Mother Blame. Working Paper No. 4. http://workingfamilies.berkeley.edu/papers/4.pdf.

Giroux, H. (1994). *Disturbing Pleasures: Learning Popular Culture.* New York: Routledge.

Goldman, R. (1992). *Reading Ads Socially.* New York: Routledge.

Greider, W. (1992). *Who Will Tell the People? The Betrayal of American Democracy.* New York: Touchstone.

Griffin, C. (1993). *Representations of Youth: The Study of Youth and Adolescence in Britain and America.* Cambridge, MA: Polity Press.

Grossberg, L. (1995). What's in a Name (One More Time). *Taboo: The Journal of Culture and Education*, 1, Fall, pp. 11–37.

Hammer, R. and Kellner, D. (Eds.) (2009). *Media/Cultural Studies: Critical Approaches.* New York: Peter Lang Publishing.

Hengst, H. (2001). Rethinking the Liquidation of Childhood. In M. du Bois-Reymond, H. Suenker, & H. Kruger, *Childhood in Europe.* New York: Peter Lang.

Kasturi, S. (2002). Constructing Childhood in a Corporate World: Cultural Studies, Childhood, and Disney. In G. Cannella & J. Kincheloe (Eds.), *Kidworld: Childhood Studies, Global Perspectives and Education.* New York: Peter Lang.

Kellner, D. (1992). Popular Culture and the Construction of Postmodern Identities. In S. Lash & J. Friedman (Eds.), *Modernity and Identity.* Cambridge, MA: Blackwell.

———. (1990). *Television and the Crisis of Democracy.* Boulder, CO: Westview Press.

Kenway, J. & E. Bullen (2001). *Consuming Children: Entertainment, Advertising, and Education.* Philadelphia: Open University Press.

Kincheloe, J. (2004). *Critical Pedagogy.* New York: Peter Lang.

———. (2001). *Getting Beyond the Facts: Teaching Social Studies/Social Sciences in the Twenty-First Century.* New York: Peter Lang.

———. (2008). *Knowledge and Critical Pedagogy.* The Hague: Springer Press.

———. (2002). *The Sign of the Burger: McDonald's and the Culture of Power.* Philadelphia: Temple University Press.

———. (2003). *Teachers as Researchers: Qualitative Paths to Empowerment.* 2nd Ed. London: Falmer Press.

———. (1995). *Toil and Trouble: Good Work, Smart Workers, and the Integration of Academic and Vocational Education.* New York: Peter Lang.

———. (1993). *Toward a Critical Politics of Teacher Thinking: Mapping the Postmodern.* Westport, CT: Bergin and Garvey.

Kunzle, D. (1992). Dispossession by Ducks: The Imperialist Treasure Hunt in the Barks-Disney Comics. (Unpublished Paper.)

Lincoln, Y. (1995). If I Am Not Just One Person, but Many, Why Should I Write Just One Text? Paper Presented at the American Educational Research Association. San Francisco. April 13.

Lipsky, D. & A. Abrams (1994). *Late Bloomers.* New York: Times Books.

Mason, J. & B. Steadman (1997). The Significance of the Conceptualisation of Childhood for Child Protection Policy. *Family Matters*, 46, pp. 31–36.

McLaren, P. (1994). *Critical Pedagogy and Predatory Culture.* New York: Routledge.

McLaren, P., R. Hammer, D. Sholle, & S. Reilly (1995). *Rethinking Media Literacy: A Critical Pedagogy of Representation.* New York: Peter Lang.

Mumby, D. (1989). Ideology and the Social Construction of Meaning: A Communication Perspective. *Communication Quarterly*, 37, 4, pp. 291–304.

Nations, C. (2001). How Long Do Our Children Have to Wait? Understanding the Children of the Twenty-first Century, http://pt3.nmsu.edu/edu621/cynthia 2001.html.

Nelson, C., P. Treichler, & L. Grossberg (1992). Cultural Studies: An Introduction. In C. Nelson, P. Treichler, & L. Grossberg (Eds.), *Cultural Studies*. New York: Routledge.

Nightingale, C. (1993). *On the Edge: A History of Poor Black Children and Their American Dreams*. New York: Basic Books.

Ottosen, M. (2003). Children as Social Actors: A Critical Comment. Paper presented at the Danish Sociology Conference, Aalborg, Denmark.

Pascal, F., M. Stewart, & Y. Hu (1993). *Ellen Is Home Alone*. New York: Bantam.

Paul, W. (1994). *Laughing and Screaming: Modern Hollywood Horror and Comedy*. New York: Columbia University Press.

Polakow, V. (1992). *The Erosion of Childhood*. Chicago: University of Chicago Press.

Postman, N. (1994). *The Disappearance of Childhood*. New York: Vintage Books.

Scott, D. (2002). What Are Beanie Babies Teaching Our Children? In G. Cannella and J. Kincheloe (Eds.), *Kidworld: Childhood Studies, Global Perspectives, and Education*. New York: Peter Lang.

Seiter, E. (1993). *Sold Separately: Parents and Children in Consumer Culture*. New Brunswick, NJ: Rutgers University Press.

Spigel, L. (1998). Seducing the Innocent: Childhood and Television in Postwar America. In H. Jenkins (Ed.), *The Children's Culture Reader*. New York: NYU Press.

Steinberg, S. (2001). *Multi/Intercultural Conversations*. New York: Peter Lang.

———. (2007). Introduction. In *Media Literacy: A Reader*. Macedo, D. & Steinberg, S.R. (eds.). New York: Peter Lang.

———. (2007). Reading Media Critically. *In Media Literacy: A Reader*. Macedo, D. & Steinberg, S. R. (eds). New York: Peter Lang.

———. (2010). *19 Urban Questions: Teaching in the City*. New York: Peter Lang.

———. (2010). Not the Real Thing: A History of Hollywood's TV Families. In Marsh, M. and Turner-Vorbeck, T. (Eds.) *Learning to Listen to Families in Schools*. New York: Teachers College Press.

Steinberg, S. and J. Kincheloe (1997; 2004). *Kinderculture: The Corporate Construction of Childhood*. Boulder, CO: Westview Press.

Thiele, L. (1986). Foucault's Triple Murder and the Development of Power. *Canadian Journal of Political Science*, 19. June, pp. 243–260.

Ventura, M. (1994). The Age of Endarkenment. *Utne Reader*, 64. July/August, pp. 63–66.

Vogel, J. (1994). Throw Away the Key. *Utne Reader*, 64. July/August, pp. 56–60.

Vieira, C. (2001). Alt.cyberkid: Contingencies of the Technological Child.

Warde, A. (1994). Consumers, Identity, and Belonging: Reflections on Some Theses of Zygmunt Bauman. In R. Keat, N. Whiteley, & N. Abercrombie (Eds.), *The Authority of the Consumer*. New York: Routledge.

Wartenberg, T. (1992). Situated Social Power. In T. Wartenberg (Ed.), *Rethinking Power*. Albany, NY: State University of New York Press.

Chapter 2

TEENS AND VAMPIRES: FROM *BUFFY THE VAMPIRE SLAYER* TO *TWILIGHT'S* VAMPIRE LOVERS

Douglas Kellner

Since the appearance of the 1992 film *Buffy the Vampire Slayer* (hereafter *BtVS*) and the popular 1997–2003 TV series based on it, Buffy has become a cult figure of global media culture, with a panorama of websites, copious media and scholarly dissection, academic conferences, and a fandom that continues to devour reruns and DVDs of the 144 episodes. The series caught its moment and its audience, popularizing Buffyspeak, the Buffyverse (the textual universe of the show), and Buffypeople, who dedicated themselves to promoting and explicating the phenomenon and exemplified the British cultural studies ideal of the active audience, able to quote and interpret while citing episode and season. By the time the series reached its apocalyptic conclusion in the summer of 2003, it was widely recognized around the globe as one of the most striking cult TV shows of the epoch.[1]

In the 2000s and up to the present, there have been a proliferation of movies and TV series centering on vampire characters, suggesting that the traditional monsters resonate with contemporary fantasies, fears, and desires. Traditionally, vampires represented fears of and attraction to extreme sexuality and were also caught up in Christian religious problematics, as the "undead" threatened the Christian scheme of redemption and salvation; in classical vampire stories and films, the cross was thus a potent weapon against vampires.

Post-1960s vampire fiction and films featured female and black vampires, gay and lesbian ones, gangs of vampire youth, and an assorted array of vampire figures who represented different sorts of societal fears or transgressions. In general, media culture articulates in allegorical forms fears, fantasies, and dreams of a given society at a particular point in time (Kellner, 1995). Reading popular fantasy TV like *The X-Files* and *BtVS*, or popular films like the *Star Wars* cycle, provides access to social problems and issues and hopes and anxieties that are often not articulated in more "realist" cultural forms.[2] The richness of allegorical structure and content in these shows allows the production of meanings and identities beyond more conventional media culture, and can help generate a wealth of different readings and appropriations.

In this chapters, I first argue that *BtVS* functions as an allegorical spectacle about contemporary life and provide a diagnostic critique concerning what the series tells us about life in the United States and the situation of contemporary youth during its epoch. Then I look at the films released so far in the series adapting Stephenie Meyer's *Twilight* novels, which portray a young teenage woman, Bella, falling in love with a vampire and becoming involved in the destiny of her love, Edward, and his vampire family. I will argue that these texts provide particular ideological interventions into specific historical situations and that their allegories provide varying and often contrasting moral and ideological messages.

BUFFY THE VAMPIRE SLAYER AS ALLEGORY

BtVS features the adventures of Buffy Summers (played by Sarah Michelle Gellar), a sixteen-year-old high school student who, when the series opens, has just transferred to the small town of Sunnydale from Los Angeles, where she got into trouble with school authorities for her erratic behavior (which we learn was fighting vampires). Buffy's parents are divorced, and she and her mother attempt to begin life anew, a theme of renewal and change that will become central in the unfolding episodes.

In the series mythology, Sunnydale High School is located on the Hellmouth, a portal to nether regions that demonic forces enter to threaten everyday life and wreak havoc, portending apocalypse. The opening episode introduces a hideous Master who plans to open the Hellmouth to legions of monsters who will unleash their fury. Buffy learns that she is the Chosen One, with the powers to fight evil monsters, and bonds with the bookish Willow (Alyson Hannigan) and awkward but loyal Xander (Nicholas Brendon), who are tutored by the English librarian Rupert Giles (Anthony Stewart Head). Giles possesses a vast collection of books that identify the various monsters who emerge in Sunnydale, and he serves as Buffy's "Watcher," providing guidance and mentorship to help her deal with her occult powers. Giles's figure provides a rare TV image of a nurturing mentor able to relate to and work with youth.

Buffy's "Scooby gang," named after the *Scooby-Doo* cartoon series featuring young detectives, fight various vampires and demons each week, while grappling with their own personal and interpersonal problems. Encompassing realist, mythological, and allegorical levels, *BtVS* offers a polysemic and complex hermeneutical challenge to contemporary criticism to depict how the series works and how it presents a startling diversity and intensity of themes. The series combines the genres of horror and fantasy, gothic romance, teen dramas, soap operas, and epic adventure tales. It is a pastiche featuring the perennial figures of the vampire, werewolf, witch, and a panorama of traditional monsters, while adding some new ones. Mixing comedy and drama, *BtVS* offers social satire and illuminating insight embodied in a wide array of compelling characters, engaging narratives, and clever commentary on contemporary culture.

On the *realist level*, the show presents down-to-earth and revealing relations between teenagers, and between young people and parents, teachers and mentors, and a diverse range of authority figures. *BtVS* engagingly deals with social relationships, love, rejection, loss, and all the complexities of family, school, work, constructing identity and finding oneself, growing and evolving, or failing and regressing as a human being.

BtVS is particularly realistic and boundary-breaking in its depiction of sexual relations, with a considerable amount of gay and lesbian sexuality and quite frank and explicit depictions of an extensive variety of sexualities. The series abounds with steamy sex and mutating relations where hate turns to love and violence to erotic entanglement. Playing with S&M and taboo-breaking eroticism to a degree hitherto unseen on U.S. television, *BtVS* sizzles and titillates with throbbing music, yearning looks, passionate kisses, and more. In addition, the series depicts typical relationships and problems, such as teen and young adult angst; needs for love, acceptance, identity, and community; and a panorama of teen desires and fears. It engages painful and heavy problems like rejection and loneliness, drugs and addiction, violence, gangs, rape, destructive behavior, death, and a range of other issues that concern young people and adults, although it often does this, as I argue below, in the mode of allegory rather than movie-of-the-week-style realism. It deals with the hell of high school, with its group conformity, hierarchies, ostracisms, anti-intellectualism, oppressive authority figures, and meaningless rules and regulations. Moreover, *BtVS* deals with existential crises like coping with parents' divorce, creating a relationship and life with one's single mother, and then dealing with the death of a parent or loved one.

Families are presented as essentially dysfunctional in Buffy's world. Mothers are largely ineffectual or perhaps destructive, fathers are mostly absent, and divorce appears to be a norm. Depicting ways to cope with the problems of contemporary life, the series shows how teenagers and young people often have to forge alternative families and in effect create friendships and communities as traditional families disintegrate. Clearly, Buffy's "Scooby gang" offers its members a substitute family they can count on in times of trouble, as well as a cadre of friends and lovers with whom viewers can vicariously experience the agonies and ecstasies of growing up and becoming initiated into life's pleasures and disappointments.

One of the series' most distinctive themes concerns how individuals with exceptional powers and abilities can develop these capacities and find and cultivate love, friendship, affirmation of difference, and identity. The show's grappling with difference, otherness, and marginality is a major theme and puts on display its affinity with postmodern theory.[3] It affirms certain types of difference and otherness, as it shows the main positive characters as outsiders who refuse to conform to the dominant teen subculture and who cultivate their individual powers and abilities while relating to others in respectable ways. But the series also shows how certain types of otherness, embodied in the various monsters, threaten school, community, and everyday life and must be stood up to and dealt with. The dialectic of otherness is complicated further, as I will note, by showing slippages between "good" and "bad" otherness, as, for example, when the vampires Angel and Spike exhibit abilities to do both significant good and evil and are forced to make important moral choices.

In addition, Buffy can be read, on a more traditional narrative level, as a female *Bildungsroman*—that is, a coming-of-age and growing-up story focused on a young woman. It provides a fantasy of an empowered woman able to control her environment and to hold off and defeat forces of evil. While the *Bildungsroman* is associated with Goethe, Thomas Mann, and novels about young men coming of age,[4] Buffy is different and groundbreaking in having a female protagonist. Indeed, the series exhibits perhaps the most fully developed female *Bildungsroman* narrative in the history of popular television and earned a cult following and incredibly dedicated audience.

The theme of how to cultivate exceptional abilities and deal with monstrosity obviously takes us to the level of the series' *mythology*, as Buffy is a vampire slayer and her antagonists are often demons and monsters of a certain pop-cult-genre type. I'm using "mythology" as series creators Chris Carter did in relation to *The X-Files* and Joss Whedon did with *Buffy*, as the particular mythical universe and narrative of the series, rather than in the traditional sense of mythology, which I'll argue takes us more to the allegorical level (which I'll come to shortly). The series' mythology compromises the particular supernatural powers that the characters possess, the demons they fight, and the conflicts they are involved in within particular story arcs and narrative sequences.

Series creator Joss Whedon introduced the *BtVS* mythology in the 1992 film *Buffy the Vampire Slayer*, on which he is credited as writer and Fran Rubel Kuzui is credited as director (she would serve as longtime producer on the TV series). The film opens with the portentous narrative frame: "Since the dawn of man the vampires have walked among us, killing, feeding. The only one with the strength or skill to stop the heinous evil is the Slayer . . . Trained by the Watcher, one Slayer dies and another is chosen." A caption reads "Europe: The Dark Ages," and the screen shows the vampire slayer emerging; then after the titles, the picture cuts to the title "Southern California: the Lite Ages." Buffy and her friends are introduced as valley girls who are into cheerleading, shopping, boys, and the prom. But the Chosen One, Buffy (Christy Swanson), has dreams of dark events in the past involving vampires, and her Watcher, Merrick (Donald Sutherland), tells her of her "birthright" and initiates her into the art of vampire slaying. Buffy resists her calling at first, but as the vampires invade the student prom, she displays her mythical powers and slays the Evil Ones.

The film sets up the Buffy mythology and displays its blend of humor, horror, and social satire, but the TV series that appeared on the fledgling Warner Bros. WB channel in 1997 went much further in developing a complex mythology, set of characters, and plot lines that generated a genuine pop culture sensation. The WB channel was looking for programming that would appeal to a youth market and was willing to gamble on more offbeat and idiosyncratic programming that would give the fledgling network buzz, publicity, and ratings in the competitive world of network television.[5] Although *BtVS* was never a major ratings hit, as was *The X-Files* for some years, it picked up enough viewers so that a new, smaller network like the WB would be inclined to promote and renew it.

Joss Whedon called his company Mutant Enemy, and the corporate logo that appeared at the end of the show featured a squiggly animated character tearing across the screen and screeching Grrrr . . . Arrgh![6] The logo codes the series as subversive and offbeat, and the show, at its best, has dissident and oppositional features, although, as I will show, it also reproduces dominant ideology and has flaws and blemishes.

On the series mythology level, *BtVS* creates stories about vampires and the vampire slayer, monsters, various forms of evil, and their defeat; the mythology follows story arcs, as does the realist narrative level of the series. From our retrospective position at the end of the series, we can see that the first three seasons dealt with high school and introduced the mythology; Season Four dealt with college life; and Seasons Five through Seven dealt with work, college and postcollege life, and initiation into adulthood.

The two-part premiere, "Welcome to the Hellmouth" and "The Harvest," introduces viewers to Buffy and her friends, who are positioned as outsiders and nonconformists who bond together in a close community. The episodes unfold the mythology of the Hellmouth and introduce an aging vampire demon, the Master, who opens the Hellmouth to an invasion of demons, threatening the apocalyptic destruction of the community.

Season One put on display a series of salient fears of contemporary youth and won a devoted audience by providing characters, situations, and narratives that embodied contemporary worries and anxieties.[7] It is remarkable that the series resists the assaults on youth and demonization of the young that is a major theme of many films, media representations, academic studies, and political discourse.[8] Instead, *BtVS* presents images of youth who are intelligent, resourceful, virtuous, and able to choose between good and evil and positively transform themselves, while also dealing with their anxieties and grappling with the problems of everyday life.

In Season One, Episode Three ("Witch") deals with the fears of an overbearing and manipulative mother wreaking havoc on her daughter. Episode Four ("Teacher's Pet") shows Xander falling in love with a beautiful substitute teacher who is actually a She-Mantis, displaying fears of being overpowered by a seductive and destructive sexuality. Several episodes deal with fears of dating (1005, "Never Kill a Boy on the First Date"), and Episode Seven introduces the mysterious Angel, with whom Buffy falls in love and who reveals himself to be a vampire, exhibiting the fear of falling for someone bizarre and potentially destructive.

"The Pack" (1006) portrays fears of group conformity leading to teen brutality and violence, while Episodes Nine ("The Puppet Show") and Eleven ("Out of Sight, Out of Mind") portray alienated teens turning viciously on their schoolmates, as had happened in the Columbine shooting and other well-publicized episodes of high school violence. Episode Eight ("I Robot . . . You Jane") exhibits fears of computers and the Internet while ultimately valorizing the technology as a powerful instrument for research and knowledge.[9] Episode Ten ("Nightmares") exhibits fears of one's worst anxieties materializing, while Episode Twelve

("Prophecy Girl") unleashes a coterie of monsters wreaking havoc in the community, articulating fears of uncontrolled gang violence.

I'll return to some of the specific mythologies of the series, but I want to argue that *BtVS* also has an *allegorical level* that makes it more interesting than just a self-contained vampire-slayer narrative and mythology or conventional story of growing up in the contemporary United States. The allegorical level builds on the previous levels I've mentioned and has its own complexities.

In general, a complex and multidimensional allegory like *BtVS* has a theological and religious dimension that copes with life and death; sin, guilt, and redemption; the choice between good and evil; and how to understand and deal with life and an afterlife.[10] There are also moral and philosophical allegories that present ethical lessons, ranging from children's stories to philosophical treatises like those of Kant, Hegel, and Marx, which convey specific ethical or social and political ideals or lessons, as when the Brothers Grimm terrify their young audiences into accepting conservative German values or the Disney factory indoctrinates its audiences into proper white middle-class American small-town morality. More sublime philosophical allegories would include Kant's presenting the Enlightenment as a mode of emancipation and social progress, or Marx positing the proletariat and socialism as solutions to the damnation and evils of capitalism and modernity. As critics ranging from Georg Lukacs to Fredric Jameson tell us, literature can also be read as allegory about life in specific milieus in particular historical periods that conveys concrete sociohistorical truths. And finally, popular culture can be allegorical in a sociopolitical mode; it can tell stories about contemporary life in a symbolic and narrative structure, providing specific life lessons as well as commentary and critique of contemporary life and specific events, institutions, and types of people.

Although popular culture allegory can provide a vehicle for ideology, reproducing the values and prejudices of the dominant class, race, and gender, it can also resist and subvert the dominant ideology, valorizing outsiders and resistance to hegemonic norms, and can present alternative ways of relating, living, and being, as I'll argue in the succeeding analysis. Thus, reading complex texts like *BtVS* involves both critique of its ideologies and politics of representation as well as presentation of its critical and subversive moments.

I might note here that I got this notion of the use of the category of allegory for interpreting media culture from Jameson's work, including the article "Class and Allegory in Contemporary Mass Culture: *Dog Day Afternoon* as a Political Film" (2000 [1977]), which presents the 1970s film as an allegory about class, sexuality, the media, the police, the city, and other central aspects of contemporary American life. Unlike social realism, allegory uses symbolic representation to comment on, interpret, and provide a vision of a historical moment without the pretenses of realism that portend a direct representation of reality. Allegory has multiple dimensions of meaning and there is no claim to capture the real in a clear and straightforward way, although allegory may better capture, Jameson suggests, the complexities and ambiguities of a contemporary situation than realism.

Applying this model of allegory, I wrote an article in 1983, "Fear and Trembling in the Age of Reagan: Notes on *Poltergeist*," in which I argued that the *Poltergeist* films, as well as *The Amityville Horror* and other horror/fantasy films of the era, depicted fears of losing one's home, economic downward mobility, the family falling apart, and other fears of the era. These truly horrifying problems were too distressing and traumatizing for a realist aesthetic depiction, but horror and fantasy could represent the themes in ways that allowed audiences to deal with them. Horror and fantasy films could also allegorize themes such as the corruption of capitalism or opposition to patriarchy more accessibly and less threateningly than more realist films.

BtVS can be read the same way as an allegory about contemporary life, with its monsters as metaphors for societal difference and threats, and Buffy and her friends' special powers can be read as metaphors for how knowledge, skill, and courage can help solve problems and dispatch evil. Classically, monsters like vampires symbolize predatory sexuality; werewolves connote bodily energies and forces exploding out of control; witches signify traditional female powers, including sexuality, which threaten the rational patriarchal order; while a wide range of demons signify various sorts of deviance and threats to contemporary order and security. In the current situation, for instance, many of the demons on

BtVS point to the dangers of drug addiction, and the gangs of monsters signify the dangers of gang violence. Obviously, many of the monsters are figures for alienated teens who strike out at their classmates with violence and often murder.

The vampire as addict was clearly depicted in the figures of Spike (James Marsters) and Drusilla (Juliet Landau) in the second season. In the episodes introducing her, Drusilla appeared zoned out on hard drugs like heroin, and the show's creators contend that the duo was modeled on the characters from *Sid and Nancy*, a popular film of the era based on the lives of Sid Vicious, the heroin-addicted punk rocker with the Sex Pistols, and his girlfriend, Nancy. Spike and Drusilla's need for blood is a clear metaphor for drug addiction, and their sexual nihilism and ambiguous ménage à trois with the vampire Angel suggest sexual degradation associated with addiction and amorality.

As Gregory Erikson suggests (2002), vampires have a historical specificity as well as more universal connotations. Early vampires in European folklore were peasants who emerged from the grave to avenge grievances, while by the time of Bram Stoker's novel *Dracula*, it was aristocrats who embodied vampiric evil and would require elaborate rituals to destroy. The representation of vampires in German expressionist horror films of the 1920s like *Nosferatu* was disturbingly similar to the representation of Jews, such as in the anti-Semitic *Jude Suss*. In contemporary U.S. culture, vampires have been largely represented as anarchic individuals, who can emerge from any class, age, or social grouping.

The allegory of *BtVS* is that all of these teen monstrosities create a conflictual and dangerous situation for youth today that must be dealt with skillfully and successfully to defeat the evils of the contemporary era. Buffy's method of dispatching vampires is literally "dusting" the creatures with a stake or sharp weapon, turning them into dust and avoiding the blood-squirting associated with more traditional vampire-slaying. The series provides positive characters and models who embody a creative otherness and difference and are able to overcome and destroy the more monstrous threats to community and security.

The term "allegorical" is in some ways honorific and suggests that *Buffy* is more than both a realist narrative about teen angst and growing up and a vampire slayer mythology that constructs its own world and system of meanings. Although it does both of these things, I would argue that the series is interesting and important because it also produces an allegorical system of meaning that connects it with traditional religion, philosophy, mythology, literature, and popular culture. Allegory, more than metaphor, points to a complex structure and polysemic depth of meaning in an artifact that demands levels of interpretation. It is allegory, then, that provides the structure and levels of meaning for the series as a whole, as well as holding together the various story arcs and narrative sequences. Yet the allegory of *BtVS* does not produce a seamless whole or convey a unified system of messages, as does Christian allegory; rather, it provides a more fragmented and contradictory postmodern set of meanings.

The characters and plot situations of *BtVS* are highly unstable and transformative, as seemingly bad characters show themselves to be good, good characters turn bad, and many flip from good to bad in a specific episode and thus display themselves to be highly ambiguous and mutable. Hence, while traditional allegory had stable and fixed meanings and provided a consistent and unified allegorical tale and system—concerning the Christian salvation narrative in Dante or Milton, for example—the postmodern allegory of *BtVS* is highly fragmented, insecure, complex, and subject to constant change and transformation. The characters of the series thus exhibit flexible and transformative postmodern selves valorized in some contemporary postmodern theory as opposed to the fixed, unified, and stable selves valorized in some forms of traditional culture.

Hence, the concept of allegory calls attention to what *BtVS* does as a series and how it relates to the whole world of culture and contemporary society. In conclusion, I want to note that *Buffy*, like all popular artifacts, has progressive and regressive ideological features. I have stressed here the subversive and critical aspects of the *Buffy* allegory, although it also has more conservative elements. As Susan Douglas notes (2010), while Buffy represents an icon of empowered young women, she also embodies a classical ideal of beauty as blond, thin, attractive, well-dressed, and traditionally feminine, with her warrior persona a rupture with the "normal" teenage girl Buffy. In addition, it is unfortunate that quasi-feminist representations of empowered women had to take the woman warrior persona that legitimates militarism and uses violence to solve social problems. Yet compared to the regressive representations of women presented in the *Twilight* novels and films, Buffy was a subversive figure within the mainstream of media culture.

TWILIGHT'S DELIRIOUS VAMPIRE LOVE

While Buffy fell prey to dangerous vampire love in her relations with Angel and Spike, she was generally the central character and center of multiple romances and adventure. *Twilight*, by contrast, positions the central female character as subordinate to her one true love in a highly romantic scenario of male-dominated extreme passion and love.

Twilight emerged as a cultural phenomenon perhaps even transcending the *Buffy* cult and craze of its era.[11] Stephenie Meyer's novels sold millions of copies, multiplying significantly with the release of the initial films based on her stories, and gave rise to a cult following that became intense and much discussed in the media with the 2008 release of the *Twilight* film.

The initial film in the *Twilight* saga was directed by former production design creator Catherine Hardwicke. Her debut film, *Thirteen* (2003), which interrogates the lives of Southern California girls as they enter the perilous teen years, was itself a media sensation that has become a cult classic. Hardwicke's second film, *Lords of Dogtown* (2005), explores the milieu of 1970s skateboarding subculture along the Santa Monica and Venice Beach piers, where a popular form of the highly complex and athletic art of urban skateboarding was born. In a highly unpredictable turn, Hardwicke took a biblical excursion into *The Nativity Story* (2007), where she immersed herself in reverential Christianity in a pious retelling of the birth of Jesus, before taking on the challenges of vampires in *Twilight*. Not surprisingly, the film focuses on the human lives, frailties, and adventures of Mary and Joseph, although three wisecracking Magi who venture to Bethlehem for Jesus' birth are thrown in for comic relief.

Hardwicke's *Twilight* continues her exploration of teen culture as she moves from Southern Californian and Middle Eastern teen adventures to a vampire story in the Pacific Northwest. The film, however, focuses more on teen romance than vampire mythology, from which she departs in significant ways. *Twilight* presents a faithful version of Meyer's best-selling novel to promote male-centered romance and a puritanical (actually Mormon) attitude toward sexuality.[12] The story centers on a teenage girl, Isabella Swan (Kristen Stewart), who comes to live in a small Northwestern town with her divorced father, who is sheriff, after her mother in Arizona takes up with a minor-league baseball player, who wants the mother to travel with him.

Bella's mother is shown as confused and passive, and her father exhibits little affection for or interest in Bella, leading her to say, "One of the best things about Charlie is that he doesn't hover." The students at school are equally unappealing to the romantic Bella, although one of the guys shows interest in her. All of this changes when she first views the glamorous Cullen family and especially the brooding and handsome Edward, whom she sits next to in biology class. Bella learns that the Cullens are vampires but of a breed unto themselves, not eating human flesh but animals.

The film's ideological scenario is contradictory: On one hand, *Twilight* valorizes difference and mocks conformity and bourgeois life. The young heroine Bella does not want to be like her family or fit in with the conformist teen subcultures she encounters; she wants something different and better, and as it turns out, vampire hunk Edward Cullen (Robert Pattinson) offers her that "something more." The film thus embodies a romantic female fantasy of finding someone completely different who can transport you to the highest possibilities of romantic love. Here, however, *Twilight* takes a conservative turn, as Edward renounces both biting Bella and making her one of his own and taking her virginity away. Hence, the film embodies a very conservative fantasy in which men are the gatekeepers of morality and purity and women are subordinate. Throughout, Edward has to intervene and protect Bella from a possible car accident; assault by thuggish young men in an alley; and threats to Bella from a "bad" vampire clan, which puts both Edward and his family in a male protector role, another highly conservative patriarchal fantasy. Likewise, Edward must protect Bella from her own budding sexual passions, playing the role as sexual regulator and embodiment of control, as well as the overpowering object of female desire.

Like *Buffy*, *Twilight* divides vampires into "good" and "bad," with the aristocratic Cullen family representing the cultured and tightly knit family unit standing in for good family values, while the trailer-trash vampires who threaten Bella represent delinquent and dangerous underclass youth out of control. The Cullens are upper class, with highly cultivated aesthetic tastes, and they exhibit the benefits of wealth and education; they also valorize whiteness as an aesthetic ideal with their skin pallor and white clothes and brightly lit, sun-drenched modernist house (in the *Twilight* version, aristocratic vampires do not fear the sun). Indeed, characters of color tend to be the "bad" figures in a thoroughly racist iconography, just as the film is classist in its depiction of a good middle-class and upper-class life, opposed to the underclass ruffians and predatory vampires who threaten Bella, as if the working class and people of color are a threat to the white middle and upper class.

Both Bella and her mother are portrayed as weak and vacillating women who need to be protected by men. Indeed, the story is as much a romance in the Harlequin novel genre,[13] as the vampire tale provides a delirious romantic fantasy of dangerous romantic love and a tale of star-crossed lovers in an impossible situation. Edward is a very Edwardian romantic figure, and Pattinson became a major teen heartthrob as the film quickly attracted a large cult following. While vampires have traditionally and recently served as metaphors of extreme sexual attraction and threat, representing really dangerous sex, the *Twilight* saga, by contrast, appropriates vampire figures to push sexual abstinence.

This conservative appropriation of vampire mythology can be contrasted with the HBO TV series *True Blood*, which premiered in 2008 and concluded its third season in the fall of 2010. The series presents vampires as not only sexy but highly attractive and sexually active. The central character, Sookie Stackhouse (Anna Paquin), is smitten by the sexy vampire Bill (Stephen Moyer), and *True Blood* features a variety of sexual relations and connections between vampires, werewolves, other creatures, and humans, valorizing sexual diversity in cautionary pro-sex narrative mythologies.

Likewise, the TV series *The Vampire Diaries* (2009–) provides a sharp antithesis within the vampire genre to the *Twilight* films. The two recent TV series portray the ultraerotic themes central to the vampire myth, but also the bizarre, grotesque, and savage elements. Like *Twilight*, *The Vampire Diaries* and *True Blood* distinguish between "good" and "bad" vampires, but unlike the *Twilight* films so far released, the heroines of the TV series have highly sexualized love affairs with the vampires, with *True Blood* in particular celebrating extreme erotic love between vampire and human characters.

Thus, while *Twilight* exploits the extreme romanticism and transcendent side of a hopeless vampire-human love, *True Blood* displays the horrific side of vampirism. Both *True Blood* and the *Twilight* films display an extreme type of romantic love, but whereas the latter enacts abstinence, the former travels to extremes in portraying the connections between the vampire myth and hypereroticism, as well as the perverse and bizarre aspects of vampirism, going totally over the top by combining horror motifs with pornography, tropes, and generic forms avoided like the plague in *Twilight*.

Although *Twilight* centers its narrative attention and energy on Edward, the Cullen family, and Bella's relationships with the vampires, in the sequel, *New Moon* (2009), directed by Chris Weitz, Edward is drained of life and energy, listless, with an absence of affect; he is shown brooding and sullen throughout the film. While Bella is heartbroken that Edward has left her to protect her from the price of vampire love, she takes on some of the energy and depth of Edward, showing a willingness to take risks, to seek thrills, and to gain experience to transcend the limits of the boring teen world and broken family life into which she is thrown.

In this sense, *New Moon* has a quasi-feminist dimension, showing a strong woman seeking experience and gratification, although subsequent films in the series, following the sequence of the novels, focus more centrally on the Edward-Bella relation and the subordination of Bella to Edward's will and fate. Some reviews of *New Moon*, however, were savagely negative, and parts of its fan base obviously wanted to see hot Bella/Edward romance and not a lifeless and brooding vampire who pushes Bella away, although this obviously sets up reconciliation in further episodes of the saga.[14]

In certain ways, *New Moon* is more interesting than *Twilight*, as it deals with Bella's nightmares and cultural monsters like vampires and werewolves, and how they haunt and threaten everyday life, just as out of control sexual drives (vampires) and brutal, animalist aggression (werewolves) threaten normality and social existence. *New Moon* also depicts Bella as having romantic choices (between a werewolf and a vampire!), as her Native American friend Jacob, who has developed into a highly buffed werewolf, pursues Bella's affections—a triangle developed in the third entry of *The Twilight Saga: Eclipse* (2010). Yet Bella seems fated to being a vampire lover, a destiny spelled out in the succeeding novels and forthcoming films in the series.

CONCLUDING COMMENTS

The cycle of vampire literature, films, and TV series shows the continuing fascination in the culture with the experiences and dynamics of extreme sexuality and romance. The vampire is a symbol upon which to project societal fears and fantasies, just as *Buffy the Vampire Slayer* presented a fantasy that violent erotic and aggressive impulses could be tempered and held in control and virtuous teens would counter them and protect societal norms and stability. While the *Twilight* films explore dangerous love more aggressively than previous artifacts of popular culture (it was always a subtext of *Buffy*), they also advocate more conservative models of love and romance and in particular male-dominated love and patriarchal institutions as the societal norms. A critical media/cultural study is challenged to interrogate these figures, to assess the politics of representation and cultural-ideological effects, and to help illuminate what these popular texts tell us about contemporary societal issues and obstacles to a freer, happier, and more egalitarian society.

References

Benjamin, W. (1977). *The Origins of German Tragic Drama*. London: New Left Books.

Best, S. & Kellner, D. (1991). *Postmodern Theory: Critical Interrogations*. London and New York: MacMillan and Guilford.

———. (1997). *The Postmodern Turn*. London and New York: Routledge and Guilford Press.

———. (2001). *The Postmodern Adventure*. London and New York: Routledge and Guilford Press.

———. (2003). Contemporary Youth and the Postmodern Adventure. *The Review of Education/Pedagogy/Cultural Studies*, Vol. 25, Nr. 2. April–June, pp. 75–93.

Douglas, S. J. (2010). *Enlightened Sexism: The Seductive Message That Feminism's Work Is Done*. New York: Times Books.

Erickson, G. Sometimes You Need a Story: American Christianity, Vampires, and *Buffy*. In Lavery & Wilcox, 2002.

Giroux, H. (1996). *Fugitive Cultures: Race, Violence, and Youth*. New York: Routledge.

———. (2000). *Stealing Innocence: Youth, Corporate Power, and the Politics of Culture*. New York: Saint Martin's.

———. (2002). *Breaking in to the Movies*. Hoboken, NJ: Wiley-Blackwell.

———. (2003). *The Abandoned Generation: Democracy Beyond the Culture of Fear*. New York: Palgrave Macmillan.

Jameson, F. (2000 [1977]). Class and Allegory in Mass Culture: *Dog Day Afternoon* as a Political Film. In Hardt. M. & Weeks, K. (Eds.), *The Jameson Reader*. London and Malden, Massachusetts: Blackwell.

Kellner, D. (1983). Fear and Trembling in the Age of Reagan: Notes on *Poltergeist*. *Socialist Review*, No. 54, pp. 121–134.

———. (1984). *Herbert Marcuse and the Crisis of Marxism*. Berkeley and London: University of California Press (USA) and Macmillan Press (England).

———. (1995). *Media Culture*. London and New York: Routledge.

———. (2000). New Technologies/New Literacies: Reconstructing Education for the New Millennium. *Teaching Education*, Vol. 11, No. 3, pp. 245–265.

———. (2003). *Media Spectacle*. New York: Routledge.

———. (2010). *Cinema Wars: Hollywood Film and Politics in the Bush/Cheney Era*. Malden, Massachusetts, and UK: Blackwell.

Kellner, D. & Ryan, M. (1988). *Camera Politica: The Politics and Ideology of Contemporary Hollywood Film*. Bloomington, Indiana: Indiana University Press.

Lavery, D. (2002). Emotional Resonance and Rocket Launchers: Joss Whedon's Commentaries on the *Buffy the Vampire Slayer* DVDs. *Slayage* Six, November. http://www.slayage.tv/.

Lavery, D. & Wilcox, R. (Eds.) (2002). *Fighting the Forces: What's at Stake in Buffy the Vampire Slayer*. Lanham, Maryland: Rowman and Littlefield.

Males, M. (1996). *The Scapegoat Generation*. Boston: Common Courage Press.

Marcuse, H. (1978 [1922]). *Der deutsche Kunstlerroman*, in *Schriften* 1. Frankfurt: Suhrkamp.

Radaway, J. (1991). *Reading the Romance: Women, Patriarchy, and Popular Literature*. Chapel Hill, North Carolina: University of North Carolina Press.

Turnball, S. & Stranieri, V. (2003). *Bite Me*. Victoria, Australia: The Australian Centre for the Moving Images.

Wilcox, R. V. (2002). "Who Died and Made Her the Boss?" Patterns of Mortality in *Buffy the Vampire Slayer*. In Lavery & Wilcox, 2002.

Chapter 3

IS DISNEY GOOD FOR YOUR KIDS?
HOW CORPORATE MEDIA SHAPE
YOUTH IDENTITY IN THE DIGITAL AGE

Henry A. Giroux and Grace Pollock

WHILE THE "EMPIRE OF CONSUMPTION" has been around for a long time (Cohen, 2003), American society in the past thirty years has undergone a sea change in the daily lives of children—one marked by a major transition from a culture of innocence and social protection, however imperfect, to a culture of commodification. Youth are now assaulted by a never-ending proliferation of marketing strategies that colonize their consciousness and daily lives. Under the tutelage of the Walt Disney Company and other megacorporations, children have become an audience captive not only to traditional forms of media such as film, television, and print, but even more so to the new digital media made readily accessible through mobile phones, PDAs, laptop computers, and the Internet. The information, entertainment, and cultural pedagogy disseminated by massive multimedia corporations have become central in shaping and influencing every waking moment of children's daily lives—all toward a lifetime of constant, unthinking consumption. Consumer culture in the United States, and increasingly across the globe, does more than undermine the ideals of a secure and happy childhood: It exhibits the bad faith of a society in which, for children, "there can be only one kind of value, market value; one kind of success, profit; one kind of existence, commodities; and one kind of social relationship, markets" (Grossberg, 2005). But corporate-controlled culture not only exploits and distorts the hopes and desires of individuals: It is fundamentally driven toward exploiting public goods for private gain, if it does not also more boldly seek to privatize everything in the public realm. Among U.S. multimedia megacorporations, Disney appears to be one of the least daunted in attempting to dominate public discourse and undermine the critical and political capacities necessary for the next generation of young people to sustain even the most basic institutions of democracy.

The impact of new electronic technologies as teaching machines can be seen in some rather astounding statistics. It is estimated that the average American spends more than six hours a day watching video-based entertainment, and by 2013 the numbers of daily hours spent watching television and videos will match the numbers of hours spent sleeping.[1] The American Medical Association reports that the combined hours "spent in front of a television or video screen is the single biggest chunk of time in the waking life of an American child" (cited in Hazen and Winokur, 1997). Such statistics warrant grave concern, given that the messages provided through such programming are shaped largely by a $263 billion a year U.S. advertising industry (Bryce, 2005), which sells not only its products but also values, images, and identities largely aimed at teaching young people to be consumers.

A virtual army of marketers, psychologists, and corporate executives are currently engaged in what Susan Linn (2004) calls a "hostile takeover of childhood," seeking in the new media environment to take advantage of the growing economic power wielded by children and teens. Figures on direct spending by young people have dramatically increased in the past ten years, to the point where it is now estimated that each year preteens and teenagers marshal $200 billion in spending power (Molnar and Boninger, 2007). And this is not all. Young people also exert a powerful influence on parental spending, offering up a market in which, according to Anap Shah (2008), "Children (under 12) and teens influence parental purchases totaling over . . . $670 billion a year." Because of their value as consumers and their ability to influence spending, young people have become major targets of an advertising and marketing industry that spends more than $17 billion a year on shaping children's identities and desires (Golin, 2007).

Exposed to a marketing machinery eager and ready to transform them into full-fledged members of consumer society, children are conscripted by a commercial world defined by the Walt Disney Company and a few other corporations, and the amount of time spent in this world is as breathtaking as it is disturbing. Children typically see about "40,000 ads a year on TV alone," and by the time they enter the fourth grade, they will have "memorized 300–400 brands" (Rideout, Roberts, and Foehr, 2005). In 2005, the Kaiser Family Foundation reported that young people are "exposed to the equivalent of 8½ hours a day of media content . . . [and that] the typical 8- to 18-year-old lives in a home with an average of 3.6 CD or tape players, 3.5 TVs, 3.3 radios, 2.9 VCRs/DVD players, 2.1 video game consoles, and 1.5 computers" (Rideout et al., 2005). There was a time when a family traveling in a car might entertain itself by singing or playing games. Now, however, many kids have their own laptops or cellphones, and many family vehicles come equipped with DVD players. Family members need not look to one another or the outside world for entertainment when a constant stream of media sources is at their fingertips.

Today's kids have more money to spend and more electronic toys to play with, but increasingly they are left on their own to navigate the virtual and visual worlds created by U.S. media corporations. In what has become the most "consumer-oriented society in the world," Juliet Schor (2004) observes, kids and teens have taken center stage as "the epicenter of American consumer culture." The tragic result is that youth now inhabit a cultural landscape in which they can increasingly recognize themselves only in terms preferred by the market. Multibillion-dollar media corporations, with a commanding role over commodity markets as well as support from the highest reaches of government, have become the primary educational and cultural force in shaping, if not hijacking, how youth define their interests, values, and relations to others.

Given its powerful role among media-driven modes of communication, the Walt Disney Company exercises a highly disproportionate concentration of control over the means of producing, circulating, and exchanging information, especially to kids. Once a company that catered primarily to a three- to eight-year-old crowd with its animated films, theme parks, and television shows, Disney in the new millennium has been at the forefront of the multimedia conglomerates now aggressively marketing products for infants, toddlers, and tweens (kids ages eight to twelve).[2] Websites, video games, computer-generated animation, Disney TV, and pop music—developed around franchises like *High School Musical, Hannah Montana*, and the Jonas Brothers, and accessible online with the touch of a button—are now sustaining Disney fans into their teenage and young adult years. Allied with multimedia giant Apple, Inc. (Apple CEO Steve Jobs is the single largest shareholder in Disney) and the cutting-edge animation studio Pixar, Disney is beyond doubt a powerful example of the new corporate media at the beginning of the twenty-first century.

Disney not only represents "one of the best-known symbols of capitalist consumerism" (Lyne, 2004) but also claims to offer consumers a stable, known quantity in its brand-name products. Understanding Disney's cultural role is neither a simple nor a trivial task. Like many other megacorporations, it focuses on popular culture and continually expands its products and services to reach every available media platform. What is unique about Disney, however, is its titanium-clad brand image—synonymous with a notion of childhood innocence and wholesome entertainment—that manages to deflect, if not completely trounce, criticism at every turn. As an icon of American culture and middle-class family values, Disney actively appeals to both conscientious parents and youthful fantasies as it works hard to transform every child into a lifetime consumer of Disney products and ideas. Put the corporation under scrutiny, however, and a contradiction quickly appears between a Disney culture that presents itself as the paragon of virtue and childlike innocence and the reality of the company's cutthroat commercial ethos.

Disney, like many corporations, trades in sound bites; the result is that the choices, exclusions, and values that inform its narratives about joy, pleasure, living, and survival in a global world are often difficult to discern. Disney needs to be addressed within a widening circle of awareness, so we can place the history, meaning, and influence of the Disney empire outside its own narrow interpretive frameworks, which often shut down critical assessments of how Disney is actually engaged in the commercial carpet-bombing of children and teens. Understanding Disney in 2010 requires that we draw attention to the too-often hidden or forgotten corporate dimension surrounding the production, distribution, and consumption of Disney culture and, in so doing, equip parents, youth, educators, and others with tools that will enable them to critically mediate the ways they encounter Disney. In 1999, Disney was a $22 billion profit-making machine (Giroux, 1999). Ten years later, Disney is generating more than $37.8 billion per year and quickly expanding the market for its products in countries such as China, where the latest Disney theme park—Hong Kong Disneyland—opened in 2005, and another park is slated for development in Shanghai (Iger, 2008). Now a worldwide distributor of a particular kind of cultural politics, Disney is a teaching machine that not only exerts influence over young people in the United States but also wages an aggressive campaign to peddle its political and cultural influence overseas. As global capital spreads its influence virtually unchecked by national governments and the international community, citizenship becomes increasingly privatized, and youth are educated to become consuming subjects rather than civic-minded and critical citizens. If today's young people are to look ahead to a more rather than less democratic future, people everywhere must develop a critical language in which notions of the public good, public issues, and public life become central to overcoming the privatizing and depoliticizing language of the market.

DISNEY'S MARKETING JUGGERNAUT

One measure of the corporate assault on kids can be seen in the reach, acceleration, and effectiveness of Disney's marketing and advertising efforts to turn kids into consumers and childhood into a salable commodity. Every child, regardless of how young, is now a potential consumer ripe for being commodified and immersed in a commercial culture defined by brands. The Walt Disney Company spares little expense in generating a coherent brand image and encapsulating its many products and services within the seductive symbolism of childhood innocence and wholesome family fun. The company's approach makes Disney a particularly useful case for understanding corporate strategies directed at youth in the new media environment. At the same time as Disney represents nostalgia and tradition, it has become a global leader in transforming digital technologies into profit-making platforms and developing a consumer-centered discourse that softens and deflects criticism away from what can only be called boldly commercial self-promotion. Disney, with its legion of media holdings, armies of marketers, and omnipresent advertisers, sets out not just to exploit children and youth for profit; it actually constructs them as commodities while promoting the very concept of childhood as a salable commodity. Childhood ideals increasingly give way to a market-driven politics in which young people are prepared for a life of objectification that will simultaneously drain them of any viable sense of moral and political agency. This is especially true in the current consumer society, in which children more than ever mediate their identities and relations to others through the consumption of goods and images. No longer imagined within the language of responsibility and justice, childhood begins with what might be called the scandalous philosophy of money—that is, a corporate logic in which everything, including the worth of young people, is measured through the potentially barbaric calculations of finance, exchange value, and profitability.

Disney, perhaps more than any other corporation, has created a marketing powerhouse that uses the pivotal educational force of children's culture in combination with new digital media technologies. Kids can download enormous amounts of media in seconds and carry around such information, images, and videos in a device the size of a thin cigarette lighter. Moreover, media technologies "are morphing and merging, forming an ever-expanding presence throughout our daily environment" (Rideout et al., 2005). Mobile phones alone have grown "to include video game platforms, e-mail devices, digital cameras, and Internet connections," making it easier for marketers and advertisers to reach young people (Rideout et al., 2005). Kids of all ages find themselves in what the Berkeley Media Studies Group and the Center for Digital Democracy call "a new 'marketing ecosystem' that encompasses cell phones, mobile music devices, broadband video, instant messaging, video games, and virtual three-dimensional worlds," all of which provide the knowledge and information that young people use to navigate their place in families, schools, and communities (Chester and Montgomery, 2007). Disney, along with its researchers, marketing departments, and purveyors of commerce, largely defines and controls this massive virtual entertainment complex, spending vast amounts of time trying to understand the needs, desires, tastes, preferences, social relations, and networks that characterize youth as a potential market.

The disconnect between market values and the ethical responsibility to care for children is on full display in Disney's almost boastful use of research to mine the inner lives and experiences of young children. That Disney's insidious strategies receive front-page coverage in the *New York Times* and are presented without so much as a critical comment is a testament to how commercial values have numbed the public's ability to recognize the danger such values often present to children. According to the *New York Times*, Disney is at the forefront of finding ways to capitalize on the $50 billion spent worldwide by young boys between the ages of six and fourteen (Barnes, 2009a). As part of such an effort, Disney seeks the advice of educators, anthropologists, and even a research consultant with "a background in the casino industry" not only to study all aspects of the culture and intimate lives of young boys, but to do so in a way that allows Disney to produce "emotional hooks" that lure young boys into the wonderful world of corporate Disney in order to turn them into enthusiastic consumers (Barnes, 2009a). Disney's recent attempts to "figure out the boys' entertainment market" enlisted the services of Kelly Pena, described as "the kid whisperer," who attempts to uncover what makes young boys tick by using her anthropological skills to convince young boys and their parents to allow her to look into the kids' closets, go shopping with them, and pay them $75 to be interviewed. Ms. Pena, with no irony intended, prides herself on the fact that "Children . . . open up to her" (Barnes, 2009a). Given Disney's desire to expand into boys' culture, the company's announcement in 2009 that it had purchased Marvel Entertainment came as no surprise. Marvel's comic book empire owns the licenses to approximately 5,000 superhero characters. The *Wall Street Journal* remarked that by "bringing in macho types such as Iron Man, Thor, and Captain America, the Marvel deal would expand Disney's audience, adding properties that appeal to boys from their preteen years into young adulthood" (Smith and Schuker, 2009).

It is even more disturbing that Disney and a growing number of marketers and advertisers now work with child psychologists and other experts who study young people in order to better understand children's culture so as to develop marketing methods that are more camouflaged, seductive, and successful. Disney claims this kind of intensive research pays off in lucrative dividends and reinforces the Disney motto that in order to be a successful company, "You have to start with the kids themselves" (Barnes, 2009a). Several psychologists, especially Allen D. Kanner, have publicly criticized such disingenuous practices.[3] Disney's recent attempt to corner the young male market through the use of sophisticated research models, ethnographic tools, and the expertise of academics indicates the degree to which the language of the market has disengaged itself from moral considerations and the social good. It is clear that Disney's only goal is to win over the hearts and minds of young people so as to deliver them to the market as both loyal consumers and commodities. In such unscrupulous strategies, the contradiction becomes visible between Disney's public relations image as a purveyor of wholesome entertainment and the hidden reality of Disney as a political and economic power that promotes ideology conducive to its own corporate interests, thereby impoverishing the imaginative possibilities of youth and dismantling the public foundations for a thriving civic culture.

CHILDHOOD, INC.

Corporate culture is rewriting the nature of children's culture, a trend that becomes visible in the various ways traditional boundaries once maintained between the spheres of formal education and entertainment are collapsed. According to Lawrence Grossberg, children are introduced to the world of logos, advertising, and the "mattering maps" of consumerism long before they can speak: "Capitalism targets kids as soon as they are old enough to watch commercials, even though they may not be old enough to distinguish programming from commercials or to recognize the effects of branding and product placement" (Grossberg, 2005). In fact, researchers have found that while children as young as three years old recognize brand logos, not until they are around eight years old do they understand advertising's intention to manipulate their desires (Fischer et al., 1991).[4] But this has not stopped corporations from exposing kids from birth to adulthood to a consumer blitz of advertising, marketing, education, and entertainment that has no historical precedent. There is now even a market for videos for toddlers and infants as young as three months old. Not surprisingly, this is part of a growing $4.8 billion market aimed at the youngest children—an area of multimedia culture into which Disney recently expanded (Molnar and Boninger, 2007).

In 2000, Disney purchased the Baby Einstein Company from its founder, Julie Aigner-Clark, who had created a line of products and toys known to mesmerize these youngest television watchers by displaying, for example, vibrant moving objects while playing a soundtrack of classical music selections. The marketing of the products suggests that parents can purchase toys and videos that will not only enable their children to develop good taste in music but also make them capable of great intellectual achievements. (Disney/Pixar's 2004 film *The Incredibles* plugs the Baby Einstein franchise shamelessly when one character exclaims, "Mozart makes babies smarter.") Despite objections to the marketing of baby videos as educational media by organizations such as the Campaign for a Commercial-Free Childhood, Disney persists in using clever packaging for the videos that implies they are, at best, beneficial learning tools to be used in a child's most formative years and, at worst, harmless distractions for infant audiences. And the marketing strategy works. A 2007 survey by the Kaiser Family Foundation found that 48 percent of parents believe that baby videos have "a positive effect on early childhood development" (Rideout, 2007). The news that baby DVDs and videos actually impair infants' cognitive development broke in 2007, when researchers at the University of Washington published a study in the prestigious *Journal of Pediatrics* that concluded infants eight to sixteen months old who were exposed to one hour of viewing baby DVDs and videos per day displayed slower language development: Those children understood on average six to eight fewer words for every hour of viewing than infants who did not watch the videos (Schwarz, 2007). Reading to a child once a day, by contrast, produced an observable increase in vocabulary (Zimmerman, Christakis, and Meltzoff, 2007).

How did Disney respond to the researchers' findings? President and CEO Robert Iger demanded that the University of Washington immediately retract its statements on the grounds that the study's assessment methodology was faulty and the publication of the results was "misleading, irresponsible, and derogatory."[5] Disney's main objection was that the study did not differentiate between brands when it tested the effects of baby videos on language development. Mark Emmert, president of the University of Washington, refused to comply with Iger's demand for a retraction and instead articulated the need for more "research aimed at helping parents and society enhance the lives of children."[6] While this research was clearly not enough to deter Disney from marketing its Baby Einstein wares as beneficial for babies and toddlers, other researchers have found that one of the greatest costs associated with surrounding very young children with screen media is a reduction in the time they spend engaging in creative, unstructured play. In a 2007 report, the American Academy of Pediatrics lamented that "time for free play has been markedly reduced for some children" (Ginsburg, 2007).[7] Yet Disney continues to foster the idea that parents should not only accept the ubiquitous presence of screen culture in their babies' lives but view it as an inevitable fact of life, one pointless to criticize and impossible to change.[8] In an utterly cynical gesture, the Baby Einstein website cites a 2003 finding by the Kaiser Family Foundation that "in a typical day, 68% of all children under two use screen media" (Rideout, Vandewater, and Wartella, 2003). This statistic is not presented as something that should alarm concerned parents and encourage different parenting practices; on the contrary, it becomes simple proof of "the reality of today's parents, families and households" and an indicator of how the American Academy of Pediatrics, which discourages television viewing for children under two years old, is simply stuck in the past.[9]

Disney's marketing tactics utilize the idea that parents who want their kids to keep up in a highly competitive world must supply them with every available product that purports to nurture young minds. In 2007 Disney launched an educational website for parents, DisneyFamily.com, which offers parenting advice "in a manner that is compelling, comprehensive, entertaining and, most importantly, objective." The website taps into the growing parenting industry, claiming to target "the more than 32 million moms that are online in the U.S."[10] Given Disney's attempt to refute work by leading researchers in children's health, it is unclear what the website intends to publish as "articles from experts in the parenting field." But if the so-called expertise is not useful to parents, they can at least download a coupon from the "Family Tool Box."[11] The website also features the "Disney Family Learning Center," developed in collaboration with Sony Electronics and Powered, Inc., an online education provider that also happens to specialize in social marketing. Disney finds ways to promote Sony's and its own products when advising parents on child development, entertainment options, and other "family-relevant information" in its online courses, such as "Traveling Light with Kids and Technology" and "Contact Management for the Busy Mom and Dad."[12]

The Internet's commercial potential is certainly not lost on Disney; as Steve Wadsworth, president of the Walt Disney Internet Group, stated, "There is massive opportunity here" (Barnes, 2007). Harnessing the power of virtual space is a strategy openly championed by Iger, whose stated goal is for the company to establish "clear leadership in the kids and families online virtual worlds space around the globe."[13] Disney views online media as an opportunity not so much to enhance children's lives as to make money for shareholders, enjoy low overhead costs, and keep the company's film and television franchises profitable. The Disney.com site, redesigned in 2007, includes video games, social networking, customized user content, and videos on demand. As of the summer of 2009, approximately 16 million users have designed customized fairy avatars that inhabit Pixie Hollow at DisneyFairies.com.[14] Websites offering cooperative games and social networking to children seem like a relatively innocuous option in a media culture currently exploiting every imaginable angle to populate reality television's competitive worlds of winners and losers. It is far less innocuous, however, that these sites help Disney collect and use personal information to assail consumer groups with targeted, cross-promotional advertising. Web-based social media not only acculturate children to being constantly bombarded with advertising but give them the illusion of control while they are actually being manipulated.

Disney's interest in capturing the attention of very young people through the Internet has also involved the acquisition of Club Penguin, a web-based virtual world, in a $700 million deal in 2007. Club Penguin targets kids ages six to fourteen and provides each user with an animated penguin avatar that interacts in a snow-covered world, chats with other users, and earns virtual money to purchase items such as pets, clothing, and furnishings for an igloo home. Users can play for free but must pay $5.95 per month for access to certain features. As an interactive and "immersive environment," Club Penguin enables Disney to train children in the habits of consumption—merchandise, such as stuffed penguins, is advertised on the site—while making direct contact with its global consumer base through the online network. Similarly, Disney's Pirates of the Caribbean Online, for children under ten, lures kids into a virtual world of consumers that is predicted to include 20 million children by 2011 (Barnes, 2007). As Brooks Barnes (2007) points out in the *New York Times*, these electronic malls are only superficially envisioned by developers as entertainment or educational sites. Their main purpose, he states, is to enable media conglomerates to "deliver quick growth, help keep movie franchises alive, and instill brand loyalty in a generation of new customers."

In order to tap further into the youth market, Disney's recent strategy has involved spending $180 million on video game development. Disney-branded online space includes the Internet's first multiplayer game for kids, Toontown Online. As Sara Grimes (2008) points out, multiplayer online games "construct entire cultural experiences based around beloved characters, fantasy and play [but] entry into these worlds is only possible through a perpetual cycle of consumption." Another video game, Epic Mickey, revamps the character of Mickey Mouse in an alleged effort to make him more appealing to today's generation of youth. The mouse will no longer embody a childlike innocence and generosity but will instead be "cantankerous and cunning" and will exhibit "selfish, destructive behavior" (Barnes, 2009b). With Mickey's popularity in decline in the United States, Disney's market-driven agenda is visible not only in its willingness to transform the hallowed icon upon which its corporate empire was built but also in the very way it has transformed the character. Although Disney representatives suggest that this reimagining of Mickey Mouse merely reflects what is currently popular among young people, it seems more aligned with the current ideology of a ruthless economic Darwinism (also evident in reality TV shows) that has little to do with the needs of children and a great deal to do with a survival-of-the-fittest view of the world perpetuated by market-centered culture. The recent moves by the Walt Disney Company to give edge to the characters it incorporates into its cultural offerings should be seen as less a demystification of the brand image of Disneyfied innocence and more a signal of the company's desire for a growing compatibility between its public pedagogy and a commercial culture's ethos of egocentric narcissism, social aggression, and hypermasculinity.

The issues surrounding Disney culture as a source of identity for young people are complex. Adult existence, according to Zygmunt Bauman (2007), involves "changing one's ego" through "an unending series of self-focused pursuits, each episode lived through as an overture to the next." Whether or not this is a dramatic departure from the way life was lived in the past, it is nevertheless becoming clear that today's youth are also caught up in negotiating shifting identities through processes that involve a constant engagement with educational sites throughout the culture. How much more challenging, then, will young people who are just embarking on the process of identity development find the navigation of a commercialized culture that appears to offer limitless choices in terms of selfhood yet effectively limits the choices that both children and adults can make in extending their sense of personal and collective agency?

One sign of how the Walt Disney Company seeks to intervene in children's lives by shaping their identity narratives was evident in the company's 2009 announcement that it would be redesigning its chain of 340 Disney Stores to mirror a theme park design. Based on the prototype, called Imagination Park, the renovated stores will be entirely networked with interactive technology to create a multisensory recreational experience that encourages consumer participation and emphasizes community through collective activities (Barnes, 2009c). The goal of the refurbishment project, which will cost approximately $1 million per store, "is to make children clamor to visit the stores and stay longer" (Barnes, 2009c). By enabling visitors to generate a narrative for their own consumption, the stores will offer the illusion that kids are the producers of meaning and have the capacity to customize their identities through the stories that are created around Disney products and places. Such power is not necessarily false, and it is undoubtedly seductive in a world of narrowing opportunities for agency and expression—perhaps even more so for children and youth for whom such opportunities are few and for whom the spectacular has not yet lost the appeal of novelty. At the same time, it confines the imagination and any corresponding sense of community to the narratives on offer, which ultimately all lead back to immersing the individual in fun, conflict-free processes of consumption designed to generate corporate profits.

The ease with which Disney's conventional fantasy formula for young adults—recently updated and reissued in films like *High School Musical*—reduces unpleasant and contradictory lived experiences to the "trials and tribulations" of well-off kids who "just want to fit in" and can easily do so by participating in consumer culture, is astounding. Elayne Rapping (1995) observes a similar thematic message in the design of Disney World, which, not unlike the world of the *High School Musical* films, is "uniform in its middle-American, asexual, uninflected sameness," all of which works to embody a "sense of classless luxury and unthreatening sameness . . . a synthetic spirit of democracy" that promises a kind of belonging free from the "stress of competition." The Disney celebrity factory has long been masterful at churning out clean-cut teen idols who symbolize these wholesomely bland American values. Miley Cyrus (a.k.a. Hannah Montana) is one of the latest incarnations of Disney's star-making power. According to a *New York Times* article, for many people, but especially for those "parents unnerved by the spectacle of the Spears family," Miley Cyrus represents a positive role model for "millions of girls still figuring out how they feel about boys" (Sanneh, 2007). Cyrus plays the character Miley Stewart in the Disney TV show *Hannah Montana* alongside her real-life father, country singer Billy Ray Cyrus. The show focuses on the story of a teenage girl who wants to lead a totally normal life at home and school and therefore decides to keep it a secret that she is also the superstar pop singer Hannah Montana. She achieves this goal by changing her clothing and hair color. On the show, then, the lead character, Miley Stewart, has a rock-star alter ego named Hannah Montana, and in real life Disney aggressively markets Miley Cyrus as a pop icon by producing her music CDs and funding concert tours. As one reporter for the *New York Times* commented, Disney's public relations' ingenuity ensures that consumers get "three girls for the price of one" (Sanneh, 2007). It seems that in a world increasingly defined by fragmentation and instability, *Hannah Montana* taps into the fantasy of celebrity, offering young people the lure of agency through an endless reinvention of the self. A tween girl might identify with the family dynamics depicted on the show, but she need not stop there when she can also transform herself among her classmates and achieve the chic look of a rock starlet merely by purchasing Hannah Montana clothing at Walmart. According to the Disney formula, self-expression is once again reduced to what a young person can afford to buy. And Disney is expert at reinforcing such cycles of brand promotion by generating relationships between its media offerings and consumer products. As Mike Budd (2005) explains, the company exhibits "highly developed corporate synergy in which every Disney product is both a commodity and an ad for every other Disney commodity." The comment from the *New York Times* about Miley Cyrus being a good role model for kids should be considered within this context of consumerism and what it teaches young girls in terms of their identities, values, and aspirations. Hannah Montana is not a superhero but merely a superstar whose only responsibility in life is to entertain her fans and make money. Miley Stewart's raison d'être is to deceive the people around her so that she can live her life unencumbered by the social responsibilities attendant on being a well-known public figure. Finally, does not Miley Cyrus, as the real-life embodiment of "three girls for the price of one," represent the most commodified of role models, severely and insidiously proscribing the imaginative possibilities for a generation of young women who are sadly being encouraged to view their bodies as objects, their identities as things to be bought and sold, and their emotional and psychological health as best nurtured through "retail therapy" (shopping)?

Concepts of self and society are undoubtedly shifting as we witness the "growing interpenetration of the economic and the cultural" (Bryman, 2004). Spaces that were once constructed through "forms of public culture," as noted by Sharon Zukin (1995), have now become privatized, controlled, and framed by corporate culture. These spaces, from suburban shopping malls to tourist spots to city centers, encourage leisure while also "priming the young for consumerism" (Bryman, 2004). While colonizing multiple cultural spaces, corporations like Disney are increasingly looking to virtual space in order to provide "enhanced" experiences for a consumer class that wants to maximize its leisure time. Developing virtual online worlds gives Disney, to a greater extent than at any previous point in history, more global corporate control over the "production of subjectivity that is not fixed in identity but hybrid and modulating" (Hardt and Negri, 2000). Paradoxically, though, Disney gains access to children and adults by selling the illusion of fixity. Disney not only represents "one of the best-known symbols of capitalist consumerism" (Lyne,

2004) but also claims to offer consumers a stable, known quantity in its brand-name products. In other words, Disney culture acts as a temporary salve to growing feelings of uncertainty and insecurity produced by economic dislocations and social instability on a national and global scale. It is no small irony that while offering people what Ernst Bloch called the "swindle of fulfillment" promised by rampant consumerism (cited in Rabinach, 1977), multinational corporations such as Disney are one of the globalizing forces largely responsible for the instabilities and upheavals facing contemporary nation-states.

Indeed, the sovereignty of national governments is increasingly challenged by the power of multinational corporations and the logic of the marketplace they embody; governments are downsized and their services are privatized or gutted; corporations receive incentives in the form of huge tax breaks or bailouts with taxpayers' money; legislation is passed that further deregulates the market; and democratically elected governments fail in their responsibilities to foster a just and equal society. Given these conditions, it is no wonder that individuals find comfort in the stable meanings they can ascribe to Disney and turn to consumption for even the semblance of personal agency. Multinational corporations such as Disney have become "the aristocratic articulations" of a global monopoly of power and coercion that is imposed from above and that achieves control through circuits that do not reveal themselves because they operate on the "terrain of the production and regulation of subjectivity" itself (Hardt and Negri, 2000)—that is, in the realm of cultural production and consumption. According to Jeremy Seabrook (1998), capitalism adapts to local cultures and conditions in ways that secure its profit-making power: "The market does not simply obliterate all earlier traditions. It is opportunistic. It will enhance and concentrate on those features of a society which turn a profit or change them in such a way that they will make money." Consequently, everything potentially becomes a commodity, including, and perhaps most especially, identity. Global capitalism manages and controls diversity by commodifying and selling different identity positions, while also encouraging self-commodification—particularly of youth—through various marketing trends and technologies that become increasingly ubiquitous in the lives of the adults, teens, and the very youngest children alike (Chester and Montgomery, 2008).

CONCLUSION

Children are not born with consumer habits. Their identities have to be actively directed to assume the role of consumer. If Disney had its way, kids' culture would become not merely a new market for the accumulation of capital but a petri dish for producing new commodified subjects. As a group, young people are vulnerable to corporate giants such as Disney, which makes every effort to expand inwardly into the psyche and emotional life of the individual in order to utilize human potential in the service of a market society (Rutherford, 2008). Virtually every child is now vulnerable to the many advertisers and entertainment providers who diversify markets through various niches, most recently evident in the use of mobile technologies and online social media. Complicit, wittingly or unwittingly, with a global politics defined by market power, the American public offers little resistance to children's culture being expropriated and colonized by large multimedia conglomerates and Madison Avenue advertisers. Eager to enthrall kids with invented fears and lacks, corporate media culture also entices them with equally unimagined new desires, to prod them into spending money or to influence their parents to spend it in order to fill corporate coffers.

The potential for lucrative profits to be made off the spending habits and economic influence of kids has certainly not been lost on Disney and a number of other multinational corporations, which under the deregulated, privatized, no-holds-barred world of the free market have set out to embed the dynamics of commerce, exchange value, and commercial transactions into every aspect of personal and daily life. Wrapping itself in the discourse of innocence and family-oriented amusement in order to camouflage the mechanisms and deployment of corporate power, Disney uses its various entertainment platforms, which cut across all forms of traditional and new media, in a relentless search for young customers to incessantly bombard with a pedagogy of commerce. In the broader society, as the culture of the market displaces civic culture, children are no longer prioritized as an important social investment or viewed as a central marker for the moral life of the nation. Instead, childhood ideals linked to the protection and well-being of youth are transformed—decoupled from the "call to conscience [and] civic engagement" (Adatto, 2003)—

and redefined through what amounts to a culture of excessive individualism and the numbing of public consciousness.

Rather than participate mindlessly in the Disneyfication of culture, we all need to excavate the excluded memories and silenced voices that could challenge the uncomplicated commodified identities offered to young people by Disney in the name of innocence and entertainment. As one of the most influential corporations in the world, Disney does more than provide entertainment: It also shapes in very powerful ways how young people understand themselves, relate to others, and experience the larger society. It is not difficult to recognize tragedy in the fact that a combination of entrenched social inequality and a lack of resources means that kids disappear literally into foster care institutions; teachers are overwhelmed in overcrowded classrooms; and state services are drained of funds and cannot provide basic food and shelter to growing numbers of kids and their families. Yet corporations such as Disney have ample funds to hire a battalion of highly educated and specialized experts to infiltrate the most intimate spaces of children's and family life—all the better to colonize the fears, aspirations, and futures of young people.

Disney's commodification of childhood is neither innocent nor simply a function of entertainment. The values Disney produces as it attempts to commandeer children's desires and hopes may offer us one of the most important clues about the changing nature of our society and the destructive force behind the unchecked economic power wielded by massive corporations. Strategies for challenging the corporate power and the consumer culture Disney propagates in the United States and increasingly across the rest of the globe must be aligned with a vision of a democracy that is on the side of children and youth. It must enable the conditions for young people to learn and develop as engaged social actors more alive to their responsibility to future generations than those adults who have presently turned away from the challenge.

References

Adatto, K. (2003). Selling Out Childhood. *Hedgehog Review,* 5:2 (Summer), 24–40. www.iasc-culture.org/HHR_Archives/Commodification/5.2DAdatto.pdf.

Barnes, B. (2007). Web Playgrounds of the Very Young. *New York Times,* December 31. www.nytimes.com/2007/12/31/business/31virtual.html.

———. (2009a). Disney Expert Uses Science to Draw Boy Viewers. *New York Times,* April 14. www.nytimes.com/2009/04/14/arts/television/14boys.html.

———. (2009b). After Mickey's Makeover, Less Mr. Nice Guy. *New York Times,* November 5. www.nytimes.com/2009/11/05/business/media/05mickey.html.

———. (2009c). Disney's Retail Plan Is a Theme Park in Its Stores. *New York Times,* October 13. www.nytimes.com/2009/10/13/business/media/13disney .html.

Bauman, Z. (2007). *Liquid Times: Living in an Age of Uncertainty.* London: Polity.

Bryce, R. (2005). Click and Sell. *University of Texas at Austin News*, August 15–22. www.utexas.edu/features/2005/advertising/index.html.

Bryman, A. (2004). *The Disneyization of Society.* London: Sage.

Budd, M. (2005). Introduction: Private Disney, Public Disney. In M. Budd and M. Kirsch (Eds.), *Rethinking Disney: Private Control, Public Dimensions* (pp. 1–33). Middletown, CT: Wesleyan University Press.

Chester, J. & Montgomery, K. (2007). *Interactive Food and Beverage Marketing: Targeting Children in the Digital Age.* Berkeley, CA: Media Studies Group; Washington, DC: Center for Digital Democracy. http://digitalads.org/documents/digi MarketingFull.pdf.

———. (2008). No Escape: Marketing to Kids in the Digital Age. *Multinational Monitor* 30, no. 1 (July/August). www.multinationalmonitor.org/mm2008/072008/ chester.html.

Cohen, L. (2003). *A Consumer's Republic: The Politics of Mass Consumption in Postwar America.* New York: Vintage.

Fischer, P. et al. (1991). Brand Logo Recognition by Children Aged 3 to 6 Years: Mickey Mouse and Old Joe the Camel. *Journal of the American Medical Association* 266, no. 22, 3145–3148.

Ginsburg, K. (2007). The Importance of Play in Promoting Healthy Child Development and Maintaining Strong Parent-Child Bonds. *Pediatrics* 119, no. 1 (January), 182–191. www.commercialfreechildhood.org/pdf/aapplay.pdf.

Giroux, H. (1999). *The Mouse That Roared: Disney and the End of Innocence.* Lanham, MD: Rowman & Littlefield.

Golin, J. (2007). Nation's Strongest School Commercialism Bill Advances Out of Committee. Common Dreams Progressive Newswire, August 1. www.common dreams.org/cgi-bin/newsprint.cgi?file=/news2007/0801–06.htm.

Grimes, S. (2008). Saturday Morning Cartoons Go MMOG. *Media International Australia* 126 (February), 120–31. www.commercialfreechildhood.org/pdf/ satammmog.pdf.

Grossberg, L. (2005). *Caught in the Crossfire: Kids, Politics, and America's Future.* Boulder: Paradigm Publishers.

Hardt, M. & Negri, A. (2000). *Empire.* Cambridge, MA: Harvard University Press.

Hazen, D. & Winokur, J. (Eds.) (1997). *We the Media.* New York: New Press.

Iger, R. (2008). Letter to Shareholders, Part II. *The Walt Disney Company 2008 Annual Report.* Disney Investor Relations. http://corporate.disney.go.com/investors/ annual_reports/2008/introduction/letterToShareholdersII.html.

Linn, S. (2004). *Consuming Kids: The Hostile Takeover of Childhood.* New York: New Press.

Lyne, J. (2004). Hong Kong Disneyland Tops Out Centerpiece Structure. *The Site Selection Online Insider,* October 10. www.siteselection.com/ssinsider/snapshot/sf041014.htm.

Molnar, A. & Boninger, F. (2007). Adrift: Schools in a Total Marketing Environment. *Tenth Annual Report on Schoolhouse Commercialism Trends: 2006–2007.* Tempe: Arizona State University.

Rabinach, A. (1977). Unclaimed Heritage: Ernst Bloch's *Heritage of Our Times* and the Theory of Fascism. *New German Critique* (Spring), 5–15.

Rapping, E. (1995). A Bad Ride at Disney World. *The Progressive* (November). findarticles.com/p/articles/mi_m1295/is_n11_v59/ai_18008842/.

Rideout, V. (2007). *Parents, Children and Media: A Kaiser Family Foundation Survey.* Kaiser Family Foundation, June. www.kff.org/entmedia/upload/7638.pdf.

Rideout, V., Roberts, D. F., & Foehr, U. G. (2005). *Generation M: Media in the Lives of 8–18 Year-Olds.* Washington, DC: Kaiser Family Foundation, March.

Rideout, V., Vandewater, E. A., & Wartella, E. A. (2003). *Zero to Six: Electronic Media in the Lives of Infants, Toddlers and Preschoolers.* Kaiser Family Foundation, Fall. www.kff.org/entmedia/upload/Zero-to-Six-Electronic-Media-in-the-Lives-of -Infants-Toddlers-and-Preschoolers-PDF.pdf.

Rutherford, J. (2008). "The Culture of Capitalism." *Soundings* 38 (Spring), 8–18. www.lwbooks.co.uk/journals/soundings/articles/02 s38 rutherford.pdf.

Sanneh, K. (2007). 3 Girls for the Price of One (If You Could Get a Ticket). *New York Times,* December 31. www.nytimes.com/2007/12/31/arts/music/31hann .html?_r=1&oref=slogin.

Schor, J. B. (2004). *Born to Buy: The Commercialized Child and the New Consumer Culture.* New York: Scribner.

Schwarz, J. (2007). Baby DVDs, Videos May Hinder, Not Help, Infants' Language Development. *University of Washington News,* August 7. http://uwnews.washington .edu/ni/article.asp?articleID=35898.

Seabrook, J. (1998). Racketeers of Illusion. *New Internationalist* 308 (December). www.newint.org/issue308/illusion.htm.

Shah, A. (2008). Children as Consumers. *Global Issues,* January 8. www.global issues.org/TradeRelated/Consumption/Children.asp.

Smith, E. & Schuker, L. A. E. (2009). Disney Nabs Marvel Heroes. *Wall Street Journal,* September 1, A1.

Zimmerman, F. J., Christakis, D. A., & Meltzoff, A. N. (2007). Associations Between Media Viewing and Language Development in Children Under Age 2 Years. *Journal of Pediatrics* 151, no. 4 (October 2007), 364–68.

Zukin, S. (1995). Learning from Disney World. *The Cultures of Cities.* Malden, MA: Blackwell.

Chapter 4

SELLING SUBCULTURE: AN EXAMINATION OF HOT TOPIC

Sarah Hanks

Teenagers, as a targeted market, are increasingly important because of their relative expendable capital. What is consumed with this capital often confers with the taste and identity of the consumer. Youth's participation in taste cultures facilitates socialization "into a knowledge of (and frequently a belief in) the likes and dislikes, meanings and values of the culture" (Thornton, 1996, p. 3) and is reflective of their position in the social system. They become centered on aesthetic judgments, particularly "shared taste in music . . . consumption of common media and, most importantly . . . preference for people with similar tastes" (Thornton, 1996, p. 3). Aesthetic judgments are thereby simultaneously tied to commodities and the identity of the teenage consumer within a larger cultural context.

Historically, music and fashion have been the media by which the play of identity within consumption is approached. "Music is primary, preceding and leading to related subcultural affiliation" (Muggleton, 2000, p. 69). In a youth survey of a small town in England, Simon Frith found music "served as the badge of individuality on which friendship choices could be based . . . music was taken as a symbol of a cluster of values" (Frith, 1981, p. 208). Though the importance of music is emphasized by teenagers, their affiliation with a lifestyle associated with a style of music is not fixed or permanent. Correlating fashions are imbibed with meaning by both the dominant culture and subculture; as such, they become a means by which to "articulate identity and difference" (Hebdige, 1988, p. 30). Because marketers then respond to the use of such commodities by marketing resistance back to the subculturalists, meanings in style can become vague, obfuscated, or abandoned.

Within music-based taste cultures, status can be explored through "subcultural capital," a term coined by Sarah Thornton, which "confers status on its owner in the eyes of the relevant beholder" (Thornton, 1997, p. 202) or peers of the same age group. This form of distinction not only supports teens' need for individuality, "affirm[ing] that they are not anonymous members of an undifferentiated mass," but also "fuels rebellion against, or rather escape from, the trappings of parental class" (Thornton, 1997, pp. 201, 204) through generational conflict. Traditionally, subcultures have been examined as cultures that take place in "an antagonistic relation to the prevailing culture and ideological practices" (Willis, 1977, p. xiii). This "antagonism" is ambiguous, at best, in that it is expressed through meaning and interpreted by its practitioners and the public at large in numerous ways. These themes are enacted outside ideological practices, however, and occur within the capitalist setting. The social power of teenagers is thus gained and lost through distinctions particular to teenage lifestyles and relates to both peer groups and consumption practices.

The importance of consumption in subculture can be explored through both objectification in material objects and internalization through self-perceived attributes of individuality. Objectification of subcultural capital in material objects leads to the consumption of objects that hold more capital than other objects. These can include the stylistic cues of subcultural identity, "fashionable haircuts and carefully assembled record collections" (Thornton, 1997, p. 203). The status conferred through material objects is often held in tension with the internalization through self-perceived attributes of individuality. This internalization is both the perception of subcultural identity and the knowledge required for such an identity. The identity must then be a reflection of individuality and natural to the individual. "Being 'in the know,' using (but not over-using) current slang and looking as if you were born to perform the latest dance styles" becomes a way of asserting both natural belonging to a group and belonging as a product of individuality (Thornton, 1997, p. 203). If one attempts an identity and it is judged unnatural, the person is considered a "poser," a follower who lacks capital and whose participation is limited to stylistic copying. Because every individual would then distinguish him/herself as an authentic member, no objective measurement of authenticity can be established.

In the process of mass production, fashion is removed from its original context. The meaning of objects is argued to defuse, whereby "the subversive potential of subcultural style is sanitized, commercially, through . . . commodification . . . into mainstream fashion" (Muggleton, 2000, p. 132). Within this alteration process, genre boundaries are often crossed in order to increase profitability, and messages are often altered. Simultaneously diffusion, or "the . . . geographical and social dispersal of the style from the original nucleus of innovators to new and mass publics," is carried out through mass media forms as well as local shopping venues (Muggleton, 2000, p. 132). Media catalysts to this process include such forms as MTV, with a need for large appeal and increased profitability leading to the crossing, meshing, and creating of genre and related style. These items then can be consumed within venues such as the mall. Consisting of a multitude of chain stores, malls function to bring an array of current trends to centralized locations within suburban sprawls. The "forbidden content" in "forbidden forms" is no longer forbidden; "they become codified, made comprehensible, rendered at once public property and profitable merchandise" (Hebdige, 1979, p. 96). This process is not linear, however; a constant dialectic occurs between resistance and incorporation.

The tensions between resistance and incorporation, authenticity and consumption, and individuality and group identity can all be seen in the case of Hot Topic. Through this mall-based fashion retailer we can see how companies target and market products, particularly apparel, to "alternative" youth taste cultures. Using fair-trade disclosures, annual reports, print advertisements, casual observations as a shopper, and articles from business and finance press, I will examine the general profile of Hot Topic, its target consumers, store environment, research, strategies, product lines, and competition.

The agency and articulations of the shoppers must also be acknowledged, however critically examined. I utilize discussions on open-access Internet message boards in order to explore the store in light of subcultural and postsubcultural theory concerning topics such as the combination of rebellion and consumption, the creation of the store's identity and relation to music, how the store relates to traditional notions of subculture, and the teenage consumers' relationship to the store.

THE HOT TOPIC CHAIN

Hot Topic is an American-based company focusing on apparel, accessories, and gift items related to pop culture. More specifically, the company, whose tag line is "everything about the music," sells items directly related to or influenced by "alternative" music and artists and musicians, as opposed to pop music. Started in 1989, Hot Topic was one of the first and most successful stores relating the lifestyle represented through the new media form MTV to potential youth consumption. Though popularly considered a goth, punk, and/or emo subculture-oriented store, the company caries music-related lifestyle genres ranging from punk to rave to industrial. Items previously unavailable in suburban areas, or at least unavailable in a premade form, were brought into the mall setting. The seeming contradiction of "alternative" genres within a mainstream venue is carefully policed by the company, which tries to draw the largest possible number of consumers while simultaneously maintaining its identity as an "alternative."

The company has been successful enough in this balance to be ranked number four on Forbes magazine's "Hot Shots: 200 Up & Comers" and number six on BusinessWeek's "Hot Growth List" in 2003 (Fluke and Kump, 2003; Weintraub, 2003). With store productivity ranging from roughly $579 per square foot in 1996 to $602 per square foot in 2004, with a high of $650 per square foot in 2003, the retailer has higher productivity than most other stores within its competition (Pfaff). Its success has led to rapid expansion to all fifty states and Puerto Rico, with 668 stores by February 2005, 115 of which are under one year old ("10K 05," 2005). Regionally, the West Coast is the birthplace of the store and the location of its corporate headquarters; along with the South and Southeast, it has been one of the more successful regions of operation, as opposed to the Northeast, which has had less success ("FD Q2 05," 2005; "FD Q3 05," 2005).

Consumer

From the store's inception, the targeted consumers have remained males and females between the ages of twelve and twenty-two. Though the teen customer is not considered loyal (Shinkle, 2003), Hot Topic has reported that customers continue to visit the store through their twenties ("FD Q4 03," 2003). Partially perhaps because of the customers' ages and items carried, the average transaction as of 2003 was approximately $22.50. The company argues that its customers are socially and economically varied because of the media forms MTV, music distribution, television, movies, and magazines; however, there is a stereotype of a "customer base [of] . . . angst-ridden suburban teens" (Alva, 2003). This section of the population is often "underserved" by chain stores (Pfaff), considering roughly "20% of teens identify with Hot Topic's alternative teen niche" (Alva, 2003).

Store Environment

The store is designed to create an "alternative" space within the mall and draw in the teen consumer. The average size of a Hot Topic store is smaller than that of many other retailers, approximately 1,700 square feet as opposed to 3,500 square feet ("10K 05," 2005; Allers, 2003). The entrance evokes "the electric space of most suburban rock: the metropolis," with an industrial-looking partial circle and sometimes faux brick along the sides of its exterior walls (Frith, 1997, p. 277). The store has transitioned its look over time, however, with a general move within the past five years away from a more thematic and genre-specific "gothic-rich design" to a more general modern "warehouse-like space of post-industrial materials" (Chain Store Age, 2001). "Alternative" music is played more loudly than in most stores within the mall setting. In contrast to a brightly lit mall in pastels and creams, Hot Topic distinguishes itself through general dim lighting and the use of red filtered lights. Its primary colors, used with the logo, shopping bags, and wall colors, are red and black. This setting, combined with very crowded wall and floor space, give the location an urban boutique ambiance more often associated with locally owned or independent stores (Cooney, 2004).

Within this environment, the employees play an important role in evoking a similar "alternative" aesthetic. Allied with the ages of the average store customer, most employees are quite young, with store managers' average age falling between twenty-one and twenty-two ("Aberdeen"). With higher percentages than most national chains, Hot Topic employs 47 percent minorities and 61 percent females (Fortune, 2005). While the store's percentages of females and minorities may point to fair hiring practices, there is a question of the "type" of employees hired. Whether the store hires employees who display an interest in taste similar to that reflected by Hot Topic or those who apply self-select, or are more likely to apply for such positions, they often "fit in" to the environment. Unlike other mall-based stores, employees are able to and often do have hair dyed "unnatural" colors such as blue, green, and red; piercings and other forms of body modification; and tattoos. Perhaps because of these allowances, as well as other benefits to be discussed further in following sections, Hot Topic was ranked number twenty in best midsized companies to work for by Fortune magazine in 2005.

"Street Up" Research

Hot Topic argues that it does not determine fashion trends but instead keeps a close connection to what is happening within various "alternative" music settings through a multitude of means. Music videos, music magazines, music sales, radio, and fashion and music trade journals are consulted in order to find the next large trend (Cooney, 2004; Pfaff). In addition, comment cards are collected in stores and online from customers, and the opinions of store employees are collected through Internet communications. Store employees also are reimbursed for concert tickets in exchange for fashion reports (Chain Store Age, 2000; Pfaff; Cooney, 2004; "Aberdeen," 2005). An example of success with this system is Faygo soda:

> This year employees noticed the feverish response to Insane Clown Posse band members spraying liter after liter of Faygo—a cheap pop from their hometown of Detroit—on concertgoers. Three weeks later

Hot Topic had one-liter bottles of Faygo soda in its stores for $1.99. That's twice what it sells for in Detroit. But for a rabid ICP fan in, say, suburban Iowa, it's worth it. (Allers, 2003)

Because trends pass quickly, the store is also able to change inventory quickly, with a roughly six- to eight-week time frame from conception to store shelves by using domestic vendors, as compared to other retailers, which require six to nine months (Allers, 2003).

Products

The merchandise consists primarily of apparel, accessories, and gift or novelty items for both men and women. Products include hair dye, makeup, body jewelry, CDs, corsets, books, stationery, T-shirts, skirts, pants, intimate wear, and shoes. Roughly half of Hot Topic's products are "music-influenced and music-licensed items," while the rest primarily consist of private-label or other popular culture–related licenses (Pfaff). Overall, licensed items make up a large portion of Hot Topic's items, many of which are short-term "four-to six-month exclusive agreements" (Allers, 2003).

One of the store's most consistently strong areas of sales is music-licensed items, particularly T-shirts. While sales have remained strong overall, Hot Topic has reported a recent trend toward carrying a broader array of artists, a "diversity of all the genres," with individual artist sales going down slightly ("FD Q1 05," 2005). Some replica vintage shirts are carried, such as Led Zeppelin, Jim Morrison, Jimi Hendrix, and Bob Marley (surprisingly, one of the strongest sellers); however, stronger sales occur with recent "alternative" bands, including NIN (Nine Inch Nails), HIM (His Infernal Majesty), Good Charlotte, Newfound Glory, Weezer, Korn, My Chemical Romance, Green Day, Fallout Boy, Slipknot, ICP (Insane Clown Posse), and the Used ("FD Q1 05," 2005). The availability of products related to bands and music fluctuates according to the market, with shipment to stores possible within two weeks ("FD Q1 05," 2005). CDs and DVDs, which are carried to different degrees within different stores, have had less successful sales, on the other hand, and the store cites weak music and film releases for the failure ("FD Q1 05," 2005; "FD Q3 05," 2005).

Other popular culture licenses have also been quite profitable for Hot Topic. Beginning with *South Park* in 1997 (Cooney, 2004), *West Coast Choppers* (a motorcycle-related line), *The Nightmare Before Christmas*, *Napoleon Dynamite* (an MTV production and one of its most successful licenses), *Office Space*, *Harry Potter*, *The Punisher*, *Happy Bunny*, and *Family Guy* have all at one time been popular lines of merchandise. More recently, the company has begun to enter into licenses of different anime (animation) programs it feels "fit . . . very much into the Hot Topic vibe" ("FD Q1 05," 2005). Hot Topic's policy of short-term licenses has been quite successful in allowing the company to temporarily carry new items. Once these items become older or other companies such as Walmart enter into license agreements with them, Hot Topic discontinues the product. Hot Topic has also looked to licenses from previous decades, particularly within toy items. Ghostbusters, Rainbow Brite, Smurfs, Teenage Mutant Ninja Turtles, Strawberry Shortcake, Care Bears, and My Little Pony are all licenses the retailer has carried (Tkacik, 2003; Cooney, 2004).

Private-label items by Hot Topic consist of roughly 25 percent of sales ("FD Q4 03," 2003). Some labels include Morbid Metals (body jewelry), Morbid Makeup (cosmetics), Morbid Threads (men's and women's apparel), Morbid Adornments (accessories), MT:2 (men's and women's apparel), and Ugly Shirt. Hot Topic plans to expand private-label accessories in the future because of weaker brand association than apparel. In general, these items are not endorsed by or directly attributed to a specific musician or artist, but they are influenced by the style of such genres and artists often seen appearing in music videos (Fortune, 2003).

Women's apparel influenced by pop culture has thrived, while men's has struggled within the past two to three years. Two primary influences in women's fashion are punk and feminine gothic styles. Punk-style pants and skirts, typically consisting of plaids or solid black with zippers and straps, have sold well, with musical artists such as Gwen Stefani of ska-pop band No Doubt wearing similar items in recent music videos. A new line called Dark Romance has also proven quite popular. This line is made up of primarily dark and feminine items, such as corsets, with musical artists such as Amy Lee of goth-pop band Evanescence as an inspiration. Music-influenced men's clothing has struggled, however, with no strong trends appearing on MTV in fashion bottoms; some funding and floor space is being pulled for unisex items. Music T-shirts make up most sales within men's apparel.

While Hot Topic is receptive to following trends within music and popular culture, it does draw limits in its defining of "alternative" and what its core customers would want. In doing so, the company maintains its identity as that which is not "mainstream." This has proven to be a particularly difficult problem for trends in men's bottoms. Hot Topic identifies the current trend as "plain, basic . . . non-descript . . . doesn't have a fashion element to it" ("FD Q4 03," 2003) and has therefore been forced to wait and test products over the past two years until another trend is found. Different regions have also found success with different types of fashion; "dark bottoms . . . that have lots of hardware and chains" are being sold in the Northeast yet are not in stock in stores in California ("FD Q2 05," 2005). Hot Topic has also had difficulty carrying denim products, such as men's and women's jeans. These items are acknowledged as an important part of the shopper's wardrobe, but the store must also maintain its identity as distinct from other denim-selling stores ("FD Q2 05," 2005). Concerning trends toward bohemian and hip-hop styles, Hot Topic has stated these are not "appropriate" for its core customer and has no plans to approach either ("FD Q4 04," 2004). Despite this need to maintain an edgy, rock music–related identity, the store must also maintain a balance to avoid offending the public or creating controversy. An example of such is the store's policy not to "sell T-shirts emblazoned with curse words, with racist or sexist messages, or with anything that promotes alcohol or drug use" (Allers, 2003).

While Hot Topic competes with other stores for teenage customers, the store has limited competition within the mall setting. Rags and Gadzooks are two mall-based retailers also focusing on popular culture items; however, studies have shown that their presence does not affect Hot Topic sales ("FD Q4 03," 2003). Other teen-oriented mall-based stores include Abercrombie & Fitch, American Eagle Outfitters, Pacific Sunwear, Spencer's, and Claire's. Unlike many of these stores, however, Hot Topic's products are roughly 80 percent exclusive to the store, limiting its competition for such items ("FD Q4 03," 2003). And while larger chains such as Walmart carry some basic items that may be used by teenage consumers, Hot Topic faces little large-scale competition within its price range over its music-inspired fashions.

Limited competition leads Hot Topic to spend little on advertising. One form of advertising the store often uses is sponsorship of tours. Hot Topic sponsors the second stage at Ozzfest, an annual tour featuring Ozzy Osbourne and many other metal, goth, and industrial bands and the "up-and-coming" stage at the annual Vans Warped Tour, which features many punk, ska, and emo bands ("FD Q1 05," 2005). More recently, the store has also begun to sponsor what it terms "baby tours," where there may be one relatively larger, more well-known band and two or three "up-and-comers," for a duration of roughly two months in small venues ("FD Q2 05," 2005). These tours cost little to sponsor and can be promoted through local Hot Topic stores. Larger bands have included Take Action, Taste of Chaos, Footnote, Lamb of God, My Chemical Romance, and Slipknot. Hot Topic views this form of marketing as "a very authentic way to do it . . . it's not a real slick way," and it also benefits through rising sales of those bands' T-shirts at local stores ("FD Q2 05," 2005).

Other than tour sponsorship, Hot Topic employs little recognized advertising. Some print advertisements are placed within AP (Alternative Press) and Revolver, large-distribution "alternative" music-related magazines. Ads in these magazines often promote new CDs and tours, DVDs, or fashion items, though the label Hot Topic is only apparent through a small logo typically on the lower portion of the page. Additional local radio and print advertising is used when a new store has opened, though this is discontinued after a certain period ("FD Q1 03," 2003). In comparison to other mall-based chains such as the Gap and JCPenney, Hot Topic's advertising expenditures are relatively minute.

HOT TOPIC'S APPEAL TO YOUTH

In order to examine Hot Topic's success within the youth market, one must examine the discourse of youth and/or shoppers surrounding the store and its subcultural representations. Specifically, the medium of open-access Internet message boards allows for open and candid discussion of the topic without the need for interjection as a social scientist. The message boards utilized within this examination existed previous to the commencement of research. While no further information is known about those participating on such message boards, this examination is in no way suggesting those posting consist of a representative sample for any level of quantitative accuracy. These public discussions instead display knowledge of Hot Topic and discourses among youth and/or shoppers that are prevalent within their taste or subcultures. The themes that arise out of the postings include Hot Topic's authenticity, including discussions of its relationship to more traditional notions of subculture, its status as "mainstream" or "underground," and its relationship to music. The perceived authenticity of the store is then directly related to the perceived authenticity of the shopper, with shoppers discussing changing perceptions of Hot Topic, and shoppers and non-shoppers defending their status and subcultural capital.

PERCEPTION OF HOT TOPIC

By its very nature Hot Topic has created a space of seeming contradiction whereby resistance, to use a word from early subcultural theory, co-exists with consumption. "Hot Topic has taken that anti-establishment vibe and put it in, of all places, the suburban mall" (Allers, 2003). By placing a business on the fine line between youth rebellion and mainstream consumption, an inherent risk is built into Hot Topic. Not only do youth need to be interested in the popular or "alternative" objects being sold and have purchasing power; they also must accept this seeming contradiction in order to purchase an item. Profits from rebellion are placed back into a corporation, and this is not lost on its consumers.

Hot Topic is aware of this contradiction and attempts to lower its risk by carefully policing its identity in the eyes of potential consumers. The store acknowledges its "great pains to not be seen as 'corporate'" and to create a distinct identity from other stores (Allers, 2003). Parallel with the creation of individual identity, the store distances itself from "mainstream" stores and creates an image around exclusivity. Simultaneously, as a commercial enterprise, the store must remain popular to as many shoppers as possible. Recently, the need to appeal to a broader audience has become a problem for Hot Topic, with trends often involving "preppy clothes and denim" (Clark). Hot Topic's identity is in opposition to these looks and, as such, isolates those shoppers who might not identify with the store's aesthetic. "'It scares me,' said [a] 19-year-old student . . . 'They tend to sell a lot of Goth, and that's totally not my style'" (Earnest, 2004). On the other hand, others may find Hot Topic to be too mainstream and trying too hard to be alternative. On numerous message boards, participants discussed the store as "mainstream" ("Spank"; "Gurl"), "try[ing] to cash in on popular things" ("Horror"), "a sell-out . . . [catering to] the media punk rock clothing" ("Urban"), "way too commercial" ("Gurl"), and having "a contrived commercial vision of a style" ("Vegan").

Ultimately Hot Topic must attempt to remain "authentic" to its customers. The store's primary selling of clothing and fashion products within a generally "alternative" aesthetic leads some youth to discount it as marketing the material objects associated with subcultural identity and individuality out of context of the internalization of the values associated with the aesthetic. The store is accused of marketing "pre-packaged 'individuality' to droves of teenagers . . . who really want to be just like everybody else" ("Urban"), indicating that in its popularity, Hot Topic and the items it sells are unauthenticated as mainstream. The subcultures associated with these styles are often heralded as originators, whereby shoppers "are trying to become accepted into some 'sub-culture' by purchasing their desired 'look' off a store shelf" ("Gothic"). The shoppers' perceived ability to purchase "punk in a box" ("Urban"), or a fabricated and marketed identity, leads many to label Hot Topic as a store for posers ("Urban"), "not [being] about the music it's about the clothes" ("Gurl"), emphasizing shoppers' perceived attachment to the style of particular subcultures as opposed to more internalized attributes and knowledge.

The store's focus on an "alternative" aesthetic traditionally associated with subculture leads many to compare the "mainstream" venue to its perceived "real," "underground," and therefore authentic, predecessors. Overall there is a strong discourse of the store's destroying of subcultures and scenes, often based around arguments prizing the idea of an authentic subculture possessing stronger and rightful claims to particular material objects and aesthetics as their perceived originators. "I used to wonder how pissed the Skins were about the Doc Wearers" ("Vegan"), implying that the authentic Skinheads had a rightful claim to Doc Martens as opposed to others who would wear the brand of boots. These arguments also privilege some venues, such as locally owned or independent stores, secondhand stores, and concerts, as sites of authentic consumption over mainstream stores. These locations are said to arise organically from within the authentic subculture and have stronger ties to the subculture and the music associated with it. They are also valued as selling more unique items and only one of each item, reflecting the shopper's individuality and uniqueness ("Gurl"). "The former skater who opened his own store to cater to the punks watches as his business grinds down because all the kids are . . . spending their money at Hot Topic" ("Barbelith").

While some view Hot Topic as an "alternative" option to "preppy" stores ("Gurl"), it is often conceived as "mainstream" and is not differentiated from other corporate stores. Many commented on the rumored ownership of Hot Topic by the most mainstream of mall stores, the Gap. However popular, this rumor is unsubstantiated and untrue; Hot Topic is its own publicly traded entity. Comparisons were drawn with other large chain stores such as McDonald's, referenced as "McGothkids" ("Urban," "Barbelith"), Kmart ("Urban"), Walmart ("Horror"), as well as other mall-based retailers such as Abercrombie & Fitch ("Urban").

Hot Topic attempts to separate itself from this corporate image by placing great emphasis on being "authentic" through its affiliation with music. The music associated with the store symbolizes the entire set of values and lifestyle marketed by Hot Topic, as well as the identity of the store itself. Hot Topic is very often associated with different subcultures (emo, punk, and/or goth), the result of intentional effort on the part of the store. This strategy appeals to some customers; "i can dress goth/ punk/raver wutever i want" ("Spank"). For some youth, however, the store can be too emo, punk, or goth ("YM," "Gurl"), or, on the other hand, not punk or goth enough, or attacked as "mainstream" goth ("Gothic") or emo ("IGN," "Horror").

Because fashion and stylistic elements are emphasized, some youth argue that music, the most important element of the marketed lifestyle, is not enough of a focus. Some cite Hot Topic's lack of CDs at all of its chains; "my a** it's about the music 2 words CIRCUIT CITY" ("Gurl"). Others argue the band T-shirts and music-inspired fashions do make the store music-focused ("Gurl"). The store notes such concerns and attempts to cultivate authenticity by establishing close ties with music through "Street Up" research (for which employees often attend music concerts) and advertising (by emphasizing the music group over the store in print advertising and by integrating itself into "start-up" and local music scenes through tour sponsorship).

The opinion youth hold of Hot Topic often changes over time, as do their perceptions of authenticity. There are many discussions about outgrowing the store—"I used to shop there (in like, junior high)" ("Urban")—and about how the store has become more mainstream. "Hot Topic has . . . forgott[en] it's core demographic (Urban countercultureists from ages 16–25, who are into music groups that are considered to be too bizarre and raw to go mainstream . . .) in order to appeal to a new demographic (Suburban youths, ages 11–15, into such musical groups . . . who have toned down sounds . . . and received mainstream appeal)" ("Urban"). The store "used to be cool until about two years ago" ("Urban," "Horror") and "used to be about music" ("Gurl"). While Hot Topic has changed over time in order to continue targeting fashion surrounding popular music, these changes have not been as drastic as the discourse suggests, with urban populations never having been the target market and no strong change in approach by the store to music and music-related products. In asserting the change in the store's authenticity, ex-shoppers can then explain their previous patronage and assert the superiority of their taste over current shoppers.

PERCEPTION OF HOT TOPIC SHOPPERS

The perceived authenticity of the store reflects upon the perceived authenticity of the shopper. While some shoppers assert their authenticity by not shopping at Hot Topic, others shop at Hot Topic while critical of the store, and yet others claim empowerment to choose identity and even authenticity through their consumption at Hot Topic.

For some, Hot Topic is inauthentic and the individual's authenticity is asserted through not shopping there. One theme of this assertion is the distancing of self from the material and stylistic objects of a subculture and asserting authenticity through internalized attributes of individuality. Membership is established as "merely a state of mind and not how you physically present yourself to others" ("Gothic"); it is "the way you think and act (not fake acting or thinking however). It's not about the clothes and the objects or the style" ("Spank"). Subcultural group affiliation then becomes based on natural, internal attributes and individuality as opposed to stylistic displays.

When the aesthetic of subculture is discussed, the process of creating fashion as opposed to purchasing premade fashion is characterized as authentic. The process of clothing modification or creation is prized as requiring creativity in playing with meaning and aesthetics. Second-hand stores are often viewed as acceptable venues for purchase of items for modification. "It's cheap, so you won't feel like you're wasting your money . . . [and] without that feeling of wasting expensive stuff" ("Gothic"). The association of DIY (do it yourself) with uniqueness means "authentic" members are drawn to DIY as opposed to buying premade subcultural items. "True goth punk or emo kids make most of thier own clothes and accesories or the go to trift shops and find real vintage clothes and accessories" ("Gurl"); "if you want the punk look, get off your butt and get to a thrift store and do it properly" ("Gurl"). Hot Topic is considered to lack the creativity required by DIY and is instead uniform and uncreative, reflecting upon the lack of individuality of the shopper. "If you are punk then you buy your clothes second hand and custom them, you do not buy them from an overpriced chain store with ready-made everyone-owns-one punk clothing" ("Gurl"). Within this context, shoppers are labeled as "clones" ("Urban," "Gurl") and as easily identifiable through their "uncreativ[ity]" ("Barbelith") and "look[ing] like they have come straight out of a hot topic catalog" ("Gurl").

Some critics of Hot Topic did place value on premade material objects but felt as though they had claims to the objects through their association and authenticity within their subculture. Such items, it is then argued, should remain exclusive to true members. The selling of the objects through Hot Topic is framed as an invasion into the culture whereby nonfans will have access to previously privileged knowledge and meanings. "Now any jackass can get Naruto gear" ("IGN"). Some members prefer not having access to premade material objects affiliated with their subculture as long as nonfans will also lack access; "having to make own Futurama gear is a small price to pay when the alternative is over-merchandising and non-fans wearing it" ("Futurama").

Critics of Hot Topic expressed a need to distinguish themselves from those who shop there. The authenticity and subcultural capital of the non–Hot Topic shopper is established through the labeling and stereotyping of the Hot Topic shopper. Particular qualities are targeted as relating to the shoppers' lack of subcultural capital and authenticity from the point of view of nonshoppers. Shoppers are not only labeled with terms such as "brain-dead emo kids" ("Futurama") but are discussed as wanting to be goth or punk ("Gurl") or claiming to be so through purchases ("YM," "Urban"). The shoppers are then constructed as posers ("Barbelith," "Urban") as opposed to "genuine" members who "wouldn't even_SHOP_at a store" ("Gurl").

The quality most associated with the Hot Topic shoppers' lack of capital is age, with preteens and younger teenagers possessing less capital than older teenagers. Throughout the comments the ages attacked as that of the typical Hot Topic shopper ranged from eight to sixteen, with eleven being the age mentioned most often. "Hot Topic is annoying, and has produced an army of 11–15 year olds who think they are so 'punk rawk' or so 'gawth' that I want to put my head through a wall . . . " ("Vegan"). They are said to have a "feeling of 'I'm 11 and I am hardfuckingcore'. No. You are JUST 11" ("Vegan"). Comments such as these are often made in conjunction with asserting the authenticity of older participants in subcultural aesthetics; "when you see say a twenty six year old . . . then you've got yourself a full fledged goth" ("Gothic").

The attack of shoppers as unauthentic on the basis of age is often paired with attacks based on gender, with females possessing less subcultural capital than males. The image of the young female is often evoked as the symbol of "poser." The store is argued to be "frequented by 12-ish year old females that like to express themselves by wearing net-sleeved shirts" ("Urban") and possess "things for the 11 yr old girls who think they are so punk/goth" ("Urban").

Class, "suburban" status, and "preppiness" are also cited markers of Hot Topic shoppers' lack of subcultural capital. The store is thought by many to be overpriced ("Spank") and therefore said to require the shopper's "rich daddy's money" for purchases ("Urban"). It is cited as a "safe place where mom can drop you off in the minivan" ("Barbelith") and sell "overpriced crap to the suburban kiddies" ("Gothic"), denigrating the store as a sanitized form of subculture for stereotyped suburban teenagers. Hot Topic is also characterized as a store where "preps," a teen status based on a combination of class and suburban milieus, can "try to be 'punk'" ("Gurl"). Such groups are said to possess ingenuine angst and to be attempting, unsuccessfully because of their unauthentic qualities, to be rebellious. These discourses concerning shoppers are brought to extremes, with shoppers being characterized as blond cheerleaders, a symbol of stereotypical preppy-ness, and eight-year-olds, an age group that is younger than the target market ("Gothic").

Another basis on which the authenticity of the Hot Topic shopper is questioned is knowledge of the subcultural field in which they find aesthetic pleasure. Shoppers are labeled as lacking knowledge and natural association with the subculture; their interest is limited to aesthetics, and they lack status as true fans. "I think if anyone wants to claim they are 'Punk' that they should study some history and get the facts because people are getting a mis conception" ("Spank"). Some place the need for knowledge above all other subcultural capital factors, such as age, pointing out that "even someone in their twenties who dresses like a Goth could be totally ignorant of the music, beliefs, and history that go with the image" ("Gothic"). Others connect subcultural factors such as age with the level of knowledge attainable; "at 33 if I wore a Ramones or a CBGB's tee I'd be accused of not dressing my age when I have more right to wear it than some kid who couldn't tell you the title to a Ramones song if you put a gun to his head" ("Horror").

Still supporting these subcultural hierarchies, some self-identified sub-culturalists do shop at Hot Topic; however, their consumption is explained through subcultural logic. Several shoppers under this category claim specific items of purchase determine the status of the shopper. Hot Topic is then discussed through seemingly contradictory statements: "in which posers shop . . . I bought an eyebrow barbell there, and a T-shirt at one point" ("Urban"). Consistency of identity and categorizations is not required through such attempts at defining one's subcultural status. Generally the store is said to "sell . . . a lot of poser stuff. But they do sell some cool band t-shirts, and CDs" ("Urban," "Gurl," "Spank"). Some also attribute their enjoyment of the store to their individuality and opinion, as opposed to others who shop there. "True a lot of posers shop there, but whatever . . . i shop there because i like the clothes and wear the clothes" ("Spank").

Even if Hot Topic is considered an acceptable venue for specific purchases, some consumers also attempt to purchase items that are not obviously from Hot Topic in order to not look as though they are trying too hard, thereby depleting subcultural capital. Critics of Hot Topic often argue that "it's easy to tell" someone who is wearing the clothing sold at the store ("Gothic"). In the text *What Is Goth*, which is sold at Hot Topic stores, Voltaire cautions against such unnatural-appearing constructions, to "choose [purchases] wisely—you don't want to look like a Hot Topic store exploded on you while you walked through the mall" (Voltaire, 2004, p. 19).

Many youth identify with Hot Topic and associate the store's selection of products with their own tastes. Some shoppers attribute their choice to shop at Hot Topic as having to do with their individual identity and liking what the store carries. "Its who we are! and we kinda like to stand out a little instead of being sucked into the mass producers of polos and capris" ("Gurl"). The process is reduced to individuals purchasing items they like as individuals. The label of "poser" is denied from their relative position, often bringing into question the definition of the term. "We dress the way we want to express ourselves" ("Gurl"), "we aren't posers . . . we are unique" ("Gurl"). Sometimes the shopper goes so far as to assert his or her authenticity and specific group identity as directly correlating with consumption. "I used to be a big time goth and that was my fav store" ("Gurl").

Many shoppers defend the store as making available items not previously available for purchase, particularly within more rural areas. Previous to the chain store, the "alternative" aesthetic was not widely popular outside major U.S. cities, much less in smaller suburban locations across the country and among other major retailers. "Hottopic is the only place where we can get clothes like that" ("Gurl"); it is "the only decent store in town" ("Gurl"). Hot Topic then carries "things that you can't usually get in normal stores" ("Gurl"), and in doing so becomes "the only store . . . that doesn't suck" ("IGN"). The availability of items diminishes the seeming contradiction of selling "alternative" aesthetic items within the mall setting.

Some shoppers attribute their ability to take on temporary identities and different subcultures to Hot Topic. These allow for a multidimensional self-concept whereby stability within a singular identity is not essential. "Now we have a hot topic and i can dress goth/punk/raver wutever i want to. i love it love it" ("Spank"); it is "good for the few days I go all Queen of Darkness" ("YM"). The store then provides the ability to purchase "name brand clothes that match your mood" ("Gurl"). The individual's internal attributes and creativity are the basis for claims of authenticity as opposed to more permanent identification with a particular subculture. And for some, shopping is merely a starting point for further alterations, as Muggleton predicted, for continued customization and subversion. "I make my clothes OUT OF HT clothes" ("Gothic"); "if you're truly original you can buy something cool from there and match it with some thrift co[u]ture to make something truly cutting edge" ("Urban"). Previously invested subcultural meanings can then be enhanced, altered, and blurred.

Those viewing Hot Topic as a venue for authentic subcultural practice then often police the space and their conceptions of authenticity. Specifically, there is a discourse of disliking what are viewed as preppy kids invading and changing their subculture's space by frequenting Hot Topic. "It's being invaded by a bunch of preppy princesses" ("Gurl"); "Gosh, Go Back To Your Abercrombie! I can't stand when the 'Preppies' go in there though. They act like it's so ***ing cool to go in there" ("Gurl"). The group identified as preps are viewed as mainstream and posers entering subcultural space. "They start to assimilate into our culture and corrupt it from within" ("Gothic"). These shoppers are then asserting their identity and consumption practices at Hot Topic hierarchically above the identity and consumption practices of identified preps at other mall-based stores.

CONCLUSION

Members of subcultures have a great fear of the popularization of a particular lifestyle. This fear leads to policing of boundaries (what is punk versus what isn't), labeling, and the need to differentiate one's identity from others. Involved in this is a defining of self against "mainstream" and therefore attempts to avoid becoming "mainstream." This distancing is related both to fears of perceived forms of mainstream media and mainstream consumption; however, defining of the self and mainstream is relative to different self-identified members.

The transformation of taste cultures into lifestyles greatly appeals to the teenage consumer's need for both group identity and differentiation from the mainstream. Items within the taste cultures experience a change of meaning and context when placed within mass marketing. In distancing the self from the mainstream through such "alternative" products, the subculturalist is ultimately reconnecting with mainstream ideology and systems of distinction. In the case of Hot Topic, marketing an "alternative" lifestyle within a capitalist mall venue displays the dilemma of youth consumption. The simultaneous action of the market and the creator/consumer illustrates the constant dialectic over the power of culture.

References

Allers, K. L. (2003, October 27). Retail's Rebel Yell. *Fortune.*

Alva, M. (2003, February 13). Endless Supply of Trendy Teens Keeps This Chain in the Money. *Investor's Business Daily.*

Book of the Dead. HorrorWatch!: Horror Forum [message board]. www.horror-watch.com/modules/newbb/viewtopic.php?topic_id=2172&forum=13 [2005, November 22] ("Horror").

Chain Store Age. (2000, November). 76.11, 72–74.

———. (2001, March). 77.3, 148–150.

Clarke, J. et al. (1976). Subcultures, Cultures and Class: A Theoretical Overview. *Resistance Through Rituals: Youth Subcultures in Post-War Britain.* London: Harper Collins, 1976.

Cooney, J. (2004, January). Hot Topic: 2003 Retailer of the Year. *License!: Where Concepts Come to Market.*

Fluke, C. J. and Kump, L. (2003, October 27). Hot Shots: 200 Up and Comers. *Forbes.*

Fortune. The 100 Best Companies to Work For. (2005, January 24).

————. The 100 Fastest Growing Companies. (2003, September 1).

Frith, S. (1996). *Performing Rites: On the Value of Popular Music.* Cambridge, Mass.: Harvard University Press.

————. (1981). *Sound Effects: Youth, Leisure, and the Politics of Rock 'n' Roll.* New York: Pantheon Books.

————. (1997). The Suburban Sensibility in British Rock and Pop. In Silverstone, R. (Ed.), *Visions of Suburbia.* New York: Routledge.

Hebdige, D. (1988). *Hiding in the Light.* New York: Routledge.

————. (1979). *Subculture: The Meaning of Style.* New York: Routledge.

Hot Topic. (2005). Annual Report on Form 10-K for the Year Ended January 29, 2005. ("10K 05," 2005).

————. (1997). Form 10-K for the Fiscal Year Ended February 1, 1997. ("10K 97," 1997).

————. (2005). Fair Disclosure Wire Q1 2005. ("FD Q1 05," 2005).

————. (2005). Fair Disclosure Wire Q2 2005. ("FD Q2 05," 2005).

————. (2005). Fair Disclosure Wire Q3 2005. ("FD Q3 05," 2005).

————. (2003). Fair Disclosure Wire Q4 2003. ("FD Q4 03," 2003).

————. (2004). Fair Disclosure Wire Q4 2004. ("FD Q4 04," 2004).

————. (2005, October 5). Fair Disclosure Wire Hot Topic Sales Conference Call, ("FD 05," 2005).

Hot Topic!. Futurama: Employee Lounge [message board]. www.peelified.com/cgi-bin/Futurama/15–000668–1/ [2005, November 22] ("Futurama").

hot topic!!!. Spank Mag! Youth and Teen Culture Online [message board]. www.spankmag.com/f/d.cfm/cc.67455/o_r.261/p.htm [2005, November 15] ("Spank").

Hot Topic. Gothic.net [message board]. www.gothic.net/boards/archive/index.php/t-498.html [2005, November 15] ("Gothic").

Hot Topic Definition. Urban Dictionary [message board]. www.urbandictionary.com/define.php?term=hot+topic [2005, November 15] ("Urban").

Hot Topic: Dig it or Dis it. Gurl [message board]. www.gurl.com/react/dod/dilemmas/0,,605410_622880–8,00.html [2005, November 15] ("Gurl").

A Hot Topic for Lawson Software: Providing a High-Performance IT Platform for Retail Growth. Aberdeen Group. www.lawson.com/library/collateral/IRET-WP 6039.pdf [2005, December 30] ("Aberdeen").

Hot Topic Has Redeemed Itself. Vegan Porn [message board]. www.veganporn.com/1052274269.html [2005, November 15] ("Vegan").

Hot Topic Shopper? Barbelith Underground: Subcultural Engagement for the 21st Century [message board]. www.barbelith.com/topic/37 [2005, November 22] ("Barbelith").

Hot Topic Stores Are Now Selling Naruto Swag. IGN Boards [message board]. http://boards.ign.com/Message.aspx?topic=100934255&replies=30 [2005, November 15] ("IGN").

Muggleton, D. (2000). *Inside Subculture: The Postmodern Meaning of Style*. New York: Berg.

Pfaff, K. Edgy Hot Topic on a Hot Streak. International Council of Shopping Centers. www.icsc.org/srch/sct/current/sct0401/page1c.php?region [2005, December 30].

Shinkle, K. (2003, September 3). Give Us Your Hipsters, Your Punks and Goths. *Investor's Business Daily*.

Thornton, S. (1996). *Club Cultures: Music, Media and Subcultural Capital*. Hanover, N.H.: University Press of New England.

———. (1997). "The Social Logic of Subcultural Capital." *The Subcultures Reader*. New York: Routledge.

Tkacik, M. (2003, June 11). Many 1980s Icons Still Have Toy Appeal. *Wall Street Journal*.

Voltaire. (2004). *What Is Goth: Music, Makeup, Attitude, Apparel, Dance, and General Skullduggery*. Boston: Weiser Books.

Weintraub, A. (2003, June 9). Hotter Than a Pair of Vinyl Jeans. *BusinessWeek*.

Who Likes Hot Topic. YM [message board]. http://boards.ym.com/message.jspa?messageID=5493606 [2005, November 22] ("YM").

Willis, P. (1977). *Learning to Labor: How Working Class Kids Get Working Class Jobs*. New York: Columbia University Press.

Chapter 5

QUEER EYE FOR THE STRAIGHT-ACTING GUY: THE PERFORMANCE OF MASCULINITY IN GAY YOUTH CULTURE AND POPULAR CULTURE

Dennis Carlson

W HEN HE PUBLICLY "CAME OUT" at a press conference in 2006, Lance Bass, former star in the "boy band" *NSYNC, told reporters:

> I want people to take [from my coming out] that being gay is normal. That the stereotypes are out the window. . . . I've met so many people like me that it's encouraged me. I call them the SAGs—the straight-acting gays. We're just normal, typical guys. I love to watch football and drink beer. (quoted in Rice, 2006, 88)

There is much to unpack in these few sentences about the meaning of masculinity among adolescent and young adult males. At first glance, the reader may well applaud Bass's affirmation that many gay young men do not fit the stereotype created for them in popular culture and within "straight" America and are asserting that they are not effeminate and not feminized men. They are "real" men, just like "straight" men, and they like football, drinking beer, and hanging out with their buddies just like straight men do. Certainly this normalization of gayness has been a dominant theme in the modern gay and lesbian rights movements, and one that at least offers some advantages to gay folks. If "normal" people (i.e., "straight" people) view "straight-acting" gay people as almost straight but not quite, as almost "normal," they are likely to be more tolerant and accepting. When gay people are treated as "normal" rather than psychologically disturbed and psychopathic, they are less likely to be made the subject of efforts to "cure" them or "save" them. They are also less likely to be represented in popular culture in a stereotypical manner—reduced to a one-dimensional stereotype, an objectified "other"—and more likely to be represented as people whose lives are not too different from other people's lives. This is all well and good, and perhaps gay people need to be normalized in this way as part of a struggle to be humanized and treated as deserving of basic human and civil rights.

But the project of normalization will only take us so far, as the social theorist and historian Michel Foucault (1980, 1995) has helped us see. To normalize is to correct that which is deficient, to bring it into the normal or relegate it to the status of the abnormal "other." This binary opposition of "normal" and "abnormal" is clearly still taken for granted in Bass's comments, and it is linked to the binary of "straight" (normal) and "gay" (abnormal). This binary associates "real" masculinity with exclusive heterosexuality, to be sure, but it also associates real men with aggressive sports, competition, and a jock culture that historically has objectified and "othered" women, homosexual men, and all gender nonconforming men. If gay men now claim entrance to the halls of jock culture and the real man, is it only to distance themselves from what they consider to be gay men who act a bit feminine, or what is considered feminine within the dominant culture? Will they participate, like their straight brothers, in the bullying and exclusion of these other gay men—in locker rooms, and on and off the playing field—who do not meet their standards for how a real man should act?

These are questions I want to address, if not resolve, in what follows. I am not so much interested in "straightness" and "gayness" as sexual orientations, or even sexual behaviors, although this is part of what is referenced by these binary oppositional terms. Rather, I am interested in acting straight and acting gay, that is, in how straightness and gayness get represented and performed in popular culture and youth culture. Bass's comments indicate, among other things, that straightness is performed in everyday life, and this performance is not a sexual performance so much as it is a way of acting masculine. By implication, gayness is associated with a form of masculinity that is feminized or effeminate—and so the ultimate "other" within this type of "straight" masculinity is still women. Consequently, it is a very limited agenda to represent gay people in popular culture as "straight-acting" rather than in terms of the traditional stereotypes. A more transformative and liberatory agenda, I argue, would engage young people in a critical, deconstructive reading of the performance of masculinity in popular culture texts, to examine how hegemonic masculinities are dependent on oppressive "othering" practices and also to analyze alternative representations and performances of masculinity that are consistent with commitments to equity, inclusive communities, and social justice.

I want to suggest some of what a critical reading of masculinities in popular culture might look like by providing my own reading of several popular "indie" films produced over the past decade or so and targeted to a primarily gay, white, young adult, male audience, all of them dealing in one way or another with the relationship between gay male identity and jock culture. The gay male market niche has grown exponentially since the mid-1990s, and one might think that because these films are generally made by gay directors and producers, and targeted to gay young men, that they would provide counterhegemonic images and performances of masculinity. I argue, however, that while these films partially demystify the reigning narratives of hegemonic masculinity and mythologies of the "real man," they also take these narratives and mythologies for granted in a way that is deeply contradictory. Thus, many indie films targeted to a young gay audience are of the romance genre, and a significant number of these are about a rather one-sided and unfulfilled romantic attachment between an "out" gay adolescent (represented as having many stereotypically feminine traits) and a straight-acting jock who represents the "real" man of his dreams, who also abuses and deserts him. I call this, with a nod to popular culture, the "queer eye for the straight-acting guy" narrative. To develop this general line of argument, I look at two popular gay romance films from 1998 (*Get Real* and *Edge of Seventeen*), and then analyze a gay documentary that has been popular among young gay males—*Straight Acting* (2005), about gay young men who play aggressive contact sports.

Progressive teachers, other educators, and public intellectuals can play an important role in helping young people unpack films such as these as part of a study of gender and masculinity (McLaren, Hammer, Sholle & Reilly, 1995; and Nowak, Abel & Ross, 2007). To engage in this kind of pedagogic work, helping students unpack popular culture performances of gender and reflect on the performance of gender in various youthful subcultures of difference, both teacher and student must learn to rethink gender around performance theory. Consequently, before turning to a more detailed discussion of several indie films targeted at a young gay male audience, I want to say a bit more about a performance theory of hegemonic masculinities, drawing upon Judith Butler's (1990, 2007) feminist performance theory and R. W. Connell's (2000, 2005) theory of hegemonic masculinities in the emergent field of masculinity studies.

TOWARD A PERFORMANCE THEORY
OF HEGEMONIC MASCULINITIES

These are unsettling and contradictory times for young people to construct a sense of self, including a sense of who they are as gendered, raced, and classed subjects (Carlson & Apple, 1998). Particularly with regard to gender, two contradictory discourses continue to circulate, and most young men and women take elements of both for granted, although there is a good deal of variability among young people in regard to their beliefs about gender. Over much of the past century, gender has been understood by most Americans, and represented in popular culture, as having an authentic, natural, given character, with "real" masculinity and femininity naturally the opposite of each other. Indeed, essentialistic or natural theories of gender are still very influential in education, even if they are now being challenged and critiqued. Nel Noddings's (2003) work on an "authentic" model of care is grounded in a theory of gender that associates women with caring, nurturance, and cooperation. One of the problems with this theory is that by implication, "natural" masculinity gets associated with a set of negatively valued traits: aggressiveness, self-interest, competition, hierarchy, objectification, and so on. At the same time, and in a contradictory way, Noddings suggests that boys should be taught to be more caring, like girls. So gender is understood to be a social construction, open to change, and at the same time grounded in natural gendered differences. It does, I think, make sense to recognize that there is some naturalness to gender. After all, different hormonal mixes run through male and female bodies, and the fact that women are equipped physically and emotionally to bear and nurture children means that most human females have what we would call (in the animal world) maternal, caring "instincts." Human males have evolved along a somewhat different path in both prehistoric and historical times, their masculinity organized around hunting and protecting the community from external attack, with organized teamwork and athletic prowess valued in the hunt and in battle, along with organized aggression and competitiveness. If the past is never really separated from the present, we may have to accept some aspects of maleness as deeply rooted in a cultural and species history. The trouble is, even within the time frame of history and among diverse cultures, masculinity has meant different things and been performed in very different ways, as anthropologists have documented. Furthermore, the acceptance of the idea that there is an authentic or natural masculinity has been linked with a rightist cultural politics of hypermasculine authoritarianism, as in fascism in Europe and more recently in the neo-Nazi and "skinhead" movements in Europe and the United States. It is also associated with the movement among evangelical Christian men, through groups such as the Promise Keepers, to take back control of their families and reestablish a "God-given" patriarchal authority (Apple, 2006).

A second and more progressive discourse on gender—and the one that I rely on in this chapter—has emerged in cultural studies and gender studies over the past two decades, and it has radically called into question the naturalness of any performance of masculinity or femininity. In *Gender Trouble* (1990), a book that heralded the arrival of the new performance theory of gender, Judith Butler wrote, "Gender is the repeated stylization of the body, a set of repeated acts within a highly rigid regulatory frame that congeal over time to produce the appearance of substance, of a natural sort of being" (Butler, 1990, 25).

Gender is, from this perspective, not something you are but something you do. It is a verb more than a noun, a "doing" instead of a "being" (Salih, 2006, 55). But it is a doing, a stylization of the body that is highly regulated by social norms, so that those who step outside the approved bounds for the performance of gender face severe social sanctions. It is also a performance that seems natural because it has been repeated so many times, from the moment of birth, that it becomes unquestioned, as the way things are. But it is not natural, and the actor cannot hope to model his or her performance on some original, natural, authentic performance, some "real" masculinity or femininity. As Jean Baudrillard, the theorist of the postmodern age, argued, all we have left (and indeed all we have ever had) to construct a sense of self are "simulacra"—copies of copies for which no original exists, "a real without origin or reality: a hyperreal" (Baudrillard, 1994, 1). Popular culture and the mass media are engaged in marketing and circulating copies of copies of masculinity and femininity, which young people then use to do their "identity work" (Wexler, 1992). A good example of this is in the popular movie *The Bird Cage*, in which Nathan Lane, playing the part of an effeminate gay drag queen, is being coached by his partner, played by Robin Williams, on how to act like a real man by emulating John Wayne—how he talked, walked, held a fork, and crossed his legs. The Hollywood image of masculinity, John Wayne, becomes the standard for "realness," and real men seek to model their performances of masculinity after these constructed, manufactured representations of real masculinity.

This is where masculinity studies enter the picture, along with the notion of hegemonic masculinities, which has been perhaps the central organizing term within the field. The idea of hegemony is associated with Antonio Gramsci's (1971) insightful analysis of the battle over ideas and over the "common sense" that organizes and legitimates power relations within a society. According to Gramsci, a dominant power bloc (such as white, middle- and upper-middle-class heterosexual males), as part of the project of establishing its cultural and moral leadership, must ensure popular or mass consent to being governed through the production of a common-sense understanding of the world that appeals even to groups being systematically disempowered. In this case, we can say that hegemonic masculinities provide a basis for males of various racial and class backgrounds to find common ground around domination by what Connell calls "transnational business masculinity," a hegemonic masculinity that "embodies, organizes, and legitimates men's domination in the world gender order as a whole" (Connell, 2000, 46). Its "common sense" is one of a natural hierarchy of masculinities, from the real man to the feminized man, which serves to maintain control over women but also over men through its representation of gayness as feminine. A good deal of attention has been focused in masculinity studies on the notion that there is diversity within the category of hegemonic masculinity, so that it is perhaps more accurate to speak of hegemonic masculinities, all loosely aligned with a hegemonic power bloc and all developed out of struggle with counterhegemonic movements among women and subordinated males—including gay and gender-nonconforming males. Those in dominant positions strive to maintain their power by controlling the common-sense image of the real man in ways that gain the consent of subordinated males (Coles, 2009, 36). But a new common-sense understanding of masculinity, linked to a new power bloc, is always threatening to coalesce. However, the development of an opposition to hegemony may be stymied and managed indefinitely. In order for a new democratic power bloc to coalesce, Gramsci argued, public intellectuals—including, most notably, teachers—need to help young people become more critically and self-reflectively aware that what appears natural and normal actually hides power relations and interests. The ultimate aim of masculinity studies is to undo hegemonic performances of masculinity and encourage more equitable and nondominative ways of "acting like a man."

Hegemonic masculinities legitimate a patriarchal mythology of intellectual and physical superiority, with the alpha male positioned on the top of a masculinity hierarchy. A particular male's masculinity is constructed by accumulating "masculine competence" in one area to counter any perceived femininity (Visser, 2009, 370). Thus, if he is physically strong he can compensate somewhat for not having a college education; and if he is academically strong, he can compensate for not developing physical strength. These two images of hegemonic masculinity, representing the masculine mind and body, have been particularly influential among young males, although in ways that differ dramatically by class and racial identity. The hypermasculine mind is not associated with the academy as such, since the academy is associated with the sedentary passivity of femininity (Lusher & Robins, 2009, 388). Instead, the hegemonic male mind uses his smarts to become a Wall Street broker or company executive on the make. According to Christine Beasley, capitalist masculinity involves self-consciously managing the body and emotions along with money, and detaching oneself from traditional loyalties to firm, family, or nation. This is an image and performance of masculinity that has particular appeal to young, middle-class males, although it may also appeal to poor inner-city youth who aspire to have access to power and privilege. In the 1980s television series *Family Ties*, the teenage son, Alex, sought to emulate this hegemonic masculinity, and in the cultural and political climate of the Reagan era, Alex is positioned as an American hero. His Boomer parents, on the other hand, were represented as a bit old-fashioned with their '60s values. Oliver Stone's movie *Wall Street* (1987), the story of a young and impatient stockbroker on his way to the top—he believes that "every dream has a price" and trades on illegal inside information—was a scathing indictment of this performance of capitalist masculinity. Yet it remains a potent image of the real man for many adolescents and college students.

The corporate executive and Wall Street banker represent images of transnational business masculinity that celebrate the power of the male mind to turn ideas into money and to use money to accumulate objects, including women. The star athlete represents an image of hegemonic masculinity more invested in the body than the mind, although the star athlete who also gets good grades is the ideal model of masculinity. The athlete invests in "physical capital," having to do with the size and shape of the body, speech, gait, and general deportment (Coles, 2009, 38). The "jock" as a hegemonic image of masculinity is tied historically to the emergence of the high school in the early twentieth century and to competitive, interscholastic athletics. The great champion of athletics competition for boys in the early Progressive era was Granville Stanley Hall, who saw in sports a way of toughening boys and teaching them teamwork. He linked this rather directly to militaristic masculinity—borrowing from the ancient Greeks. "Most smaller Greek states," he wrote, "had athletic excursions . . . [that] sometimes even mimic warfare, to season the body and soul of youth" (Hall, 1969/1905, 259). Football was, from the start, a sport that mimicked warfare and prepared young men for military service. The influential "Muscular Christianity" movement of the early Progressive era also associated masculinity with athleticism, healthiness in mind and body, and vigorous outdoor activity (Ladd & Mathisen, 1999). Jock culture has been supported by school administrators and many parents because of its associations with school spirit, a "clean-cut" appearance, "wholesomeness," respect for authority, and patriotism. Despite a whole genre of movies, beginning with *Animal House* (1978), that parody and poke fun at jock masculinity, it continues to be hegemonic in much of the United States—as witnessed by the success of various "reality" television shows and movies about high school football over the past decade. It offers poor and working-class black and Latino males an opportunity to be popular at school. However, to the extent that boys invest more in physical capital than intellectual capital to construct their masculinity, it sets them up for subordination in the social order—except for those few school athletes who make it to the pros.

Both of these images of hegemonic masculinity historically have been associated with exclusive heterosexuality, and this is still largely the case. The image of the aggressive, competitive Wall Street broker is linked to sexual conquests with women; and so too is the image of the aggressive, competitive athlete. Gayness is then linked to the image of the unathletic, noncompetitive, fearful, overemotional "sissy" boy and to the "nerd," the academically oriented young man who lives in an intellectual world detached from direct concerns with making money and getting girls. Within this world of hegemonic masculinities, homosexual young men have two performative options. The option open to homosexual young males is to "act gay," modeling their performance of gender on hegemonic images of gayness and gay culture, which associate gayness with "acting like a girl." Young men who adopt this option may learn to excel in drama and music and stay away from the athletic field, which they view as the territory of straight men; and they may learn to associate their own gayness with traits defined as feminine. In an earlier time, some gay men even referred to themselves as "girls" and "queens" as a way of acting gay. If this is a language rarely heard today, gayness continues to be linked in both the mainstream straight and gay media to the feminine. The other option for homosexual young males is to "act straight" and try to fit in, which means conforming to the norms of hegemonic masculinity, including the norm of acting as if you are exclusively heterosexual, which means being "in the closet" rather than "out." This option has given closeted straight-acting men access to power and privilege; Lance Bass was merely asserting that "out" gay men who are straight-acting should be treated the same as their straight brothers. The linkages between hegemonic masculinities and exclusive heterosexuality are thus loosening somewhat without fundamentally challenging the hegemonic common sense that results in the "othering" and bullying of gender nonconforming males and anything associated with gayness. At the same time, to act gay, at least as popular culture has defined and represented it, has been to act within the confines of hegemonic masculinities as well. Gay men have been intelligible in the culture of hegemonic masculinities only when they perform the part they were expected to play.

QUEER EYE FOR THE STRAIGHT-ACTING GUY

In the culture of hegemonic masculinity, the gender "other" is disrespected and denied recognition as an equal, and ironically also desired, for desire is mobilized around domination and inequality. To the extent that gay-identified men have internalized the values of hegemonic masculinity, they too tend to envision romantic relationships between "straight-acting" and "gay-acting" men; as in the heterosexual world, though, these relationships are understood to be undermined by tensions and conflicts. The popular "reality" television show *Queer Eye for the Straight Guy* represents gay men who only have eyes for the straight man whom they serve and glamorize, only to turn him over to his bride-to-be. If gayness is no longer performed in quite the flamboyant way it once was, it is still associated with a romanticized desire for the straight guy or the straight-acting gay guy—in either case, for a "real" man. In many gay romance novels and films these days, this fantasy has a happy ending, as a straight-acting athlete comes out and acknowledges his love for his gay buddy. But in other romance novels and films, the gay young man has to recognize that he doesn't need the object of his desire, who disrespects and abuses him, and that as an out gay man he can find friendship and perhaps even love with other men who are out and proud, and who don't try to act straight. In this case, acting straight means acting heterosexual as well and thus living according to what Eve Sedgwick (1990) has called the "epistemology of the closet." Gay male popular culture texts thus provide at least a partial critique of the hegemonic trope of "queer eye for the straight-acting guy," although they also, in a contradictory way, continue to organize the central romantic narrative around this trope.

One of the most widely reviewed and distributed young gay male romance movies, which continues to be popular in DVD form, is *Get Real* (1998). Set in an elite British public school, the movie is about a thin, unathletic young man, Stephen, and his relationship with the captain of the school rugby team. Stephen hangs with the school newspaper crowd—a potentially supportive network of friends. But at the beginning of the movie he is still wrestling with coming out and is frequenting a public restroom where he meets "straight" men for brief sexual encounters. When Stephen sees one of these men at a social gathering with his wife and young child, the man quickly distances himself from Stephen. A second straight-acting man Stephen meets at the public restroom is one of his schoolmates, John, the most popular jock on campus as captain of the school rugby team, who is dating a popular cheerleader. They quickly develop a romantic interest in each other and find ways of being alone together, even if it means sneaking into the woods for a few moments of intimacy. John, however, is not interested in coming out about their relationship to others and has accepted the need to hide this part of his life. Later, John will even participate in bullying and kicking Stephen—to prove his straightness—when the rugby team catches them in the locker room together.

In one of the movie's most touching scenes, John breaks down and cries as he confides to Stephen about a romantic attachment he had with a fellow rugby player the year before. It becomes clear that he is still very hurt by the fact that his buddy rejected him and that they have been distant ever since. Yet this is just what John will do to Stephen, as he chooses to remain in the closet rather than acknowledge their relationship and love. John's rationale for continuing to date his girlfriend is that it provides cover. People won't suspect that he and Stephen are having a relationship, and that way they can continue to see each other secretly. Aside from this rationale for lying about his life and their relationship, John clearly is not "out" because he thinks there is something wrong with homosexuality, and he does not accept himself for who he is. He tells Stephen he went out with his girlfriend because "I needed to feel good about myself." Stephen asks, "Did you?" And John replies, almost in tears, "All I could feel is that I was going through the motions." Here straight-acting implies performing as a heterosexual, and that made John feel normal. But at the same time he recognizes it was not being true to who he "really" was. If he ultimately chooses to act "normal" rather than risk giving up all the power and privilege he exercises, and because he is ashamed of his homosexual desire, it is at the cost of happiness. A central theme of this movie, and other gay movies, is that happiness comes only through self-acceptance. In performance theory terms, we might say that some performances of self are more consistent with what we feel "inside," whereas others are more managed, more dramatic performances meant to convince people that we are something other than what we feel inside. Some performances of self are "truer" to ourselves, more open and honest, more "real," while others hide behind a mask. The climactic scene in the movie takes place at the school's annual award ceremony, where, before the assembled student body and faculty, Stephen is to be given an award for an essay he wrote in the school magazine and John is to be given an award for athlete of the year. In his acceptance speech, Stephen tells the audience that he has been given an award for writing a story about growing up "as I imagined it must be for most of you." There was to be another essay by him in the school magazine, he said, but it was censored because it was "about a young guy who just happened to be gay." Stephen almost breaks down for a few moments, then, more steadily and with conviction says, "I'm sick of feeling totally alone. I want to have friends who like me for who I am . . . not someone I pretend to be." He calls on people not to be afraid, and to accept others for who they are. Some come to his defense, including his parents and his circle of friends, while John cowers in the back and quickly leaves after receiving his own award. The film ends with Stephen beginning to develop a support network as an "out" gay man. He finds happiness, while John, the straight-acting gay man who seems to have everything, is left unhappy and with a low self-esteem, a victim of hegemonic masculinities and the epistemology of the closet.

Edge of Seventeen was released the same year as *Get Real*, and this American film is another variation on the narrative of the queer guy with an eye for the straight-acting guy. In this case, the straight-acting guy is an out gay college student majoring in hotel management, appropriately named Rod—a man who measures power in terms of sexual conquests and getting what he wants. He acts, that is, the part of young straight college student on the make, always after the next sexual conquest, using romantic pickup lines to get his way and then dumping guys who want something more. Rod performs the hegemonic masculinity of an aggressive, self-interested stud. Eric, the young gay man in this movie who falls for Rod, begins the film as a shy, skinny, awkward but otherwise "normal" high school student living in Sandusky, Ohio, in 1984. When Eric and Rod meet and spend time together that summer, working in a nearby amusement park, Rod quickly decides that this shy, innocent, just-coming-out young man will be his next sexual conquest. Eric is impressed by Rod's assertive, take-control attitude and also his romantic tenderness, and he falls hopelessly in love. When Rod moves back to Columbus and Ohio State University that fall, Eric hounds him with phone calls telling him how much he misses him—all of which irritate Rod, who has lost all interest in Eric. After being sexually used one more time, then finally dumped by Rod, Eric begins to pick himself up and realize he doesn't need what Rod represents, and that in fact they didn't have much in common. With the help of supportive parents and a butch lesbian bartender, he comes out as a gay man and finds a support network in the gay community—represented by a gay bar attended by lesbians, gay men, and drag queens, where people of different races and interests mix and perform their own interpretations of self. This is not a representative gay bar so much as a bar meant to represent a queer space of openness and acceptance of people for who they are. For Eric, that means stylizing his body as a punk body, and thus a gender non-conforming body that is also feminized. The *New York Times*, in its review of the film, noted that when Eric begins to come out, his narcissistic side comes out and he "metamorphoses . . . into a preening distillation of period British pop fashion, with flaming two-toned hair, eyeliner and Culture Club-inspired clothes" (Holden, 1999). He also begins dreaming of moving to New York City and becoming a concert pianist. His mother, who once had such dreams, is sympathetic, and when he finally does come out to her, she is his staunchest supporter. But even as an out gay man, Eric learns that he cannot afford to fall for guys who sweet-talk him and manipulate him into doing what he does not want to do. He learns how to be strong on his own, without needing the validation of these versions of straight-acting men, and to wait for a man who has more to offer, like the young man he meets at the bar who is also into punk music and styles.

A third popular gay indie film that deals with the complex and contradictory relationship between gay men and hegemonic images of straightness is a documentary rather than a dramatic romance. *Straight Acting* (2005), according to the movie's promotional materials, is "the story of one man's journey from a closeted Mormon missionary into an openly gay athlete." It is the story of the filmmaker, Spencer Windes, but mostly it is the story of men who play highly competitive contact sports in gay sports leagues and organizations—everything from rugby to ice hockey to bull riding in a rodeo. The film begins with clippings from gay newspapers, the kind of personal ads in the form: "Straight-acting GWM (gay, white, male) seeking other straight-acting GWMs for fun and possibly more." This speaks once more of a constructed desire among many gay men for "straight-acting" men, not just by gay men who do not act straight but by those who do. The ultimate desire among straight men in a patriarchal and heteronormative culture, according to Sedgwick (1985), is for other men, and this desire is played out in sports and the homosocial bonding that surrounds it. "Straight-acting" suggests some gay men are genuinely "straight" in every way other than sexual orientation, and that in an ironic way they are not acting at all. This is the position put forward by Lance Bass, of course, and as I have already said, it has its appeal, although we must also ask how innocent this performance and presentation of masculinity is, given that it is modeled on hegemonic straightness.

The narrator begins by asking a number of gay athletes what "straight-acting" means to them. One rugby player answers: "I know so many straight men who are 'nelly' as hell. So when I hear that term, 'straight-acting,' my brain fries." This works to effectively disassociate straightness from sexual orientation; as one of the other young men remarks jokingly, he is a straight man who happens to like sex with men. Yet another athlete—a man built like a professional football player, with a short black beard and sporting a black eye from last week's rugby game—remarks, "For me straight-acting is the equivalence of self-loathing." His point is that if he became an athlete just because he was trying to act like straight men, it would be a form of internalized oppression. Consequently, he does not view himself as acting straight, just being himself, a "normal" guy who happens to like competitive contact sports and hanging out with his buddies and who happens to be gay. Several of the young athletes interviewed even argue that because they do not fit into self-imposed stereotypes in the gay community, they feel excluded and marginalized within that community. Others report being turned off by media stereotypes of gay people and feeling unable to relate to these stereotypes:

> There is just a very narrow stereotype you have to fit into in gay society. . . . There's a lot of shows, like *Will and Grace* and *Queer Eye for the Straight Guy*, that depict a lot of negative attitudes about gay people. . . . That's not me and that's not anybody I know.
> The images I saw in the media were all negative. It was a guy in a dress, or a big, scary leather man on a motorcycle.
> I don't think a lot of people realize there are a lot of [here he pauses] "normal" [and he makes quote marks with his hands] gay people out there.
> It's all about breaking stereotypes and making it seem that we're just as normal as everybody else. Well, we really are, but it doesn't seem that way to some people.

These comments represent insightful critiques of media representations and performances of gayness that circulate in both the mainstream and gay media. The men refuse to be bound by these stereotypes, and their assertions that they are "normal" are meant to indicate that they do not fit into stereotypes and refuse to. The act of participating in competitive contact sports is itself a refusal to adhere to these media constructions of acting gay. Part too of what these young gay men are rejecting is the stereotype of the "gay lifestyle," organized around promiscuous sexuality and bars.

To give viewers some idea of how oppressive the controlling, hegemonic images of gay men have been, and what an impact these images have on gay men, Windes interjects scenes from an early 1970s *60 Minutes* episode in which Mike Wallace calmly reports: "Most Americans are repelled by the mere notion of homosexuality. . . . The average homosexual is promiscuous and not interested in or capable of a lasting relationship like that of a heterosexual marriage. His love life consists of a series of chance encounters at the bars he inhabits." A psychiatrist is then asked if he thinks homosexuals can be happy. He replies, "The fact that someone is a homosexual . . . automatically rules out the possibility that he will remain happy for long." Windes interweaves his own story into the text at this point. He suggests that while he was in the closet and not open about who he was, he was unhappy and unmotivated. He became overweight and out of shape, he dropped out of college and lost friends, he lost his job, and he had to move in with his parents. Then one day he saw a newspaper story about Mark Ingham, one of the 9/11 heroes who tried to take back the hijacked jet headed to Washington, D.C., and lost their lives in the process. He had been a member of a gay men's rugby team in San Francisco—The Fog. "He wasn't who I expected a gay man to be," Windes says. "I couldn't imagine a rugby team of gay guys." He finally got the courage to begin working out again and turning his life around, and ended up playing on a gay rugby team in Los Angeles.

Windes clearly means to represent "straight-acting" gay men as just "normal" men, although "normal" continues to be defined in terms of an athleticism that is organized around aggression, competition, and hierarchy, and excludes those who are not "man enough" to make the cut.

This aspect of acting straight is linked in the film to an authentic male-ness that is ultimately tribal, the rites of entrée into the male world of hunting and battle. Scenes of African "natives" with spears, their faces painted, yelling war chants (one supposes), flash on the screen. If this is supposed to be humorous on one level, it is to be taken seriously on an-other. Sports and athletic competition are sublimated forms of tribal male bonding but without the need to actually go on the warpath. The film ends up celebrating the cult of athletic masculinity—for all men, gay or straight. Again, if this makes sense on one level, it is wise to be a bit suspicious. In one of the most revealing scenes in the movie, a young rugby player is toasting his buddies at a postgame beer party. He holds his glass on high and leads the crowd in a chant, to much cheering and laughter: "Who can take a chicken? Spread its little legs, fuck it in the ass until it gives us scrambled eggs." The narrator at this point interjects, "Looking around at all these happy, healthy homos, wearing their bat-tle scars with pride, I had an epiphany. I liked these guys! They were my kind of men." The "positive" role models he seeks to emulate end up acting a lot like Rod in *Edge of Seventeen*.

What saves *Straight Acting* are the moments of critical insight, the comments by "real" gay men that reveal some of the costs of being treated as "abnormal" and out of place in the world of sports. They also reveal some of the reasons more young gay men do not take advantage of op-portunities to participate in sports in high school and college. Several men in the movie report having been harassed or bullied by jocks in their schools generally and also more particularly in locker rooms, and this meant that they stayed clear of sports and locker rooms as much as pos-sible. One ice hockey player talks about how as a boy he loved sports, along with his three older brothers, who all excelled in athletics. "But starting around junior high, because I was a boy who did his homework and paid attention in class," he says, "I started getting called the school faggot. Locker rooms in particular were a place where I got harassed a lot, so I kind of dropped out of playing sports in junior high." This is a telling comment and ambiguous in meaning. He takes for granted the notion that gay people are "brainiacs" who take their schoolwork seri-ously, as if this were some essential aspect of his gayness that was unac-ceptable in the school's jock culture. He was acting gay by taking school seriously, and that meant he could not act straight by taking athletics seriously. The consequences of "acting gay" and "acting straight" are thus significant—for both groups. And they point to the need to disrupt these reigning narratives of hegemonic masculinity.

CONCLUDING THOUGHTS

One of the effects of multiculturalism and diversity education has been to promote more "positive" images of gay people. This is all well and good if the alternative is to promote "negative" images. But as I have sought to show in this chapter, we only get so far by trying to normalize gayness in this way, to treat gay men (in this case) as just like "normal," "real," heterosexual men except for the object of their sexual desire. What gets ignored is the broader need to question or trouble the hegemonic norms of masculinity that get reproduced and legitimated through setting up "normal" and "abnormal" categories (for we cannot have one without the other), and linking them to the performance of "straightness" and "gayness." What gets ignored as well is how gayness gets linked to acting like a girl, or a "sissy," so that the battle is most directly about a hegemonic masculinity that conquers, subordinates, and distances itself from anything perceived as feminine. This points to the need to focus on discussions of sexual identity and difference within the context of gender studies and a critical pedagogy of patriarchal, phallocentric masculinity.

There is some reason to be hopeful, at least, in the fact that young people today are much more attuned to understanding identity and subjectivity as a performance, an act, something stitched together from performances in popular culture and everyday life, rather than anything essential or natural—although some performances are genuine and others are designed to hide how we feel inside. As I have said, this is potentially transformative in that it paves the way for a critical deconstruction of the reigning tropes, norms, and narratives of masculinity in popular culture, to show how they set up certain gendered power relations. Once people recognize their own and others' gendered identity in this way, it may lead them to ask how masculinity and femininity might be re-performed in subversive ways, against the grain, and so that it is not complicit in systems and structures of inequality, marginalization, and exclusion. This is the work of critical media literacy and critical pedagogy in the era ahead.

References

Apple, M. (2006). *Educating the "Right" Way: Markets, Standards, God, and Inequality, Second Edition.* New York: Routledge.

Baudrillard, J. (1994). *Simulacra and Simulation.* Ann Arbor: University of Michigan Press.

Butler, J. (1990). *Gender Trouble: Feminism and the Subversion of Identity.* New York: Routledge.

———. (2007). *Undoing Gender.* New York: Taylor & Francis.

Carlson, D., & Apple, M. (1998). Introduction: Critical Educational Theory in Unsettling Times. In D. Carlson & M. Apple (Eds.), *Power/Knowledge/Pedagogy: The Meaning of Democratic Education in Unsettling Times.* Boulder, CO: Westview Press, 1–40.

Coles, T. (2009). Negotiating the Field of Masculinity: The Production and Reproduction of Multiple Dominant Masculinities. *Men and Masculinities,* 12 (1), 30–44.

Connell, R. W. (2000). *The Men and the Boys.* Oxford, UK: Polity.

———. (2005). *Masculinities.* Berkeley: University of California Press.

Foucault, M. (1980). *History of Sexuality, Volume 1.* New York: Vintage.

———. (1995). *Discipline and Punish: The Birth of the Prison.* New York: Vintage.

Gramsci, A. (1971). *Selections from the Prison Notebooks.* New York: International Publishers.

Hall, G. S. (1969/1905). *Adolescence.* New York: Arno.

Holden, S. (1999). Film Review: Edge of Seventeen: A Many Gendered Thing, The True Nature of Love. *New York Times,* May 14.

Ladd, T., & Mathisen, J. (1999). *Muscular Christianity: Evangelical Protestants and the Development of American Sport.* Grand Rapids, MI: BridgePoint Books.

Lusher, D., & Robins, G. (2009). Hegemonic and Other Masculinities in Local Social Contexts. *Men and Masculinities,* 11 (4), 387–423.

McLaren, P., Hammer, R., Sholle, D. & Reilly, S. (1995). *Rethinking Media Literacy: A Critical Pedagogy of Representation.* New York: Peter Lang.

Noddings, N. (2003). *Caring: A Feminine Approach to Ethics and Moral Education, Second Edition.* Berkeley: University of California Press.

Nowak, A., Abel, S., and Ross, K. (2007). *Rethinking Media Education: Critical Pedagogy in Identity Politics.* Cresskill, NJ: Hampton Press.

Rice, C. (2006). The Myth of "Straight-Acting." *Advocate,* October 10, 88.

Salih, S. (2006). On Judith Butler and Performativity. In Lovass, K. & Jenkins, M. (Eds.), *Sexualities and Communication in Everyday Life: A Reader.* New York: Sage.

Sedgwick, E. (1985). *Between Men: English Literature and Male Homosocial Desire.* New York: Columbia University Press.

———. (1990). *Epistemology of the Closet.* Berkeley: University of California Press.

Visser, R. (2009). I'm Not a Very Manly Man. *Men and Masculinities*, 11 (3), 367–371.

Wexler, P., with Crichlow, W., Kern, J., and R. Martusewicz. (1992). *Becoming Somebody: Toward a Social Psychology of School.* Washington, DC: Falmer.

Chapter 6

FLUID: TEEN AND YOUTH IDENTITY CONSTRUCTION IN CYBERSPACE

Donyell L. Roseboro

As an undergraduate student in 1995, I distinctly remember my impatience with the e-mail of that era. With its slow dial-up connection (yes, it literally dialed up and sounded something like a sick fax machine) and lack of an insert feature (how many of us remember having to erase an entire e-mail to correct one spelling mistake?), it could never become a preferred means of communication, I thought, much less a way to socially network billions of people. The Internet has evolved into a vehicle for information gathering, social networking, event and travel planning, and proselytizing (to name a few). This evolution comes imbued with particular cultural implications and is understood through various cultural perspectives. The Internet is not culturally neutral, and we can't assume that its content is culture-free. Yet its capacity to influence, to reach, and to affect is undeniable. Perhaps most important to those of us who are interested in the way young people learn, the Internet further complicates the ways we discuss knowledge and identity as socially constructed. When social networks have no geographic bounds, when text talk transcends linguistic differences, when identity is disembodied, and when the meaning of time changes, our processes of constructing/learning the self take on new form.

The numbers of youth using the Internet are not surprising to those of us who work with them. According to a survey done by Princeton Research Associates International (2007/2008), 93 percent of teens use the Internet (up from 87 percent in 2004). Of those, 63 percent reported using the Internet daily; 81 percent used it to visit websites for movies, music, sports stars, or TV shows; and 65 percent used it to visit social networking sites like MySpace or Facebook. Seventy-one percent of them own a cellphone, 77 percent of them own a gaming system (e.g., Xbox, PlayStation, or Wii), and 74 percent of them own an iPod or portable music device. They are, as Kelsey (2008) has proclaimed, "Generation MySpace," with twenty-four-hour access to virtual clubs whose processes and lingo are purposefully designed to limit, restrict, and prevent parent access. 99 TOY LMIRL. What? Did you miss that? Let me translate: 99 (parent is no longer watching), TOY (thinking of you), LMIRL (let's meet in real life) (Netlingo, 2009). As a nonphysical interactive space with its own rules and discourse, the Internet allows for the construction of knowledge and identity distinct from the embodied raced, gendered, classed, and sexed personas that teens cannot escape in face-to-face interactions. Quite literally, anyone can refashion, reinvent, or rewrite themselves in cyberspace.

And while teens may believe or hope that their makeovers are independently driven, advertisers believe and hope otherwise. In 2007 companies spent more than $21 million on online advertising, and by 2009, analyst Doug Anmuth estimated, that figure would increase to more than $31 million. Anmuth also predicted that total advertising dollars would grow from $26.1 billion in 2008 to $45.5 billion in 2012 (Schonfeld, 2008). Companies use a variety of marketing strategies to reach children and teens online, most of which integrate the advertisements with some sort of game or interactive site such that young people may not even realize they are being sold a particular product. Virtual environments, often dubbed "village," "town," "clubhouse," or "planet," allow young people to interact with product representatives who appear as characters, as opposed to salespeople (Media Awareness Network, 2009, par. 7). This integration of games and advertising, often coupled with personalized greetings as young people enter the sites, represents an attempt by advertisers to transform young people into lifelong consumers.

In fact, even in social networking sites, where teens may believe they are exercising complete creative freedom, advertisers extend their wares. On MySpace, banner headlines announcing movie or music releases loom large at the top of the home page, and MySpace officials solicit advertisers by luring them with the promise of targeting more than 70 million users. They suggest to potential advertisers, "Show your ads to people interested in sports, fashion, yoga, gospel music, politics, TV shows, and over 1,100 more interests. Target ads by location, age, gender, education level, relationship status, and parental status" (MySpace, MyAds, 2009, par. 2). And the fun doesn't stop there. Once an advertiser has purchased an ad, s/he can monitor the hits of each ad and actually "pay per click," paying a set amount for each time a user clicks on an ad. In similar fashion, Facebook attracts potential advertisers by claiming that their ads could reach more than 250 million users. The company offers ways potential advertisers can "optimize" their ads by reaching more users, altering the content to make it more relevant, or making other modifications (Facebook Advertising, 2009).

The collusion of advertisers to solicit the disposable income of youth is not a new phenomenon, but it is mediated differently online. Making use of asynchronous communication and immediate communicative possibilities in cyberspace, companies can transmit their ads across wider social networks instantaneously. The larger questions I will explore in this chapter are: How might we consider the Internet as a cultural phenomenon bound by its historical evolution? How does the Internet mediate the construction of knowledge and identity for children and teens? And what are the implications for cyberspace identity construction on marginalized, oppressed, and erased groups? Of course, the final question I will address is, What does all of this have to do with teaching and learning?

FROM BOMBS TO BOOBS: THE EVOLUTION OF THE INTERNET FROM DEFENSE MECHANISM TO DISSEMINATOR OF SEX(ED) MESSAGES

In 1958 the Defense Department of the U.S. federal government initiated the Advanced Research Project Agency. DARPA, as it was later named, was created as a direct response to the Soviet Union's successful satellite launch into space (Sputnik). Once NASA took control of the civilian space program in 1960, DARPA focused more on computer processing. So the same agency that developed F-117 stealth fighters and M16 assault rifles facilitated the research and development of information-processing systems that would lead to computer networking and eventually the Internet. According to the agency, DARPA's current mission "is to maintain the technological superiority of the U.S. military and prevent technological surprise from harming our national security. We also create technological surprise for our adversaries" (About DARPA, n.d.). Although the scientists credited with developing the networking systems that would lead to the Internet were not intent on surprising, attacking, or eliminating our adversaries, the integration of their work into DARPA meant that, from the outset, it was created to demonstrate U.S. superiority, to use research and development as a means to do so, and to give us an edge in future conflicts.[1]

J. C. R. Licklider, a professor at MIT, first conceived of a "galactic computer network," one that would allow for the global accessing of data from multiple sites around the world. In 1962, the same year that Lick, as he was called, recorded his galactic network thoughts on paper, he became director of the computer research program at DARPA. In this role, he eventually worked with Ivan Sutherland, Bob Taylor, and MIT researcher Lawrence G. Roberts to design a network in which computers could share information and communicate more efficiently ("packet switching" would allow for the faster transmission of data). Once Leonard Kleinrock published his packet-switching theory in 1964, the journey toward achieving Lick's galactic networking dream was well under way (Leiner et al., 2003).

ARPANET, the first network created by the DARPA project, included four interface messaging processors (IMPs) located in four places: UCLA, Stanford University, UC Santa Barbara, and the University of Utah. By December 1969, all four IMPs were connected. Although this project began under the auspices of the Defense Department, the computer scientists involved, particularly Lick, believed that computer networks could facilitate community building; he also recognized that the politics of the era, specifically the cold war with the Soviet Union, had profound implications for the direction of science. In an interview conducted in 1988, Lick says,

> At that time, nuclear explosives were getting to be a big thing. That was 1950. I think Hartwell was in 1951 and Charles was in 1952 and 1953. So it was right at the crucial time, when the Russians were getting the . . . Everybody was kind of excited about that. I remember psychologists were wondering whether they should go into more practical, military-oriented things, or stay in research. One kid was saying, 'Well, I don't want to write the last journal paper.' There was some feeling of imminence. (Aspray & Norberg, 1988, p. 6)

From the outset, the political climate of the time led to a sense of defensive, protective urgency in the creation of computer networking. There was a clear delineation in federal policies, one that constructed an "us" versus "them" discourse fueled by a desire to extend democracy's territorial control. So while Lick and his cohorts believed in the communicative and community-building possibilities of computer networks, they also faced a political climate marked by the Red Scare and McCarthyism, both of which incited a fervor to identify anyone who was un-American.

By the 1970s the National Science Foundation had become involved with ARPANET; by 1979 Kevin MacKenzie had asked that some sort of emotion be integrated into the text of e-mail messages (this would lead to the development of emoticons); by 1980 the extended network had experienced its first serious virus; and by 1983 there were 113 IMPs on the network. In 1990 world.std.com emerged as the first commercial Internet service provider. The early 1990s saw the invasion of new types of worms that crippled systems, and by the mid-1990s other Internet service providers had emerged (e.g., CompuServe, America Online, Prodigy). People had begun to use the term "surfing the Internet," coined by Jean Armour Polly (a librarian), and by the late 1990s several countries had started to restrict people's Internet use (Zakon, 2006). What had begun as an effort by the Defense Department to develop more effective and efficient means of communication had transformed into a networking nightmare for some, with government officials, politicians, and other folks wondering how to disconnect, shut down, or resist the unseen dangers of the Internet.

Indeed, it seems that the culture of defense and protection that initially framed the network has embedded within the net a cultural expectation of danger and suspicion. As I began my research for this piece, I searched Amazon.com for any books related to teens and the Internet. Of the related texts that appeared, the first twenty-one seemed most relevant.[2] Of those, however, I noticed an interesting trend: Most of the titles depict the Internet as a thing that teens need to be protected from. Just to give you an idea, some of the titles were *Cyber-Safe Kids, Cyber-Savvy Teens: Helping Young People Learn to Use the Internet Safely and Responsibly, Online Teen Dangers: The Five Greatest Internet Dangers Teenagers Face and What You Can Do to Protect Them, How to Protect Your Children on the Internet: A Road Map for Parents and Teachers,* and *Surfing the Internet Safely: A Guide for Teens and Adults.* So, in response to the first question I posed at the start of this chapter—"How might we consider the Internet as a cultural phenomenon bound by its historical evolution?"—I conclude that one of the most relevant historical aspects of the net is its creation within a Defense Department agency whose primary mission is to protect the United States from its adversaries. As the net expanded and developers struggled with fighting off worms, viruses, and other sorts of networking parasites, these intangible adversaries compounded the fear framework already infused in the net. Once governments came online (the White House and the United Nations both joined in 1993, along with a host of others including Bulgaria, Costa Rica, Egypt, Fiji, and Ghana), the politics of networking became more complicated. How, for example, could nations establish trust online?

In response to perceived cyberspace threats, Congress passed two regulations, both intended to curb young people's access to particular content on the Internet—the Communications Decency Act (CDA) in 1996 and the Child Online Protection Act (COPA) in 1998. With both of these, legislators hoped to restrict the amount of "obscene" content and/or "material harmful to minors" (Preston, 2008, pp. 1419–1420). As expected, both of these regulations were challenged in court by the American Civil Liberties Union (ACLU). The Supreme Court ultimately prohibited the application of either regulation saying, in short, that the CDA went too far in restricting free speech and that COPA was too broad—almost any content could be scrutinized as possibly being "material harmful to minors." As a parent, I know that my behavior and speech could too often be classified as "material harmful to minors," so I understand the Court's position. Nonetheless, the Court, in rejecting both regulations, left the Internet open to teens and youth with only the possibility that public opinion would encourage companies to filter the content that was made available to young people.

In this battle over what to restrict and how to do it, I came to realize that what "they" (the infamously ambiguous group that calls for such restrictions) worry about most is content that is related to drugs or sex. So in about four decades, the enormous possibilities that were conceived of in those early days have become a seemingly widespread fear that our young people will see too much sex, cleavage, genitalia, etc., online. What began as a network to spawn more efficient communication in order to protect us from our adversaries has become a network infested with unnamed adversaries, all of whom want to offer sex to our children. Obviously I am being facetious. But do not mistake my sarcasm for a brushing over of the seriousness of this issue. Yes, there are sexual predators on the Internet whose specific intent is to lure unsuspecting young people into unsafe predicaments. I do not want those people harming anyone's children. But I do question the implication that sex is automatically obscene, an evil from which young people need to be protected.

"I'M COMING OUT, BUT AS WHAT?"
THE INTERNET AND TEEN IDENTITY DEVELOPMENT

In the second edition of *Kinderculture*, Steinberg and Kincheloe argued that we face a new paradigm for a new childhood. "Central to this new paradigm is the effort to make sure that children are intimately involved in shaping their social, psychological, and educational lives" (2004, p. 8). This authorship, this ability to script one's own story, is critical to the millennial generation's need rewrite the rules (Thielfoldt & Scheef,

2004). They have to believe that they determine their own destinies, and the Internet allows them unparalleled access to the information, the friends (friends = family), and the products to do so. They can re-create themselves as avatars, capable of slaying dragons and leading attack squadrons; they can construct virtual worlds via MySpace and Facebook, accepting some friends and rejecting others without uttering a word; the list could go on indefinitely. In a postmodern sense, identity is more than multiple; it is artfully and purposefully designed. It is, perhaps, artificial embodiment, an embodied sense self-dependent on computer-assisted technologies.

So what has the Internet done to or for the construction of the adolescent self? Two of the most prominent thinkers in child psychology, Jean Piaget and Erik Erikson, developed frameworks for our understanding of child and adolescent development. Piaget argued that children reach the formal operational stage at ages twelve to fifteen and that in this stage they learn to think logically and systematically. Erikson argued that teenagers engage in a constant questioning of the self ("identity versus role confusion" stage); those allowed to experience the world will come to a sense of self, whereas those who are consistently asked to conform to their parents' expectations will not develop a sense of independence or self-awareness.

Thus, in thinking about how the Internet, as a required medium of communication for many teens, affects the application of logical and systematic thinking, I believe it has redefined the processes that shape such thinking. Without the Internet, we understand logic and systematic thinking as linear, slow, and rather isolated processes. I envision the lone student sitting at her desk working a problem in incremental steps (which are, of course, required by a teacher who has students "show all of their work"). With the Internet and other networked technologies, the linear nature of logic and systematic analysis no longer applies. Nor do the boundaries of time confine problem-solving processes; time has no bounds on the Internet, and, as a result, logic and systematic thinking do not have to wait (so to speak) for thoughts to traverse geographic spaces.

Many who study teens and the Internet have commented on how the millennial generation adeptly multitask, but this is not the only distinction that makes their communication processing such a unique phenomenon. Their multitasking is multidirectional, discursively surface yet socially layered. They speak with, listen to, and consider information through various media simultaneously; though their readings may seem superficial given the speed at which they do them, they manage to create and maintain online friendships, communicate with each of these friends, update profiles and manage accounts, shop, and stay abreast of current films, music, etc. In many ways their surface reading of multiple sites using varied technologies facilitates their maintenance of a multilayered social network that, in and of itself, frames a new cultural paradigm.

To analyze this paradigm further, let's consider MySpace and Facebook once again. These sites make it clear who's a friend and who's not, and based on one's level, one has different access. No nonverbal cues or awkward explanations needed. Most important, the identities and friendships created on social networking sites are public identities that can be manipulated, traced, solidified, erased, embraced, and/or rejected. Social positioning in cyberspace comes with different documentation: Photos replace bodies, text lingo replaces standard language, emoticons replace touch, social networking sites replace clubs (the latter require ID), and avatar manipulation replaces name brand purchasing. Indeed, the success of MySpace was predicated on its unique profile pages; users can customize them to create a distinct online identity (Hansell, 2006).

But this identity is heavily influenced by capitalist expectations that MySpace's parent company (now Rupert Murdoch, who, by the way, acquired MySpace in his purchase of Intermix Media for $580 million) make a profit. If we believe that identity is constructed in a relationship (Tajfel & Turner, 1986) and social networking sites allow users to "friend" corporations (as does MySpace), then one's identity is bound by principles of consumerism. As Hansell (2006) analyzes the effects of consumer culture on MySpace, he says,

> More than 70 million members have signed up—more than twice as many as MySpace had when Mr. Murdoch agreed to buy it—drawn

by a simple format that lets users build their own profile pages and link to the pages of their friends. It has tapped into three passions of young people: expressing themselves, interacting with friends and consuming popular culture. MySpace now displays more pages each month than any other Web site except Yahoo. More pages, of course, means more room for ads. And, in theory, those ads can be narrowly focused on each member's personal passions, which they conveniently display on their profiles. As an added bonus for advertisers, the music, photos and video clips that members place on their profiles constitute a real-time barometer of what is hot.

This begs the question: Which comes first, the personal profile or the ad? If companies are mining personal profiles for information that will help them determine how best to market their products and then, in turn, advertising on social networking sites, this "mining-identity cycle" makes it difficult to determine who might have control in the relationship. In other words, does the ad tell the individual how to construct her/his identity or does the individual demand from the company what s/he needs to build a persona?

The marketing techniques that may go unnoticed by young people on social networking sites represent just one way that identity is controlled, manipulated, and/or influenced on the Internet. The fear framework created by adults who believe that the Internet holds imminent danger for teens and youth has created a media discourse that publicizes the Internet as an unsafe space. This publicity may actually increase the attractiveness of cyberspace to teens, who are quite naturally trying to assert their independence. After I surveyed the texts that relate to teens and youth and the Internet, I also pulled up articles (journal and newspaper) using a popular online database called EBSCOhost. Of the 250 articles I surveyed (the oldest dated back to 2000), 238 came with headlines that specifically discussed young people's use of the Internet in what I characterized as either a neutral or negative way—neutral headlines were ones that did not emotionally characterize teen or youth use of the Internet, did not impose some sort of danger motif on that use, and/or did not include terms that have historically been framed as dangerous (e.g., sex, pornography, drugs, addiction). The remaining twelve headlines focused more on the Internet and less on young people's use of it, so I characterized these as other.

Of the 238 article headlines, I perceived 122 to be neutral and 116 to be negative. Although this divide was almost even, I noticed that the balance shifted as the age of the population in question changed. For articles related to teen use of the Internet, I counted twenty neutral headlines, eight negative, and two other. For articles related to youth and the Internet, I identified nineteen neutral headlines, sixteen negative, and two other. And for articles related to children and the Internet, I identified eighty-three neutral headlines, ninety-two negative, and eight other. Apparently, the Internet becomes less of an unsafe space as one ages; thus, the need to discuss that safety diminishes. Although this examination begs for a deeper analysis of the content of those articles, I believe that headlines matter, particularly to a generation that consumes popular culture via varied technological media and at increasing speed.

Equally the language of the negative headlines captured my attention. In general, they emphasize drugs, tobacco, sex, and predatory solicitations as the most dangerous online activities for teens and youth. Here are a few examples: "Youth Internet Users at Risk for the Most Serious Online Sexual Solicitations," "The Exposure of Youth to Unwanted Sexual Material on the Internet," and "Salvaging States' Rights to Protect Children from Internet Predation: State Power to Regulate Internet Activity Under the Dormant Commerce Clause." What strikes me as interesting are the ways that cultural ideas about sex, drugs, and alcohol translate into cyberspace. The sex danger online becomes a heightened solicitation one; while young people are at risk for unwanted sexual advances in face-to-face interactions, the ability to reconstruct (or lie about, whichever phrase you prefer) one's age is easier online, and the consequences for those lies in unchaperoned cyberspace are potentially more threatening, particularly if the "predator" and the youth/teen build an extensive discursive relationship online and then arrange a face-to-face meeting.

While I recognize the threat of sexual predators online, I also question the language that is used to describe the predator and the youth or teen. In framing it as a predator (whom we presume is typically a male) seeking sex from an unsuspecting young person (whom we presume is typically a female), we assign all agency to the male predator regardless of the motivations and actions of the young lady (or young man) who may have initiated the interaction. To extend this discussion, I will borrow a line from Dave Chappelle, one of my favorite comedians and one who happens to have a profile on MySpace. In one of his skits, he asked, "How old is fifteen really?"[3] In typical Chappelle style he follows this question with a list of examples of very different decisions and circumstances for fifteen-year–olds, arriving at his final point that an individual's racial and gender status affects the sense of independence, intellectualism, and ability that others ascribe to the individual. At the same time that we punish adults for preying on sixteen-year-old white girls online, we also sentence sixteen-year-old black boys to prison.

Consider also the fact that the age of adulthood is defined differently in various countries around the world. The age of consent for sexual relations is, for example, thirteen for males in Argentina and sixteen for females, twelve for males and fifteen for females in Angola, thirteen for males and females in Burkina Faso, sixteen for males and females in Cuba, eighteen for males and females in Egypt, fifteen for males and females in France, and fourteen for males and females in China (AVERT, 2009). Though I respect the sovereignty of each nation to define its own laws and customs, I do wonder why age of consent can be different for females and males; in my interpretation, this represents a general belief that girls are in more need of protection, not able to exercise good judgment, and not as capable of acting independently. Equally important, feminist scholars (e.g., Gloria Anzaldua, Betty Friedan, bell hooks, Julia Kristeva, Chandra Mohanty, and Adrien Wing) have for decades documented the gender differences between men and women and the corresponding effect that cultural perceptions of these differences has on people's ability to act. So any beliefs that teens or youth need to be protected on the Internet can be compounded or exacerbated by one's gender with girls "in need" of more protection.

If the presentation of self is a performance, as Goffman (1959) suggested decades ago (and others since then have reemphasized, e.g., Butler, 1993), and that performance is tied to a social context, then the identities that youth and teens construct online in response to perceived dangers represent a purposeful and consistent effort on the part of the teen or youth engaged in the performance. Other scholars who have analyzed identity construction on the Internet have also suggested that this purposeful performance represents an attempt to reconstitute the self that has been further fragmented by cyberspace (e.g., Hanlon, 2001; Lambiase, 2003; Springgay, 2008). In a study of two teen chat rooms (including more than thirty-eight chat sessions and more than 12,000 utterances), Subrahmanyam et al. (2006) discovered that teens identified by gender, age, and location, with gender being the most frequently identified among participants. Most participants (55 percent) self-identified in some way, but themes related to age and sexual identification permeated the chat rooms. Participants in the monitored chat room described themselves as younger, while participants in the unmonitored chat room described themselves as older, with males describing themselves as older more often. In this particular study, gender, age, and geographic location mattered. Race and class are conspicuously absent from this study's findings.

To return to the second question that I posed at the beginning of this chapter, "How does the Internet mediate the construction of knowledge and identity for children and teens?" I suggest that there are several layers to identity construction for youth and teens in cyberspace. First, the history of the Internet as a project in the Defense Department interjects themes of danger and suspicion. Second, media representations of the Internet extend, analyze, and publicize this discourse of danger and suspicion. Third, this discourse of danger and suspicion operates differently for males and females. Fourth, cultural beliefs about gender (which, from a feminist perspective, continue to privilege men as more knowledgeable and able) shape the predatory discourse that surrounds the Internet. And finally, the presentation of self (or the performance of self) online is fundamentally shaped by advertisers who target specific populations and who mine user profiles in social networking sites to create more effective marketing campaigns.

FROM WHERE DO I SHOUT?
CYBERTYPING AND E-RACING IN A VIRTUAL WORLD

While young people find ways to put themselves back together in cyberspace, to construct or remake a particular identity, and to develop the language to support that identity, the Internet has also been hailed as the best possible space for anonymity. This anonymity affords people the opportunity to disrobe, disconnect, or erase those identity markers that are visually problematic in face-to-face interactions (e.g., race, gender, sexual orientation). In her book *Cybertypes: Race, Identity, and the Internet,* Lisa Nakamura, a pre-eminent scholar on race and the Internet, argues that technology and culture combine to create different possibilities for the ways we interpret and understand race online. Computer language translates culture for us and, in doing so, alters the ways we name, define, and extend our beliefs. She says,

> In an attempt to transcode the language of race and racialism that I observed online, I coined the term *cybertype* to describe the distinctive way that the internet propagates, disseminates, and commodifies images of race and racism. The study of racial cybertypes brings together the cultural and the computer layer; that is to say, cybertyping is the process by which computer/human interfaces, the dynamics and economics of access, and the means by which users are able to express themselves online interacts with the "cultural layer" or ideologies regarding race that they bring with them into cyberspace. (2002, p. 3)

With its possibilities for anonymity, the Internet is uniquely positioned to support the hope of many well-meaning white people who want to believe that they "don't see color" or that "color doesn't matter." But absence does not remove importance, nor does silence denote insignificance. At times, what we do not see and what we do not say are the most salient aspects of the conversation. Nakamura (2007), in a study that she conducted on the Internet, celebrity web pages, and race, determined that race does matter on the Internet and, with its seemingly infinite possibilities for information gathering and networking, that the Internet allows mixed-race people to be "outed" and their racial identities unveiled. In her analysis, Nakamura comments that James Hill, on the Black Entertainment Television website, "noted that white audiences are unaware of and unable to see stars' multiraciality." She goes on to add, "What I found amazing was the filmmaker's assumption that the average White viewer would understand the subtlety of bi-racial features that let Black folks know Vin Diesel and Jennifer Beals had 'something in 'em,' where most white folks didn't seem to notice at all" (p. 4).

Indeed, it is this issue of being "outed" or "coming out" that holds some significance to our discussion in this chapter. If teens are disclosing age, gender, and location more than race online, then what implications does that have for their understanding of race? Nakamura offers a beginning explanation by using the term "cybertypes" to remind us that "identity online is still typed, still mirrored in oppressive roles even if the body has been left behind or bracketed" (p. 4). And if the Internet is facing an increasing deluge of advertisers who continue to reproduce stereotypical raced, classed, gendered, and sexed images, then race (along with other identity constructs) is virtually present with the corresponding ideological, cultural, or linguistic codes that frame it.

Because race is one aspect of identity whose historical evolution has been documented and discussed as it relates to privilege, knowledge, and power, we know that the sociopsychological effects of racism persist. As one sphere of documented marginalization, race can serve as a point of reference to understanding how oppression operates on multiple levels; it's not just that race matters, for example; one's shade or skin color, whether one is tan, olive, brown, red, white, or black, determines how one is perceived. So when young people do not identify their race online, when their discourse ignores race, they are leaving unanalyzed the multiple layers/complexities of race and in so doing are not translating race discourse into cybertalk. Thus the less that race is discussed online, the less it is redefined and/or rearticulated using an integrated computer/cultural framework. It is, in essence, erased but not e-raced. To be e-raced, it would need to become a normative part of online/text messaging, given its own subsidiary codes, and nuanced in the transcoding process.

To address the third question that I posed at the beginning of this chapter, "What are the implications for cyberspace identity construction on marginalized, oppressed, and erased groups?" I suggest that identity markers must be transcoded in cyberspace, assigned a specific language, and used in everyday chats/texts such that the millennial generation ascribes their meaning to it. If certain identity markers are ignored or erased, the language of identity (e.g., the descriptors we use to define ourselves and the meanings those descriptors convey) has no opportunity to evolve in cyberspace, to find friends, to transcend social, cultural, and geographic spaces, and to seamlessly integrate into the linguistic fabric of the net.

CONCLUSION: WHAT DOES ALL OF THIS HAVE TO DO WITH TEACHING AND LEARNING?

As an educator, I am guided by one fundamental principle: to know my students so that I may tailor instruction to meet their individual needs. The distinctive disembodied linguistic codes that shape teen/tween talk today force me to acknowledge their creativity, their ingenuity, and their independence. They are forming a sense of self in different ways and in different forms. This self-identification is not occurring in isolation, however. They are, whether consciously or subconsciously, influenced by advertisers who friend them, media that present the Internet as a dangerous space, and adults who attempt to control their behavior without always having clear knowledge of the world in which they live. Ultimately, those of us who educate young people must learn to exist in this world; this is where they are, this is how they are constructing themselves, and this is how they learn—EOT.

References

About DARPA (n.d.). Retrieved on August 10, 2009, from www.darpa.gov/about.html.

Aspray, W. & Norberg, A. (1988). Interview with J. C. R. Licklider. Cambridge, MA. Retrieved on August 13, 2009. From http://special.lib.umn.edu/cbi/oh/pdf.phtml?id=180.

AVERT: AVERTing HIV and AIDS (2009). Worldwide Ages of Consent. Retrieved on August 13, 2009, from www.avert.org/age-of-consent.htm.

Butler, J. (1993). *Bodies That Matter: On the Subversive Limits of Sex*. New York: Routledge.

Facebook advertising (2009). Retrieved on August 13, 2009, from www.facebook.com/advertising/?src=pf.

Goffman, E. (1959). *The Presentation of Self in Everyday Life*. Garden City, NY: Doubleday Press.

Hanlon, J. (2001). Disembodied Intimacies: Identity and Relationship on the Internet. *Psychoanalytic Psychology 18*(3), 566–571.

Hansell, S. (2006, April 23). For MySpace, Making Friends Was Easy. Big Profit Is Tougher. Retrieved on July 30, 2009, from www.nytimes.com/2006/04/23/business/yourmoney/23myspace.html?_r=1.

Kelsey, K. M. (2008). *Generation MySpace: Helping Your Teen Survive Online Adolescence*. New York: Marlowe & Company.

Lambiase, J. (2003). Codes on Online Sexuality: Celebrity, Gender, and Marketing on the Web. *Sexuality and Culture 7*(3), 57–78.

Leiner, B. M.; Vinton, G. C.; Clark, D. D.; Kahn, R. E.; Kleinrock, L.; Lynch, D. C.; Postel, J.; Roberts, L. G.; & Wolff, S. (2003). A Brief History of the Internet. Retrieved on August 10, 2009, from www.isoc.org/Internet/history/brief.shtml.

Media Awareness Network (2009). Retrieved on August 2, 2009, from www.media-awareness.ca/english/resources/educational/handouts/internet/online_market_strat s.cfm.

MySpace, MyAds (2009). Retrieved on August 13, 2009, from https://advertise.myspace.com/howitworks.html.

Nakamura, L. (2007). Mixedfolks.com: "Ethnic Ambiguity," Celebrity Outing, and the Internet. Paper presented at the International Communication Association Conference (57th), San Francisco, CA. Retrieved on August 10, 2009, from Communication and Mass Media Complete Database.

———. (2002). *Cybertypes: Race, Identity, and the Internet*. New York: Routledge.

Netlingo (2009). The Netlingo List of Acronyms and Text Message Shorthand. Retrieved on August 13, 2009, from www.netlingo.com/acronyms.php.

Preston, C. (2008). Zoning the Internet: A New Approach to Protecting Children Online. *Brigham Young University Law Review 2007*(6), 1417–1469.

Princeton Research Associates International (2007/2008). Gaming and Civic Engagement of Teens and Parents. Data for November 1, 2007–February 5, 2008. Retrieved on August 13, 2008, from www.cyberethics.info/cyethics2/UserFiles/LenhartEtAl_Teens&VideoGames_Questionnaire_2008.pdf.

Schonfeld, E. (2008, August 13). Lehman's Online Advertising U.S. Forecast: Another $20 Billion in Growth by 2012 and Online Video Takes Off. *TechCrunch*. Retrieved on August 4, 2009, from www.techcrunch.com/2008/08/13/lehmans-online-us-advertising-forecast-another-20-billion-in-growth-by-2012-and-online-video-takes-off/.

Springgay, S. (2008). *Body Knowledge and Curriculum: Pedagogies of Touch in Youth and Visual Culture*. New York: Peter Lang.

Subrahmanyam, K.; Smahel, K.; & Greenfield, P. (2006). Connecting Developmental Constructions on the Internet: Identity Presentation and Sexual Exploration in Online Teen Chat Rooms. *Developmental Psychology: 42*(3), 395–406.

Tajfel, H. and Turner, J. C. (1986). The Social Identity Theory of Inter-group Behavior. In S. Worchel and L. W. Austin (Eds.), *Psychology of Intergroup Relations*. Chicago: Nelson-Hall.

Thielfoldt, D. & Scheef, D. (2004). Generation X and the Millennials: What You Need to Know About Mentoring the New Generations. Retrieved on July 3, 2009, from www.abanet.org/lpm/lpt/articles/mgt08044.html.

Zakon, R. H. (2006). Hobbes' Internet Timeline v.8.2. Retrieved on August 3, 2009, from www.zakon.org/robert/Internet/timeline/.

Chapter 7

TWEEN-METHOD AND THE POLITICS OF STUDYING KINDERCULTURE

Ingvild Kvale Sørenssen and
Claudia Mitchell

THE TERM "TWEEN" IS A FASCINATING one, starting out first as part of marketing discourse and now appearing more as an age demarcation to refer to preteenage children between the ages of seven or eight (although sometimes as young as six) and eleven or twelve (and sometimes even older). Traditionally within several fields of research invested in describing tweens, a dichotomy has been and still is evident in the various different literatures. The dichotomy is between the active, participating, savvy consumer child and the passive victim of media and peer pressure. Two common, taken-for-granted versions of the same assumption stand out within these two stances. First, especially asserted by the more pessimistic school of thought within this research field (child as passive victim), is that media (and hence consumption) are *very* powerful, and that children and young people are more vulnerable and more affected by the media and by the market through advertising than adults. The other version, voiced by the more optimistic theorists, is that media (and hence consumption) in the lives of children are *very* important and figure as tools for asserting one's individuality. Sometimes one might even get the feeling that media and consumption are all there is in children's and young people's lives. Both these views can lead to generalized, essentialist, and sentimentalized views of tweens—and a plethora of books that are directed at the parents of the children and tweens who are seen as being targeted by the marketers. The focus of much of this literature is on how to avoid the commodification of childhood, which is seen as a corruption of the natural state of childhood. In this literature children are often portrayed as "helpless victims of a kind of brainwashing" (Buckingham, 2000, 145). The titles of the various texts are often emblematic of the content: *The Disappearance of Childhood* (Postman, 1982), *Branded: The Buying and Selling of Teenagers* (Quart, 2004), *Born to Buy: The Commercialized Child and the New Consumer Culture* (Schor, 2004), *Consuming Kids: Protecting Our Children from the Onslaught of Marketing and Advertising* (Linn, 2004), *Packaging Girlhood: Rescuing Our Daughters from Marketers' Schemes* (Lamb and Brown, 2007), and *Packaging Boyhood: Saving Our Sons from Superheroes, Slackers, and Other Media Stereotypes* (Lamb, Brown, & Tappan, 2009). This anticonsumption literature highlights how children are tricked and how they have no protection against evil media and marketers. One main focus is on the children themselves, on the notion that consumption is an adult activity that children should not be exposed to, since their emotional immaturity prevents them from making rational, well-considered consumer choices, something adults apparently are experts on. The result can be dramatic: "The more advertising children see and hear, the more likely they are to be depressed and anxious and to suffer family conflict" (Horschild in Schor, 2004). The other main focus is on the industry targeting children and young people. This critique can also be rather extreme, with a starting point stating, at least implicitly, that children are all victims of marketers, advertisements, and commodities. Common to both critiques is the idea that the market is all-powerful and that children are easy targets. In the literature that specifically addresses girls and media, as we explore in a later section, there is the added component of hypersexualization. Central to this work is a deterministic and positivistic perspective.

At the same time, there is a burgeoning literature on marketing that also proclaims on the child consumer. As McNeal (1999) has estimated, in the United States alone they use their pester power to nag their parents into spending $1.88 trillion each year, adding to a $300 billion indirect influence on spending by parents, topped off with $121 billion of their own spending (Lindstrom, 2003, 47; McNeal, 1999). Hence, the marketers have defined children, and tweens in particular, as a highly lucrative market. The marketers, as the "saviors of childhood" facilitating identity work and individual freedom, tend to echo the anticonsumption literature in that they also lean toward deterministic and positivistic ideas, though their conclusions differ. Lindstrom (2003), for example, writes, "Tweens have the ability to sift through the cornucopia of ads without appearing to so much as notice them. . . . They have the situation under control. They are aware of the intention of the communication, and more importantly they're aware of its down-sides" (5). Lindstrom, who describes himself as "a branding guru," suggests that children are quite the opposite of vulnerable and easy targets; rather, they are strong and independent and have the skills to "read" commercials, and therefore cannot be persuaded to buy something that they do not already want. In other words, according to Lindstrom, tweens have grown up in this "information overload" society and are well equipped to handle the amount of information and potential market pressure. "Information overload" is a term of the past; since tweens now supposedly know how to deal with the information, "overload" is inaccurate. Recognizing the savvy of these tween consumers, Michael Thim, the CEO of Initiative Universal Media, proclaimed at a conference in Copenhagen in September 2008, "We are not in control anymore." This statement, of course, implies that marketers once had more control over children but that today's children are so media-savvy they are hard to reach, let alone trick into buying something. Indeed, in more "market liberal" literature, children are often portrayed as mercilessly critical individuals. Examples here are the books *BRANDchild: Remarkable Insights into the Minds of Today's Global Kids and Their Relationships with Brands* (Lindstrom, 2003), *The Great Tween Buying Machine: Capturing Your Share of the Multibillion-Dollar Tween Market* (Siegel, Livingston & Coffey, 2004), and *The Kid's Market: Myths and Realities* (McNeal, 1999). Here the market is presented as an arena for children to be individuals, free to be themselves regardless of parents, teachers, and other authority figures.

TRIANGULATION AND TWEEN-METHOD

From popular as well as academic literature we are then more or less left with these very polarized ideas, or controversies, on what children and childhood are. On the one hand children are objectified as something to protect from the harm of adult life in general, and on the other they are enthusiastically hailed as autonomous, free-floating citizens, or "the empowered child" (Cook, 2005). What these sides have in common is the idea of one homogeneous tween culture and also a very essentialist outlook on tweens. What is missing in both arguments noted above is a sense of the perspectives and views of children themselves as a critical component of Tween Studies. As Joseph Tobin observes, "Why do media researchers and other adults feel they can write confidently about the meaning of a text intended for children without talking to children?" (Tobin, 2000, 147). Ironically, as Mitchell and Reid-Walsh (2002) point out, even much of the literature on child research that tends to focus on the rights of the child to be heard skips over "the consuming child." Thus, in the remainder of this chapter we consider the need for a re-examination of methodologies for exploring the perspectives of the consuming child—particularly the tween. Using examples from Disney Channel's *Hannah Montana* and *High School Musical* along with earlier girl-focused texts such as Bratz and Barbie, we consider the need for what we term "tween method."

Even though there have been several voices calling for a focus on children's experiences, readings, and reflections on kinderculture—and on Disney specifically—for quite some time now (Buckingham, 1997; Drotner, 2003; Wasko, 2001), so far only Drotner seems to have taken this route. Disney *is* problematic, as Henry Giroux (1999), in particular, has highlighted. With all the analysis of the Disney Company and its ever-expanding conglomerates—Disney the man, Disney the brand, Disney the morals and values—the question "where is the Disney audience?" is a tricky one, as our discussion in the introduction demonstrates. However, as Tobin points out, "We cannot know from analyzing the contents of a movie what it will mean to a particular group of children" (Tobin, 2000, 150). This highlights an important aspect of media and childhood studies in relation to Stuart Hall's encoding-decoding model, namely the need to include audiences' voices in such studies. John Fiske's (1987) work on looking at multiple levels of textuality in studying media texts also seems particularly appropriate when considering the need to include the voice of the audience—and, in this case, the voice of the tween—along with the voice of the producer (e.g., Disney Channel) and more conventional forms of content analysis or reading the primary text (e.g., *Hannah Montana* and the various tie-in texts). Another important aspect when studying tweens and popular culture, we believe, is the need for reflexivity both externally and internally within the researcher, as there exists such a clear dichotomy in the perspectives on tweens' relations to media and consumer culture (Sørenssen, 2008).

Working with children's media texts, as Buckingham (2008) observes, entails looking at the broader use of the content and items. This again takes us back to the problematic (and complex) nature of the reading of Disney. Disney not only offers cultural products such as movies and TV series but also brings with them merchandising—a whole lot of it. Since "Team Disney" took over in 1984, with Michael Eisner and Frank Wells behind the steering wheel, the growth of Disney's merchandising has been enormous (Wasko, 2001). This can be read in, for example, Hagen (2001) and Wasko (2001). Home videos and spin-off products range from apparel and toys to furnishings and even a wedding dress line. Disney is more than a media conglomerate; it is also the third-biggest toy producer in the world, if one were to look at all the products it offers as part of one company and just in relation to licensing rights (Disney online).

Children are missing from audience research in media studies more broadly and are also absent in Disney consumer research. Actually, Disney consumer research in and of itself is lacking, with few exceptions other than in studies such as Drotner's (2003). Disney, it seems, is primarily thought of as a constructor of culture (Fjellman, 1992) and media output, and the fact that the company produces so many commodities that are such a big part of very many people's everyday lives seems to be simply overlooked. We advocate, in accordance with cultural studies approaches and the circuit of culture, that there are four arenas, or levels, of textuality that should be investigated in order to better understand the meanings and positionings of children's popular cultural phenomena such as *Hannah Montana* and *High School Musical.* Drawing from Buckingham (2008), we consider the need to look at the primary texts (media texts and/or commodities), the producer texts, the users (or audience) texts, and the environmental texts (where the primary texts are consumed).

The Primary Texts

Disney Channel has produced a number of live-action television shows and movies in the past four to five years that cater to the tween audience. The three *High School Musical* movies, in particular, have had great success. This is a Disney Channel Original Movie made for Disney Channel. With a Disney Channel premiere in 2006, *High School Musical* became a surprisingly huge success; it was followed in 2007 with the sequel, which was also highly successful. The third movie was released in movie theaters in 2008. The first movie has a type of *Grease, Romeo and Juliet,* or *West Side Story* story line in which an athletic boy meets a brainy girl and they find they share a passion for singing. In the typical high school realm, where belonging to different cliques and not overstepping the boundaries of these cliques is how stability is maintained, the boy and girl struggle with their identities and love for each other while the others try to tear them apart. Individuality and freedom prevail, and they discover that they are able to do both biology and basketball—and the school musical. Another highly successful Disney Channel tween venture has been *Hannah Montana,* a live-action sitcom about Miley Stewart, an ordinary high school student by day but pop singer by night. The series premiered in 2006, the same year as the first *High School Musical* movie. A quick look at the *Billboard* 200 gives a good indication of the show's popularity: In 2009 the *Hannah Montana* movie premiered in movie theaters, and the soundtrack, sung by Miley Cyrus (who plays Miley Stewart/Hannah Montana), reached number one; in addition, the Miley Cyrus album *Breakout* reached the number-one position in August 2008, and the double album *Hannah Montana 2/Meet Miley Cyrus* charted at number one in July 2007 (Billboard Online). The themes for this series, as in general for the Disney tween content, include identity struggles (finding one's self) and morals (what is the right thing to do?). The content in both media outputs here is live-action as opposed to traditional Disney cartoons. Strasburger, Wilson & Jordan (2008, 102) suggest that this is because of Disney's "discovery" of the niche tween audience, who are characterized by being "not yet teenagers, but . . . no longer interested in cartoons."

Both *Hannah Montana* and *High School Musical* have become popular phenomena in the Western world. There is a strong presence of media content "leaking into," as Fiske (1987) describes it, to the world of licensing. With this media content comes a whole range of products, from DVDs connected to the series and movies (both the actual series and movies and also the dance-along, sing-along karaoke versions) and CDs (which are commercially highly successful); to fabrics to decorate one's room with (curtains, carpets, bed sheets, and shower curtains); to various toys, clothing, accessories, books and magazines, and stationery. The list goes on and on, with almost any consumer item containing the images from these two media outlets. The goal of the Walt Disney Company is to make value for its shareholders, and in order to do so it tries to make media content that can easily turn into franchises. "Our job is to create franchises for Walt Disney, it's not just to create a television show" (Rich Ross, quoted in *Telegraph*, September 10, 2009).

The tween market is often described as a fickle one (Lindstrom, 2003), and while it may seem as though these tween items are everywhere, they are actually not nearly as popular and pervasive as Disney's *Princess* or *Cars* line of franchising. These two account for 20 percent of the revenues that the company makes a year, with an income from the two of around $6 billion (Disney Consumer Products online). However, Disney's tween market is growing, and tweens in general are thought by marketers to be a highly lucrative market—indeed, they are regarded by some marketers as the heart of the child market, as they are thought to have quite a lot of spending money on their own and are seen to be the segment of the youth market that has more power and influence than the others (Siegel et al., 2004; Lindstrom, 2003).

Producers and the Production Text

A number of researchers write about how Disney influences and constructs culture and social life (for example, Fjellman, 1992; Sammond,

2005; Giroux, 1997, 1999; Bryman, 1995, 2004). Much of this work is based on close readings and content analysis of the theme parks and other Disney texts. No one has talked *to* Disney, getting its side of the story. What do Disney representatives think, and what are their intentions with story lines and consumer products? Clearly, as Radway found in her work with the Book-of-the-Month Club a number of years ago, it is not easy to gain access to this type of informant, and strings may be attached if one does gain access (or the information given out may be of a somewhat sanitized, "official" account). For example, the Walt Disney Company may want the right to approve and edit. This is problematic, as it compromises the independence of the researcher and dictates what findings are legitimate. While it is beyond the scope of this chapter to "reveal all," one promising entry point to Disney has been through interviews with the Disney Channel Scandinavia and Disney Consumer Products Nordic. The company was contacted by Sørenssen. The focus of these interviews was on Disney as a corporation and its construction of "tweens," a term Disney uses frequently. Some of the issues studied in the interviews include the following: Does the view mirror the content analysis; in other words, are actions and words in coherence? Does this construction bear any similarity to the ones offered by developmental psychologists and others working in the area of children's culture? Does it resemble the tweens' own construction in any way?

User Texts

The situation beyond film studies, in the fields of social and cultural history, is much the same: a body of knowledge about the rise of consumerism but very little on children's participation in that process. In short, a gap exists in the research, a gap that prevents us from thinking as clearly as we might about Disney animation's address to children and particularly its address through the mechanisms of consumerism. (deCordova, 1994, 204)

This quote echoes Cook in his article on the missing child in consumption theory. Disney Channel has become ever present in Western children's lives, especially in Norway, where it has one of the highest penetration rates in the world, as the channel is in all the basic cable, fibrotic, terrestrial TV, and satellite packages (Econ Rapport, nr 2008–135: 16). Through the Disney Channel children learn about the CDs and DVDs that are purchasable. The live-action series and movies bear with them large quantities of merchandise, especially magazines and stationery. What does this mean for children, and how are these being put to use in a cultural context?

In a study of the users of *Hannah Montana* and *High School Musical* currently under way (Sørenssen), tweens were asked about their thoughts on the products and the TV shows reflecting on age and gender target groups, what they liked and disliked about the content, and what this might mean to them. Their responses are interesting in that even though most of the informants liked what Disney Channel had to offer, they also reported watching things on Disney Channel they did not enjoy as much partly it seems because that's what's out there and partly because of loyalty and trust in Disney Channel content.

Environmental Texts

"Most studies of media effects on children have failed to take account of the local contexts and of the fact that meanings, even of globally circulating media products, are made locally" (Tobin, 2000, 150).

Users (consumers), however, regardless of whether they are adults or children, do not just consume; they consume in a context and in a particular environment that in itself might be critical to deepening an understanding of the meaning of the experience. The inclusion of the environment as yet another text within the circuit of culture was first noted by Doyon (2010) in his "Girls Don't Do Wires" study of adolescent girls as media producers in a suburban Canadian high school. Using Fiske's work, he was able to carry out analyses of the documentaries that the girls produced (in this case, the producer texts) and a content analysis of the actual video productions (primary texts). However, something that "leaked into" both the production and primary texts was the phenomenon of "hallway culture," as he termed it. The girls' productions (unlike those of the boys) studied school life entirely through their perspectives on the hallways and other spaces in a functional 1950s "wires and plugs and cement blocks" school. These spaces both informed and, in a sense, constrained what the girls could imagine and film, so the resulting video productions, as Doyon observes, were both situated in and reflective of these spaces, and he speculates on how their videos might have been different had they filmed them in an ultramodern high-tech environment or a school reflective of Victorian architecture. In his chapter on environmental texts, Doyon draws on the socio-semiotic work of Stephen Riggins (1994) and others, using such tools as mapping and photography, in order to deepen an understanding of the spatial or environmental text. Applied to tween media texts, one might include in environmental textual studies (or children's geographies) mall-going behavior, the viewing of films in movie theaters versus in one's own home (see also Walkerdine, 1985, on the significance of bedroom culture; and McRobbie and Garber, 1991), digital bedroom (and other online) cultures (Mitchell and Reid-Walsh, 2005), and so on.

In work with the *Hannah Montana* and *High School Musical* texts, for example, data on the environmental text were included by the researcher (Sørenssen) going to (and documenting) the movie premiere of *High School Musical 3*, where there was a fashion show involving tweens modeling and walking the catwalk with *High School Musical 3* clothes on; going to a *Camp Rock* (another Disney Channel Original Movie directed at tweens) party at the TV premiere at one girl's house with seven of her girlfriends; and observing the use of online activities such as stardoll.com and disneychannel.tv and the tweens' talk of the Disney tween texts at two different after-school programs in Norway. In all of these different environments, talk and use of the tween media content offered by Disney Channel were not introduced by the researcher. Rather, these spaces offered an opportunity to observe the primary texts in relation to the users and hence gave a broader understanding of the texts in different contexts.

FOLLOWING THE FANS AS TWEEN-METHOD

"The capacity of children to establish radically opposed counter-cultures objectified in toys [and other forms of media] as vengeful insistence on their autonomy is already well documented" (Miller, 2010, 143).

Is there such a thing as tween-method? In the section above, we argue the case for working with a model of textuality that looks at layers of meaning and at what Fiske describes as a "leaking into" the various texts. In other words, it is not possible to consider primary texts (an episode of *Hannah Montana* or indeed the whole series) without considering the producers (and commodification) but also the users (tween audience), who consume *Hannah Montana* or *High School Musical* and the various tie-in texts, and of course the adults in their lives who themselves become consumers or purchasers of these products for whatever motive. Indeed, as Mitchell (2008) argues, "Some critics believe that the KGOY [Kids Growing Older Younger] phenomenon simply reflects the idea of children as status symbols, allowing parents to flaunt the idea that their toddler is computer savvy or that their pre-school [or early tween-age] daughter is wearing Baby Phat designer jeans or fashion boots" (380).

These levels of textuality, of course, are not unique to the study of tween culture and can be used to understand the consumption of football, soap detergents, and even "childhood discourses" in popular culture, as we pointed out in the references to the market that has grown up around "saving our sons" and "rescuing our daughters." It might be argued that we need to exhibit some caution in regarding the adult and child consumer as exactly the same. At the same time, however, much of the research by Alison James, David Buckingham, and others has highlighted the need to respect the child (or tween, in the case of eight- to twelve-year-olds) as being more than a passive dupe, and also as not being a member of a static category. Children grow up and move on, and as seriously as they might regard a particular popular culture text at age nine or ten, they may eschew this as being "for babies" a year later, as Sørenssen found in her interviews with tweens in Norway:

JANE: I'm not such a big fan of *Hannah Montana* any more.
INGVILD: What are you a fan of?
JANE: I don't know, there is so much. Mostly like those singers, maybe them, like Kate Perry, Beyonce, like English ones. . . .
PAUL: I think that when you are fourteen then you have your confirmation the next year, and then it's like, if you're going to start seeing *High School Musical* and *Camp Rock* and *Hannah Montana* then,

then maybe it's getting—then I think that you're getting a little too big for it.

This can be seen as part of the KGOY phenomenon: As Disney Channel is catering to the tween segment by producing more live-action, tweens are moving from traditional cartoons to more teenage/young adult sitcoms and movies in the romantic-drama genre earlier.

Earlier work with Barbie, as is argued elsewhere (Reid-Walsh and Mitchell, 1995), reveals that girls outgrow Barbie and move on, and with the downward shift in age in play with Barbie, Bratz, or My Scene dolls, they move on even earlier. Some argue, "Yes, but to what?" But the point is that fixating solely on the primary text, the size of the breasts of the dolls, the shape of the eyes, the "look," and so on, may simply have the overall effect of raising a moral panic without regard for the limited period of time that the girl interacts with the doll, the variability in the type of play, the meanings attached to the play, and so on. Our argument here is not with the value of commodified play overall, or whether a Barbie is now more wholesome than a Bratz doll, or whether watching episodes of *Hannah Montana* on the Disney Channel is less wholesome than watching the Discovery Channel, but only that a serious discussion of tween studies must necessarily insist on complexity and not simplicity. It is for that reason that we ask the question, Is there (or should there be) a tween method within social science research, and if so, what would it look like?

Two areas seem promising in advancing the area of tween studies within kinderculture (Steinberg and Kincheloe, 1997): the study of materiality and material culture, particularly drawing on Miller's study of "stuff" (2010), and empirical methods *with* tweens that seek to highlight their expertise as fully as can be seen in, for example, work around "children as producers" in relation to using various media forms such as photography and video (see also Mitchell and Reid-Walsh, 2002; Ewald, 2000).

"THINGS MAKE PEOPLE"

Stuff is ubiquitous, and problematic. But whatever our environmental fears or concerns over materialism, we will not be helped by either a theory of stuff, or an attitude of stuff, that simply tries to oppose ourselves to it; as though the more we think of things as alien, the more we keep ourselves sacrosanct and pure. The idea that stuff some-how drains away our humanity, as we dissolve into a sticky mass of plastic and other commodities, is really an attempt to retain a rather simplistic and false view of pure and prior unsullied humanity. (Miller, 2010, 5)

In *Stuff* Daniel Miller argues that "things make people just as much as people make things" (135). In offering this point, he uses the example of Barbie to trace the evolution of the growing autonomy of the child (primarily little girls) in relation to the parent (primarily mother), and simultaneously to explain some of the ways that the parent is forced to "give way" to Barbie play. Middle-class motherhood is in part about consumerism, and he reports on a study of mothers who

noted that the pleasure they had developed in buying clothes and items for themselves was transferred directly onto the infant. While in other communities, mothers are concerned to get back their figures and clothing style lost in pregnancy, these mothers tended to channel their knowledge and ability as consumers into the task of shopping for the baby. In the initial phase clothing the child became an act of pure projection. If the infant had a say in how she was dressed she might not have picked those faux peasant lace smocks. So when she does develop some sense of agency, she immediately declares war. The first battle relates to the substances which the infant is allowed to ingest. . . . As the child began to develop its own agency, the parent might expend considerable effort in trying to prevent any association with gendered toys. (142–143)

Miller then goes on to talk about the ways parents might, in a bid to ward off guns and swords, extol their sons' interest in dolls. However, he notes that Barbie comes to the ultimate admission of defeat: "This is a crushing defeat for parents who swore that their children would never succumb to such sexual stereotyping." Miller concludes that parenting is "a form of tragic practice, experienced as a series of inevitable defeats. . . .

The battleground moves to areas such as computer games, sexuality, drugs, parties and other genres of teenage life. In many of these there will be a similar tension between direct opposition or the attempt to buy back children through becoming the primary source of commodity purchase" (145). Miller offers that by doing this kind of tracing of the parent, the child, and the object, we can see in the case cited above "how Barbie dolls make people" (145).

We are interested in Miller's argument because we think that the kinderculture life of the contemporary Western tween is, in a sense, set up as a series of commodified moments that are critical to the growing autonomy of the child. On the one hand, Miller's example of Barbie, not unlike some of our own earlier work on Barbie (Mitchell and Reid-Walsh, 1995; Reid-Walsh and Mitchell, 2000), is now somewhat dated. Barbie, after all, has not been doing well in sales for some time, and it is the Bratz doll that can now claim greater revulsion from most parents. And given the downward shift in Bratz and Barbie play, Barbie is not in direct competition with the texts of *Hannah Montana* or *High School Musical*. On the other hand, however, the very argument of "shifting sands" when it comes to popularity and age of the user plays into the idea of what is termed by Mitchell and Reid-Walsh as the cumulative cultural text of popular culture (1995) to refer to such features as intergenerationality, intertextuality, and the generative and multidimensional "tie-ins" within popular culture (books, movies, T-shirts, lunch kits). While the term there is primarily applied to children's fictional series such as *Nancy Drew* and the *Hardy Boys*, *Sweet Valley High*, and *Babysitters' Club*, they also apply it to such texts as Barbie and My Little Pony (see also Weber and Mitchell, 1995). What might also be said, however—and this links back to Miller's work—is that these texts are seldom "adult-approved," and that they in part work for that very reason. The world of *Hannah Montana* (and the tie-in texts) or the world of *High School Musical* are tween worlds, and methods of studying them (production and consumption) rest on approaches that respect the inhabitants of those worlds; in order to show such respect, there is a strong need for reflexivity from the researcher as well (Sørenssen, 2008).

TWEENS MAKE THINGS: CHILDREN AS CULTURAL PRODUCERS

In the second section of this chapter we highlighted methods of triangulation and the significance of the primary text, production texts, audience texts, and environmental texts in the study of *Hannah Montana* and *High School Musical*. One of the challenges, particularly of studying the audience text—the tween—is to find approaches that are child-centered and that respect the child as expert (of the worlds of *Hannah Montana* and *High School Musical*). Conventional forms of interviewing and observation can be problematic, as we argue in *Researching Children's Popular Culture* (Mitchell and Reid-Walsh, 2002), particularly when they involve topics that are not adult-approved and that carry with them in popular discourses a general devaluing or association with issues such as hypersexualization, sexual stereotyping, or violence. Buckingham (1993) also drew attention to many of these challenges in studying television audiences (parents deliberately minimizing the amount of time their children spend watching TV or maximizing the amount of time watching nature shows; children being suspicious about what adult interviewers want to know). However, by being open (trying to leave one's own meanings at the door) and respectful in refraining from value judgements, an interview can help researchers gain access and rapport with the tweens (Sørenssen, 2008).

As a way to enrich data gathering, we are interested in how tweens' own multimodal productions (either as self-initiated or as developed within school and other adult settings) can be regarded as windows into deepening an understanding of the meanings of the texts under study. These productions might include websites (Reid-Walsh and Mitchell, 2005; Mitchell and Reid-Walsh, 2002), blogs (Mitchell, Pascarella, DeLange and Stuart, in press), "my bedroom" photos within PowerPoint presentations (St. John Ward, 2009), and social networking sites (Weber and Mitchell, 2007). They can also involve, as we have found in our work across a variety of geographic and cultural contexts, simply engaging the child-user as a type of co-researcher through the use of more conventional forms of photography. Wendy Ewald's work is one of the best examples of this, as her approach is not simply to ask children to take photos; rather, she works with them over a period of time to actually study what makes an evocative photo (Ewald, 2000). But work with eleven- and twelve-year-old children in southern African asked to photograph (and work with) issues of safety and security in their midst also demonstrates powerfully and poignantly their ability to curate what is important in their lives (Mitchell, 2009). And while the photos can be revealing and read as visual texts by the researcher, the narratives that they elicit in interviews with the participants suggest to us that there is a different power base and expert base altogether from the one that typically manifests itself in interviews.

DISCUSSION

In arguing for tween-method, we cannot overlook the fact that much of the work within tween studies draws directly on studies of girlhood, although Mitchell and Reid-Walsh (2005) raise the question of whether "tween" can refer to both boys and girls. Clearly the marketers do, as is made clear in interviews with the producers. Recently, for example, there has been an increasing focus on boys by Disney. In 2009 the company launched Disney XD, a channel mainly targeting six- to fourteen-year-old boys. According to Rich Ross, president of Disney Channels Worldwide, the goal for Disney XD is "to create this destination for boys that is still inclusive of girls" (*Daily News Los Angeles,* September 2, 2009). We do, however, see that work on girl-method (Mitchell and Reid-Walsh, 2008) explicitly feeds into much of what has been argued above, and although the interviews with *Hannah Montana* and *High School Musical* users also included boys, the media texts (and certainly the tie-in texts) primarily target tween-age girls. Girl-method seeks a girl-centered approach to research that privileges work *with* girls, *for* girls, and *by* girls, and that has an overall advocacy role that takes up the fact that girls worldwide are significantly more disadvantaged when it comes to such issues as attending school, being victims of sexual violence and poverty, and other forms of systemic inequalities. In the case of tweens and tween-method, arguably a Western phenomenon in the context of consuming behavior, we see a convergence in relation to being child-centered and respecting the voice of the tween (and hence the need for tools that facilitate this), and also simultaneously resist a fixation on pathologizing girls' bodies, as is seen in the popular discourse of hyper-sexualization and moral panics. Work with tweens and by tweens could go a long way to subverting what might be seen as a lining up of the far right and the far left (and how the arguments themselves can be filled with contradictions). This lining up can be seen in responses to girls' play with the Bratz doll (and formerly Barbie). For the right, the Bratz doll is hypersexualized through her gaze, her trashy clothing, being vaguely not-white, and so on. For the left (feminists and those working within a critical paradigm more generally), the Bratz doll represents much that is aggressively and stereotypically feminine, but at the heart of the concern is also a strong anticapitalist agenda. The Bratz consume and are consumed. Like Barbie they constantly need new outfits and girls need more of them, just like Lego (typically associated with boy-play), which equally might be associated with acquiring more pieces to construct bigger and more complex things and places. Yet nobody ob-jects to this kind of consuming behavior in relation to Lego.

To conclude, studying tween culture and its users calls for an explicit recognition of the status of the texts, the positioning of children in a commodified space, and the place of adults (marketers, producers, par-ents, and other caregiver adults). More than anything, though, as we have argued here, is the need for tools and methods that ensure that re-searchers can hang on to (and fully exploit), rather than cover over, the complexity.

References

Bryman, A. (1995). *Disney and His Worlds*. New York: Routledge.

———. (2004). *The Disneyization of Society*. Thousand Oaks, CA: Sage Publica-tions.

Buckingham, D. (2000). *After the Death of Childhood: Growing Up in the Age of Elec-tronic Media*. Cambridge: Polity Press.

———. (2008). Children and Media: A Cultural Studies Approach. In Drotner, K., & Livingstone, S. (Eds.), *International Handbook of Children, Media and Culture*. Thousand Oaks, CA: Sage Publications.

———. (1997). Dissin' Disney: Critical Perspectives on Children's Media Culture. *Media, Culture & Society*, 19, 285–293.

————. (1993). *Reading Audiences: Young People and the Media*. Manchester: Manchester University Press.

Byrne, E., & McQuillan, M. (1999). *Deconstructing Disney*. Pluto Press.

Cook, D. T. (2005). The Dichotomous Child in and of Commercial Culture. *Childhood*, 12 (2):155–159.

deCordova, R. (1994). The Mickey in Macy's Window: Childhood, Consumerism and Disney Animation. In Smoodin, E. (Ed.), *Disney Discourse: Producing the Magic Kingdom*. London: Routledge.

Doyon, P. (2010). Why Girls Don't Do Wires. Unpublished doctoral dissertation, Department of Integrated Studies in Education, McGill University.

Drotner, K. (2003). *Disney i Danmark. At vokse op med en global mediagigant*. Københanv: Høst & Søn.

Econ Rapport nr 2008–135 (2008). *Konkurransen i Markedet for TV-Distribusjon*.

Ewald, W. (2000). *Secret Games: Collaborative Works with Children. 1969–99*. Zurich: Scalo.

Fiske, J. (1987). British Cultural Studies and Television. In Allen, R. (Ed.), *Channels of Discourse*. London: Methuen. Reprinted in Allen, R. (Ed.), *Channels of Discourse Reassembled: Television in Contemporary Criticism, 2nd Edition* (1992). Chapel Hill: University of North Carolina Press.

Fjellman, S. M. (1992). *Vinyl Leaves: Walt Disney World and America*. Boulder, CO: Westview Press.

Giroux, H. (1997). Are Disney Movies Good for Your Kids? In Kincheloe, J. L., & Steinberg, S. R. (Eds.), *Kinderculture: The Corporate Construction of Childhood*. Boulder, CO: Westview.

————. (1999). *The Mouse That Roared: Disney and the End of Innocence*. Lanham, MD: Rowman and Littlefield Press.

Hagen, I. (2001). Norway: Norwegian Memories of the Disney Universe. In Wasko, J., Phillips, M., & Meehan, E. (Eds.), *Dazzled by Disney? The Global Disney Audiences Project*. London and New York: Leicester University Press.

Lamb, S., & Brown, L. M. (2007). *Packaging Girlhood: Rescuing Our Daughters from Marketers' Schemes*. New York: St. Martin's Griffin.

Lamb, S., Brown, L. M., & Tappan, M. (2009). *Packaging Boyhood: Saving Our Sons from Superheroes, Slackers, and Other Media Stereotypes*. New York: St. Martin's Press.

Lindstrom, M. (2003). *BRANDChild. Remarkable Insights into the Minds of Today's Global Kids and Their Relationships with Brands*. London: Kogan Page.

Linn, S. (2004). *Consuming Kids: Protecting Our Children from the Onslaught of Marketing & Advertising*. New York: Anchor Books.

McNeal, J. J. U. (1999). *The Kids' Market: Myths and Realities*. Ithaca, NY: Paramount Market.

McRobbie, A., & Garber, J. (1991). Girls and Subcultures. In McRobbie, A. (Ed.), *Feminism and Youth Culture: From Jackie to Just Seventeen*. Cambridge, MA: Unwin Hyman.

Miller, C. (2010). *Stuff*. Cambridge: Polity.

Mitchell, C. (2009) Geographies of Danger: School Toilets in Sub-Saharan Africa. In Gershenson, O., & Penner, B. (Eds.), *Ladies and Gents.* Temple University Press.

———. (2008). KGOY. In Mitchell, C., & Reid-Walsh, J. (Eds.), *Girl Culture: An Encyclopedia, Vol. 2.* Westport, CT: Greenwood Press.

Mitchell, C., & Reid-Walsh, J. (1995). And I Want to Thank You Barbie: Barbie as a Site for Cultural Interrogation. *Review of Education/Pedagogy/Cultural Studies* 17(2), 143–155.

———. (2008). Girl Method: Placing Girl-Centred Research Methodologies on the Map of Girlhood Studies. In Klaehn, J. (Ed.), *Roadblocks to Equality: Women Challenging Boundaries.* Montreal: Black Rose Books.

———. (1996). Reading on the Edge: Serious Series Readers of Nancy Drew and Hardy Boys Mysteries. *Changing English* 3(1), 45–55.

———. (2002). *Researching Children's Popular Culture: Childhood as a Cultural Space.* London and New York: Routledge Taylor Francis.

———. (2005). Theorizing Tween Culture Within Girlhood Studies. In Mitchell, C., & Reid-Walsh, J. (Eds.), *Seven Going on Seventeen: Tween Studies in the Culture of Girlhood.* New York: Peter Lang.

Mitchell, C., & Reid-Walsh, J. (Eds.) (2005). *Seven Going on Seventeen: Tween Studies in the Culture of Girlhood.* New York: Peter Lang.

Postman, N. (1982). *The Disappearance of Childhood.* New York: Delacorte Press.

Quart, A. (2004). *Branded: The Buying and Selling of Teenagers.* New York: Basic Books.

Radway, J. (1997). *A Feeling for Books: The Book-of-the-Month Club, Literary Taste, and Middle-Class Desire.* Chapel Hill, NC: University of North Carolina Press.

Reid-Walsh, J., & Mitchell, C. (2004). Girls' Web Sites as a Virtual 'Room of One's Own.' In Harris, A. (Ed.), *All About the Girl: Culture, Power and Identity.* New York and London: Routledge.

———. (2000). "Just a Doll"? 'Liberating' Accounts of Barbie-Play. *Review of Education/Pedagogy/Cultural Studies* 22(2), 175–190.

Riggins, S. H. (1994). Fieldwork in the Living Room: An Autoethnographic Essay. In *The Socialness of Things: Essays on the Socio-semiotics of Objects.* Berlin: Mouton de Gruyer.

Sammond, N. (2005). *Babes in Tomorrowland: Walt Disney and the Making of the American Child, 1930–1960.* Durham, NC: Duke University Press.

Schor, J. B. (2004). *Born to Buy: The Commercialized Child and the New Consumer Culture.* New York: Scribner.

Siegel, D., Livingston, G., & Coffey, T. (2004). *The Great Tween Buying Machine: Capturing Your Share of the Multibillion-Dollar Tween Market.* Chicago: Dearborn Trade, a Kaplan Professional Company.

Sørenssen, I. K. (2008). Researching Children's Popular Culture. Paper presented at the Child and Teen Consumption Conference, Trondheim, Norway, April 24–25.

Steinberg, S. R. & Kincheloe, J. L., (Eds.), (1997). *Kinderculture: The Corporate Construction of Childhood.* Boulder, CO: Westview Press.

St. John Ward, M. (2009). Girl Photographers Take Us into Their Bedrooms. *Girlhood Studies*, 2 (1) 167–172.

Strasburger, V. C., Wilson, B. J., & Jordan, A. B. (2008). *Children, Adolescents, and the Media*. Thousand Oaks, CA: Sage Publications.

Tobin, J. (2000). *Good Guys Don't Wear Hats: Children's Talk About the Media*. New York: Teachers College Press.

Walkerdine, V. (1985). Video Replay. In Burgin, V., Donald, J., & Kaplan, C. (Eds.), *Formations of Fantasy*. London: Routledge.

Wasko, J. (2001). *Understanding Disney. The Manufacture of Fantasy*. Cambridge: Polity Press.

Weber, S., & Mitchell, C. (1995). *"That's Funny, You Don't Look Like a Teacher": Interrogating Images of Identity in Popular Culture*. London and New York: Falmer.

———. (2007). Imaging, Keyboarding, and Posting Identities: Young People and New Media Technologies. In Buckingham, D. (Ed.), *Youth, Identity, and Digital Media*. Cambridge, MA: MIT Press.

Online Sources

Andrews, A. (2009). Rich Ross Helps Disney Channel "Tweens." *Telegraph*, www.telegraph.co.uk/finance/newsbysector/mediatechnologyandtelecoms/6169735/Rich-Ross-helps-Disney-channel-tweens.html (visited January 9, 2010).

Billboard Online: www.billboard.com/artist/miley-cyrus/#/search/Miley%20Cyrus (visited January 9, 2010).

Disney Consumer Products, Cars: https://licensing.disney.com/Home/display.jsp?contentId=dcp_home_ourfranchises_disney_cars_us&forPrint=false&language=en&preview=false&imageShow=0&pressRoom=US&translationOf=null&region=0 (visited January 9, 2010).

Disney Consumer Products, Princesses: https://licensing.disney.com/Home/display.jsp?contentId=dcp_home_ourfranchises_disney_princess_us&forPrint=false&language=en&preview=false&imageShow=0&pressRoom=US&translationOf=null&region=0 (visited January 9, 2010).

Disney Online: www.disneyconsumerproducts.com (visited September 10, 2009).

Nakashima, R. (2009). Disney Dealing With Its Boy Problem. *Daily News Los Angeles*, http://www.dailynews.com/business/ci_13253678 (visited September 5, 2010).

Chapter 8

FROM MILEY MERCHANDISING TO POP PRINCESS PEDDLING: THE HANNAH MONTANA PHENOMENON

Ruthann Mayes-Elma

Oɴᴇ ᴛʜɪɴɢ ᴛʜᴀᴛ ᴄᴀɴ ᴅᴇꜰɪɴɪᴛᴇʟʏ be said for Disney, that I think we can all agree on, is that it knows how to market. No age is too young or too old, no skin color is too pale or too dark (although Disney has been accused of racial/ethnic stereotyping), and no money is turned away; Disney sells to all. One of the company's most successful marketing ventures is in the form of a young girl named Hannah Montana, a.k.a. Miley Cyrus (a.k.a. Destiny Hope Cyrus—her birth name). Little girls (tweens, teens, and adults as well) who used to love the Disney Princesses now love Hannah Montana. From a hit television show on the Disney Channel to music CDs, video games, a clothing line, jewelry and hair accessories, home décor, school and party supplies, nothing is off-limits when it comes to selling Hannah Montana. At the Disney Store in Downtown Disney on the Walt Disney World property, a guest can pay to be Hannah Montana for a day. The Hannah Montana makeover package includes a Hannah Montana wig, microphone headset, guitar purse, T-shirt, makeup kit including eye shadow and lip gloss, and a photo shoot including a six-by-eight commemorative photo, and costs $109.95 plus tax. MSNBC estimated that the Miley Cyrus franchise was worth $1 billion at the end of 2008. Not bad for a sixteen-year-old.

DISNEY'S CONTROL OVER CHILDREN

The United States is the most consumer-oriented society in the world. Americans work longer hours and earn more money than workers in other countries, but they save much less. The average U.S. household has one television set per inhabitant. With all of those televisions ready and waiting to be viewed, advertising has reached an all-time high. It should be no surprise to anyone that companies spend a lot of money each year through various media advertisements to entice consumers to buy their products. What may be surprising is that kids and teens are now the epicenter of consumer culture in the United States. What kids and teens like or desire drives market trends. Their opinions shape the market. It is estimated that 25 percent of prekindergarten children have a television in their bedroom and watch more than two hours of TV per day. By the time they enter first grade they can list more than two hundred brands of products (Schor, 2004). For no company does this hold truer than Disney.

Disney's 2008 Annual Report to shareholders reported total revenue of $37.8 billion, an increase of 7 percent from 2007, making it the most revenue Disney has ever reported in a year. Disney's 2008 revenue is broken down into four main segments: Media Networks at $16.1 billion, Parks and Resorts at $11.5 billion, Studio Entertainment at $7.3 billion, and Consumer Products at $2.9 billion. All four segments grew revenue in 2008. Interestingly enough, the report repeatedly cited the *Hannah Montana* franchise as one of its leading growth contributors. "Disney's brand strength and creative successes have allowed our Consumer Products segment to expand its licensing franchise portfolio and connect to a broad range of consumers. As a result, revenue from earned royalties once again increased by double-digit percentages in 2008, with growth across multiple product categories, led by *Hannah Montana* merchandise" (9). The Disney Channel's success is also credited to *Hannah Montana*. "In the U.S. alone, the sophomore season of the hit series achieved an increase of 16 percent in total viewers over the previous year, while kids and their parents flocked to Hannah Montana concerts and fans around the world purchased soundtracks, DVDs and other merchandise to make the show a part of their daily lives" (39).

The 104-page report does not discuss the content standards of various products. It reads like the exploits and most recent conquests of the rich and pompous. The report discusses kids, from birth to teenagers, as mere consumers—there is no indication of interest in the health and well-being of the Disney constituents.

Two statements that demonstrate Disney's motivation stood out in the report: "The preschool segment continues to flourish at DCP [Disney Consumer Products]" and "DCP has a keen focus on the infant market and has identified opportunities to significantly grow the market share that Disney branded products hold in that segment" (28). Disney's public appearance has one believe that Disney cares about kids, but the product report is clear that Disney is about marketing, and children and youth are the targets. To the public, Disney proclaims, "We care about you and your family—come bask in the joyful environment that only Disney can provide." The shareholders are told that opportunity abounds.

IMAGE IS EVERYTHING

Disney has become synonymous with childhood innocence, virtue, happiness, love, and family. Many of us have childhood memories of Disney World or Disneyland, "The happiest place on Earth." What is Disney really selling to its consumers? In the case of *Hannah Montana*, Disney is selling a sixteen-year-old girl, a form of pop cultural prostitution.

No one knows better than Disney executives that in order to successfully advertise to kids and teens they need to do more than just create commercials for television; they also need to put their brand and advertisements out through other forms of media as well—the Internet, to name one. Children usually know the most about such technologies and thus introduce them to their parents. Such advertisements, music groups, television shows, have become children's social worlds. They see it everywhere they go: school, the mall, at home, at church, at sporting events. Their lives revolve around what or who is "in" and "out."

Disney's grasp on what is "in" and "out" is awe-inspiring, which is one of the reasons *Hannah Montana* is so successful. And with the success of the television show comes success in other markets as well, as was announced in Disney's 2008 Annual Report. "Disney Channel continues to build on its creative momentum, with successful series like *Hannah Montana*. These properties not only raise awareness of Disney around the globe, but also enable other businesses to generate revenue through music, concerts, theatrical film releases, video games and merchandise derived from them" (9). Disney is a genius when it comes to developing and nurturing its own ventures in multiple venues. The company has created a feeding frenzy of consumers who want nothing more than to purchase the latest "in" thing Disney has debuted, which becomes a status symbol and a symbol of that child.

Toys serving as status symbols are nothing new. Historians have reported that as early as 1870 toys began to serve this purpose, with toys becoming more and more important each year to children's perception of their own image (Schor, 2004). In order to fit in or be popular, children "need" to have these paraphernalia that have been deemed "in" by their peers. Many children or teens who do not possess these items do not feel equal to their peers who do; their self-esteem plummets (Pugh, 2009). It is no coincidence that in today's society there are more reported cases of depression, obesity, hyperactivity, gastrointestinal problems, and suicide among our youth. Juliet Schor (2004) contends, "The more they [children] buy into the commercial and materialist messages, the worse they feel about themselves" (173).

Many parents report that their children are too materialistic, but ironically, these children are just emulating what adults do. In their own way, the children "keep up with the Joneses," just as their parents do when they buy a bigger house, a better car, or seasonal wardrobes. "Children are expected to act like adults" (Giroux, 2000, 19). They should be blamed, as they often are, for what is happening in our society. Children have been taught to buy; it is their curriculum. "As culture becomes increasingly commercialized, the only type of citizenship that adult society offers to children is that of consumerism" (Giroux, 2000, 19).

Hannah Montana merchandising is everywhere. Her face is on clothing items (she has her own brand), jewelry, pillowcases, bedspreads, pencils, school binders, beach towels, dinner plates, utensils, backpacks, and electronics, not to mention all of the games, toys, dolls, etc. Disney has bombarded us with nearly everything imaginable branded *Hannah Montana*. Her hit television show and sold-out rock concerts draw viewers/participants as young as preschoolers to as old as great-grandparents. No one is left out of the *Hannah Montana* moneymaking machine.

Disney released its first in a long line of *Hannah Montana* merchandise in December 2006, just in time for the holiday season. The products included clothing, jewelry, toys, and dolls. As sales increased, Disney released more toys and dolls in August 2007, which became some of the most popular toys during the 2007 Christmas season (Pesce, 2007). In 2008, the *Daily Dispatch*'s Stephen Armstrong estimated that the television show had 200 million viewers. He jokingly stated that, "If Miley's viewers were a country, they would be the fifth largest population in the world, just ahead of Brazil" (2009).

In February 2008 the first major motion picture featuring Hannah Montana was shown in movie theaters around the United States and Canada. *Hannah Montana & Miley Cyrus: Best of Both Worlds Concert*, a 3-D movie, is a concert film. It was intended to be a limited engagement, appearing February 1–7, but it was later extended. It was shown in only 638 movie theaters throughout the United States and Canada combined. The ticket prices were on average 50 percent higher than for other movies, but that did not discourage people from purchasing tickets. The movie grossed $29 million during the first weekend alone and set a record for the highest revenue for a 3-D film in one weekend.

A recent *Hannah Montana* movie, cleverly titled *Hannah Montana: The Movie*, debuted on April 10, 2009. The movie follows Miley Stewart as she tries to figure out whether it is more important to be herself or her secret pop-star alter ego, Hannah Montana. By August 2009, the film had grossed a total of $147 million. The movie has also won three awards: the 2009 MTV Movie Award for Best Song from a Movie (for "The Climb"), and the 2009 Teen Choice Awards for Choice Movie Actress: Music/Dance, and Choice Music: Single ("The Climb"). Disney couldn't be happier.

However, Disney was not so happy with the recent stripperlike dancing Miley Cyrus did on the August 10, 2009, Teen Choice Awards. While singing "Party in the USA" Miley got up on an ice cream cart and proceeded to do a seductive pole dance. Knowing that she is most popular with tween girls (ages nine to fourteen), what message is she sending them? According to Newsday.com, a Disney representative stated, "Disney Channel won't be commenting on that performance, although parents can rest assured that all content presented on the Disney Channel is age-appropriate for our audience—kids 6–14—and consistent with what our brand values are." Miley, on the other hand, did not know what all the fuss was about. In the February 2010 edition of *Harper's Bazaar,* she stated, "People like controversy because that's what sells. My job is to be a role model, and that's what I want to do, but my job isn't to be a parent. My job isn't to tell your kids how to act or how not to act, because I'm still figuring that out for myself. So to take that away from me is a bit selfish. Your kids are going to make mistakes whether I do or not. That's just life." Fans have often been confused by the image changes that Hannah/Miley/Hannah/Miley goes through. During a photo shoot Miley posed with her father, singer Billy Ray Cyrus, for a photo that was considered sexual, and discussions of an inappropriate father-daughter relationship ensued. Posed suggestively against her father, Miley was skimpily dressed, and the pose, clothing, and demeanors of the two were much more suited to two young lovers. It is interesting to watch Disney juggle the child star in Miley and the fact that, indeed, she will grow up. One also wonders if she will fall into the usual Hollywood kid fate.

Her virtue was also blemished by her "just breathe" tattoo below her left breast, on her rib cage. Although the tattoo is the slogan for the Cystic Fibrosis Foundation and she got it in memory of Vanessa, a close friend she lost more than three years ago to cystic fibrosis, Disney representatives have "declined to comment." In the February 2010 edition of *Harper's Bazaar*, Miley discusses her tattoo: "I could never get a meaningless tattoo, but I think that if you're doing something that's important, that's significant in your life, it takes some of the pain away."

WHAT *HANNAH MONTANA*, THE SITCOM, TEACHES US

The television show *Hannah Montana* debuted in the United States on March 24, 2006, on the Disney Channel and has since been broadcast in fifty-five countries. As of January 10, 2010, eighty-two original episodes had been aired. The show is about a young teenage girl, Miley Stewart, played by Miley Cyrus, who lives a secret double life. She is an average high school student by day, but by night she transforms into a pop singer named Hannah Montana. Only her family and close friends, Oliver and Lilly, know of her secret double identity; the public at large has no clue. The show is currently in production for its fourth and final season to end in the spring of 2011, but we won't necessarily count on that.

After viewing so many episodes of the television show that I could recite the opening theme song by heart, and also hear it in my dreams, I still felt like I had viewed the same episode again and again. Every thirty-minute episode is predictable, with Miley having a problem, her father giving her unwanted advice, and the problem being solved by the time the episode is over, leaving everyone happy and fulfilled. *Hannah Montana* is a very bubble-gum, *Pleasantville*, wholesome television show that is meant to warm even the coldest heart. No bad language is used; instead Miley's signature line of "sweet nibblets" is often heard, and viewers understand that it is intended to take the place of foul language. Disney has incorporated guest spots in many of the episodes to encourage tween girls to watch the show—tween heartthrobs such as Jesse McCartney, and Kevin, Joe, and Nick Jonas, for example.

Since the series is about the life of a secret rock star and her songwriter father, each episode twists a song of the past into its title, such as "Joannie B. Goode," "Miley Get Your Gum," "More Than a Zombie to Me," "Miley Hurt the Feelings of the Radio Star," and "Everybody Was Best-Friend Fighting," just to name a few. Each episode also cleverly solves all problems within thirty minutes in a very foreseeable way. Another aspect that all the episodes have in common is that Miley tries to get out of trouble by being cute, or what she thinks is cute. I found three main characteristics that are interwoven in all of the episodes: family, friends, and self. Miley's family, friends, and self are the most important things that each episode deals with, and in turn each episode's moral/lesson deals with them. The morals/lessons being conveyed to the viewers are, of course, the overt ones that Disney perpetuates, not the subliminal ones that Disney obviously supports but would not admit to, such as the sexist way in which Miley acts during many of the episodes.

Miley plays a stereotypical female in that she twists her hair between her fingers, smiles and shows dimples, and flirts in a way that presents herself not as a strong, agentic girl but instead as an airhead. She is always forgiven and given a second chance, no matter what the situation. In one episode, "Killing Me Softly With His Height," Miley flirts in her standard fake, ditzy way in order to get a date with a boy she thinks is "gorgeous." Once he stands up and she sees that he is significantly shorter than she is, she wishes she had never talked to him. This is right after she berates her friend Oliver for not asking someone else out because the girl has big feet. Miley lectures him on looking past physical features, but when it comes to her, it is a totally different story. Viewers can foresee, though, that in this episode, like all the others, Miley will rise above this, no pun intended, and find that it truly is what is inside that counts.

Just as suspected, by the end of the date she refuses to kiss him because he is shorter. He gets his feelings hurt, which, of course, makes Miley feel like a bad person. She then goes to find him and beg him for a second chance. "I was stupid, judgmental, and wrong," she says to him upon begging for his forgiveness, which he gives (Peterman & Correll, 2008). The episode, like others, makes fun of a problem that many young people have but then acts as if the problem is solved when the thirty minutes is up. The episode's moral is Disney-approved: It is what is on the inside that counts. However, at the same time the kids make fun of short people by making the boy stand on a skateboard in order to try to kiss Miley, and making his job at the mall be as one of Santa's elves, Miley gets what she wants by setting feminism back. Young girls who watch the show see someone they look up to acting in a way that emulates the stereotypical female; which, in turn, they emulate.

In another episode, "Joannie B. Goode," Oliver begins dating a girl, Joannie, whom both Miley and Lilly hate. As a favor to Oliver, though, they try to befriend Joannie. When Lilly befriends her, Miley becomes jealous and worries that she is losing her best friends. At the end of the episode Miley realizes that she has been wrong when Lilly states, "This [meaning friendship] is strong enough to handle anything" (Green & Sheridan, 2008). Miley feels good that Oliver doesn't expect her to be Joannie's friend if she doesn't want to be; he is just appreciative that she tried. Miley then feels it appropriate to call Joannie a "wart on a big monkey butt," which everyone laughs at, and the episode ends (Green & Sheridan, 2008). Once again, young people who are watching the show see this as acceptable and at a later date may repeat such behavior.

Family, friends, and self are exacerbated in the episode titled "Miley Hurt the Feelings of the Radio Star." Oliver and Miley step in and take over a successful DJ's radio talk show when he has to leave suddenly for the hospital because his wife is having their baby. He ends up getting in an accident, so Miley and Oliver must take over his show until he returns. Even though Miley has many other commitments—schoolwork, rock concerts, and appearances and engagements as Hannah Montana—she decides to help Oliver with the radio show because he begs her to and ultimately guilts her into it by stating, "Breaks like this don't just happen. This could change my whole life" (Brown-Gallenberg & Correll, 2009). She then begins doing poorly in everything she tries to do because she is overextended but feels as if she can't let Oliver down. In the end, though, the radio station wants only Oliver to do the talk show, so Miley is off the hook. Instead of being ecstatic because now she can relax and get back to her "normal" life, she is upset that they don't want her because, after all, she *is* Hannah Montana. Of course, in the end, though, she is happy for Oliver because he is fulfilled.

The main morals or themes of the show's episodes are wholesome sayings/idioms that have been around for decades: treat others the way you want to be treated, don't judge a book by its cover, blood is thicker than water, we're all cut from the same cloth, etc. There is a platitudinal approach that is quite naïve. But these messages are not the only ones the Disney Corporation wishes to "sell" its consumers. Themes such as sexism, backstabbing, and gossip are also prominent in the show. The episodes lack people of color. Moises Arias, who plays Rico, a young Latino boy, is somewhat of a token "everything," as he is the only person who isn't white.

A LEGION OF LITTLE HANNAH MONTANAS

Kids and teens have become obsessed with trying to "be" Hannah Montana. Hannah Montana merchandise has become the "in" thing to own and separates the "in" kids from the not-so-"in" ones. Walk into any public school across the country and you will likely see Hannah Montana T-shirts on kids from kindergarten to high school. They might have been purchased at the local Target or Walmart or, if the owner is really lucky, from a recent concert. You might also see students writing their assignments in a Hannah Montana binder with a Hannah Montana pen or pencil.

These items are not just wanted by children; they are needed. It is hard enough being a child/teenager when you have the coolest and latest fashions/accessories, but it is even harder for those who do not. All kids want to fit in, and by today's standards that means having and spending money. Disney understands that kids relate what they own to who they are, and the company furthers this by sending kids subliminal messages through its various media sources. "Such marketers know how to cultivate intense affect among children and use such emotion to elicit particular consumptive and in turn ideological reactions" (Steinberg & Kincheloe, 2004, 11). Disney knows it can be very devastating psychologically and emotionally when a person is shunned by his or her peers, no matter what the age; but during the adolescent years it can be even more damaging and destructive. Disney thrives on the feelings of inadequacy and degradation that follow if a child does not have the latest product, and on the feelings of belonging and joy if a child does have it.

A six-year-old girl, Bella, spoke at length with me about Hannah Montana, her only obsession. She seemed to have everything Hannah Montana: pajamas, T-shirts, folders, pillowcases, CDs, DVDs, etc. When I asked her why she liked Hannah Montana she replied, "Because my friend at school likes her." Once again I asked her why *she* liked her, and this time she replied, "She's cool." What makes her cool, though? "She's a good singer and she's really pretty."

Hannah Montana is so cool that Bella even dressed up like her on her sixth birthday at her Hannah Montana–themed party. All the little girls at the party were in their Hannah Montana apparel. Hannah Montana music played throughout the party, and the little girls had a great time singing along and pretending to be her. Most of the presents Bella received were Hannah Montana merchandizing. The birthday cake was not a regular flat sheet cake with Hannah Montana on it; a professional baker had created a freestanding 3-D cake in the form of a concert stage, made complete with a full-sized Hannah Montana doll on top. It was a Disney dream come true!

Another young girl, Kelly, whom I spoke with about Hannah Montana, recently attended a Hannah Montana concert and became the envy of her fifth-grade classmates. She confided in me that her parents kept her home from school the day after the concert because she was out so late and too tired to go to school. "It's no big deal," Kelly said. "One day is only one day. The concert was a once-in-a-lifetime experience. School is always here. I'll just make up the work. No big deal." It was quite obvious that Hannah Montana came before school. Disney would be proud.

Hannah Montana concert tickets, the T-shirts, the jewelry, the backpacks, DVDs, CDs—all are status symbols in today's youth culture. If the children do not possess these invaluable products that Disney has peddled to children and their parents, or go to the concerts or see the movies, they are deemed unimportant, unpopular, and submissive to their counterparts who do own them. Many parents understand that owning such "popular" or "in" goods is important for their children, because it is important for them. Some remember their own childhoods, of not having the "in" goods and how it made them feel. "I always wanted a Cabbage Patch Kid," stated a mother of a twelve-year-old Hannah Montana fan. "All of the kids would bring their [Cabbage Patch] Kids to school when I was in third grade, but I never could because my parents weren't able to find one. They were sold out, and my mom was on a waiting list. I always felt like those girls [who had the dolls] were better than me, and I felt shy around them. Looking back, it is totally ridiculous, but at the time it meant so much." When asked if she purchases Hannah Montana items for her daughter, she replies that she does, but sometimes she also has her daughter purchase her own with the money she has earned through chores and baby-sitting. I was interested to know if her daughter thought twice about her Hannah Montana purchases when it was her own money and not her mother's. "Unfortunately she does not," the mother answered. "No matter what the cost, she spends it. It's like life or death that she gets the clothes or T-shirts. She didn't have enough [money] for the concert tickets, so I bought those for her."

The desire among parents to give their children possessions that they believe will help them fit into their own youth culture sometimes becomes a need rather than a want. According to Pugh (2009) lower-income parents spend more money on their children than wealthier families do because they hope that "their spending would accomplish particular presentation goals" (123). These presentation goals for parents are typically a perceived improvement in their socioeconomic status. The parents hope that their children will gain socioeconomic status through their possessions and thus cultivate their tastes through these possessions in the hopes that their children will earn more money than their parents did when they grow up. Along with lower-income families, single parents and mothers who work outside the home also spend more than affluent families on their children, but for different reasons than the lower-income families. Single parents and working mothers spend money out of guilt, the guilt of not being there twenty-four hours a day, seven days a week for their children. They spend money in the hopes of showing their children that they do indeed love them. One girl I interviewed, Amy, a freshman in high school, was the very essence of Pugh's theory. "My mom took me to see the Hannah Montana movie, and afterwards we went to Target and she got me the Hannah Montana movie CD [soundtrack]. It's great when she works a lot because when she doesn't work we do a lot together and I get a lot of stuff. Before my parents were divorced, she was really strict; now she's not. Don't get me wrong, though, I want my parents to get back together."

Lower-income working mothers and single parents might be spending more money on their children than more affluent families, but at what cost? According to the National Center for Children in Poverty there were 13.3 million children living in poverty in the United States in November 2008, which is 18 percent of all children in the country. The center also reported that there are 30.1 million children who are enrolled in a free/reduced-price lunch program at school, 8.9 million children without health insurance, and 28.2 million children enrolled in Medicaid. Clearly, the parents of these children are struggling to pay their bills, but many of them still find a way to buy their children what they want or "need," such as Hannah Montana CDs and movie tickets.

"Many low-income parents did view children's consumer culture as a problem, however, not because it was a sign their children were out of control, but rather it was dangerous. Children's consumer desires posed serious risks to the family's livelihood, to parents' ability to put gas in the car, to the odds of having food on the table" (Pugh, 2009, 122). The sad part about all of this is not the fact that these parents are purchasing goods for their children that they cannot afford, but that the companies that are selling these goods perpetuate the need for them. Disney sells its goods, such as Hannah Montana, and does not care if it is a detriment to those who are consuming these goods.

DISNEY DOMINATES EVERYTHING

This is obviously very troubling for anyone within the discourse of education. The culture that we live in, this Disney culture, has become so powerful that it now shapes the thoughts and actions of children and their parents. It is obvious that these particular parents, and you know there are many more just like them, thought nothing of keeping their children home from school in order to see Hannah Montana live in concert. It is almost a brainwashing of sorts. Disney deems itself to be wholesome, innocent, and all-American, while it should deem itself to be one of the leading brainwashers in the world. Henry Giroux (2000) once stated, "Politically, those who have the power to control the dominant machineries of cultural production set limits on what can be produced, legitimated, and distributed in a society even as they disproportionately control the conditions under which knowledge becomes accessible to specific groups and individuals. Educationally, the culture industry plays a crucial role in shaping public memory, in legitimating particular ways of knowing and specific forms of knowledge, and in producing identities and the discussions that inform them" (80). Disney is that power that dominates the culture we live in. It is no wonder that children have been trained since birth to be consumers. It is also no wonder that public schools are not teaching media literacy classes as part of the curriculum. After all, the government, which is funded in part by successful businesses like Disney, funds public schools. The government can't afford, neither figuratively nor literally, for children to actively and critically think about what is being advertised and how they are being bombarded every day by corporations seeking to expand market share.

Corporate America, watch out if our nation's children learn how to decipher these texts and begin to think for themselves. Maybe then and only then will our society's obsession with material goods change.

References

Armstrong, S. 2009. Teen Queen Is Global Brand. *Daily Dispatch*, www.dispatch.co.za/article.aspx?id=316998 (accessed July 14, 2009).

Brown-Gallenberg, M. (Writer), & Correll, R. (Director). (2009). Miley Hurt the Feelings of the Radio Star [television series episode]. In Peterman, S., & Poryes, M. (Producers), *Hannah Montana*. Los Angeles: It's a Laugh Productions.

Giroux, H. (2000). *Stealing Innocence: Youth, Corporate Power, and the Politics of Culture*. New York: St. Martin's Press.

Green, A. (Writer), & Sheridan, R. (Director). (2008). Joannie B. Goode [television series episode]. In Peterman, S., & Poryes, M. (Producers), *Hannah Montana*. Los Angeles: It's a Laugh Productions.

Kahn, R. (2009). Miley Cyrus' Pole-dancing Performance Sparks Criticism. *Newsday*, www.newsday.com/entertainment/celebrities/miley-cyrus-pole-dancing-performance-sparks-criticism-1.1360720 (accessed February 2, 2010).

Larocca, A. (2010). The Real Miley Cyrus. *Harper's Bazaar*, www.harpersbazaar.com/magazine/cover/miley-cyrus-cover-interview-0210 (accessed February 13, 2010).

National Center for Children in Poverty (2008). Children in the United States. National Center for Children in Poverty, November, www.nccp.org (accessed July 2, 2009).

Pesce, N. (2007). Bite Me, Barbie! Disney's Hannah Montana Takes Over as Most Wanted Toy. *Daily News*, www.mydailynews.com/lifestyle/2007/11/19/2007/11/19/2007–11–19_bite_me_barbie_disneys_hannah_montana_ta-2.html (accessed July 11, 2009).

Peterman, S. (Writer), & Correll, R. (Director). 2008. Killing Me Softly with His Height [television series episode]. In Peterman, S., & Poryes, M. (Producers), *Hannah Montana*. Los Angeles: It's a Laugh Productions.

Pugh, A. 2009. *Longing and Belonging: Parents, Children, and Consumer Culture*. Berkeley: University of California Press.

Schor, J. 2004. *Born to Buy: The Commercialized Child and the New Consumer Culture*. New York: Scribner.

Steinberg, S., & Kincheloe, J. (Eds.) (2004). *Kinderculture: The Corporate Construction of Childhood*. Boulder, CO: Westview Press.

The Walt Disney Company (2008). Annual Report. www.corporate.disney.go.com/investors/annual_reports/2008/index.html (accessed June 23, 2009).

Chapter 9

CORPORATIZING SPORTS: FANTASY LEAGUES, THE ATHLETE AS COMMODITY, AND FANS AS CONSUMERS

Daniel E. Chapman and John A. Weaver

They pay $2 to see a game, and they think they own you.
—Larry Cannon, American Basketball
Association player, New Orleans Buccaneers
(Street & Smith's Official Yearbook, 1980–81)

Sᴘᴏʀᴛꜱ ᴀʀᴇ ᴀ ᴄᴇɴᴛʀᴀʟ ᴘᴀʀᴛ of culture in the United States in general and youth culture in particular. Yet in the fields of curriculum studies, educational foundations, and critical pedagogy, sports are rarely researched. Perhaps it is because sports are not seen as academic enough or as beneath the interests of scholars. Whatever the reasons may be, this scarcity of research is a gaping hole in connecting curriculum and educational issues to broader cultural issues. In this chapter, we wish to look at some of the ways sports shape curriculum and educational issues. We will discuss the rise of fantasy football leagues, ownership rights of college athletes, and fans as consumers. What these themes have in common is the growing tendency to view sports as an economic transaction rather than primarily a cultural experience that connects fans with players in an aesthetic and communal manner. At least since the rise of paid baseball players in the 1850s (Dickey Pearce in 1856) and professional baseball leagues in the 1870s, economics has been a part of sport in the United States. Without sounding nostalgic, we believe there is an intensification of the role of economics in the contemporary era of sports that is unrivaled in the history of athletic competition. The consequences of this shift in primary focus from sports as a cultural experience to an economic transaction are important in order to understand how young people learn what it means to be a sports fan, athlete, and citizen of the United States.

REMEMBERING JOE

I, John, want to begin with a tribute to our colleague and friend Joe Kincheloe, because *Kinderculture* was the brainchild of Joe and Shirley Steinberg, and I first met Joe in the mid-1990s when he was unveiling their idea for the first edition. Plus, and perhaps most important, Joe was an avid sports fan. In particular, he thoroughly enjoyed college football and the Tennessee Volunteers. Whenever I would telephone Joe and Shirley, inevitably I would talk academics with Shirley. We would discuss the latest debates, book contracts, book ideas, recent academic happenings. Eventually, she would say something like, "I guess you want to talk to Joe." She always said it with a humorous twist of sarcasm because she knew the boys wanted to talk about college football. Joe loved his Volunteers. One of the first things he said to me about college football in the mid-1990s was that he was born in 1950, the year Tennessee won its second national title. Of course, soon after that conversation they won their fourth national championship in 1998, the year after Peyton Manning left for the National Football League. Joe was proud of his birth year and Tennessee's second national championship. He was proud because it was through football that he reconnected to his home state no matter where he lived. Football reminded him of where he came from and who he was. Sports marked Joe as it marks all of us.

I am not a Volunteer. I am a Mountaineer. I could relate to Joe's love of Tennessee football because I held the same endearment for West Virginia. When Joe talked about the Tennessee Volunteers, I knew some of their history, with players like Conredge Holloway and Stanley Morgan coached by Johnny Majors in the 1970s. And when I talked about West Virginia football, Joe remembered Major Harris, Don Nehlen, and Bobby Bowden. Although I was from Pennsylvania, I connected with West Virginia. I received two undergraduate degrees from a small school in Philippi, West Virginia, called Alderson-Broaddus College, and it was a 1975 West Virginia football game against the University of Pittsburgh, my third alma mater, when I was in fifth grade that shaped my decision to attend Alderson-Broaddus. When Joe and I talked about college football we were expressing our love for "our teams" but more important our love for the sport and the ways it helped us share our pride for our home or adopted states. Sports became a way for us to bond as academics, and it was a way for us to remain rooted in the working-class culture we were born into. Sports reminded us of the values Tennessee, Pennsylvania, and West Virginia taught us, and how those values contributed to our successful academic careers. We always remembered where we came from and we expressed it with pride. Sports were the medium through which we expressed this pride. I know that wherever Joe may be, and if there is such a thing as a spiritual afterlife, he is doing at least two things right now: He is trying to convince someone that his or her idea should become a book, and he is telling that person about the Tennessee Volunteers.

WHO OWNS ME?

In the summer of 2009, three former NCAA quarterbacks—Sam Keller, who played for the University of Nebraska; Ryan Hart, Rutgers University; and Troy Taylor, UC-Berkeley—sued EA Sports for using likenesses of them in a college football video game. Soon after this Ed O'Bannon, who was a starter along with Tyus Edney of the 1993 UCLA Championship basketball team, sued the NCAA for likeness infringements. All four college athletes were Division I–caliber players but never superstars, and while O'Bannon played in the NBA, none of them were able to make a living playing professionally in the United States. So can the NCAA and EA Sports use their likenesses after they received scholarships to some of the most prestigious universities in the United States and, in the case of Berkeley, the world? Does the NCAA owe an athlete anything if it provides a full scholarship? Are athletes, particularly college football and men's basketball players, entitled to anything beyond a scholarship even though it is literally because of their blood, sweat, and tears that the NCAA is able to make billions of dollars in television revenues? Clearly these athletes believe they are, and, we are sure, the NCAA and EA Sports think otherwise. The courts will determine who is correct, however, and it will be years before any final decision is rendered.

But there is one important issue in this matter that can be debated immediately: Can a person's body, let alone his or her likeness, be owned? Beyond sports, this question has already been debated in the realm of medicine and stem-cell research. In 1976 John Moore was diagnosed with hairy cell leukemia; his surgeon, aptly named David Golde, urged Moore to have his spleen removed. Moore consented to the surgery. Eight years later, in 1984, he sued Dr. Golde, the University of California Board of Regents, and some pharmaceutical companies, after he discovered that Golde had taken his spleen and harvested numerous immortal cell lines of the protein lymphokine, patented the cell line, and was making hefty profits from them. Moore originally lost his case in the California state courts, won his appeal, and lost in the California State Supreme Court and eventually in the U.S. Supreme Court. Golde, the Board of Regents, and the pharmaceutical companies involved argued that Moore was not due any compensation because although the cell line was produced from Moore it was altered in the research process, and it was this altering that led to the creation of the immortal cell line. The courts ruled that body parts could be patented if there was some kind of alteration done to the body, human or animal. They also ruled, however, that Moore, or anyone else, could not own, and therefore profit from, their own bodies.

Although many cite this case as an example of the importance of informed consent, the most important question is, Can someone own another's body part or one's own body? Neither of these positions is tenable in our eyes. A corporation, researcher, or university should not have the ability to sell and trade body parts, nor should an individual have the rights to sell parts of his or her body minus perhaps blood, eggs, sperm, and stem cells. What about likenesses? The immortal stem-cell line created by Golde and the University of California system is a likeness. The courts ruled likenesses can be sold because they are modified and that the patient is not due any compensation. What about college athletes? It is their dedication and efforts that make the sporting events possible and therefore the "lifelike" video games possible. Who owns a likeness? Is a video game image like an altered stem-cell line? If it is, then why is it that corporations seem to always benefit from the hard work of individuals, but the individuals rarely, if ever, see any just compensation?

This debate over the likenesses of athletes reveals an alarming trend in which individuals are viewed as commodities rather than as individuals with inalienable rights granted to them at birth. The athlete is now seen, perhaps more than ever, as an object to be bought and sold by his or her owner, be it a professional sports owner, a university and its board of trustees, a governing body such as the NCAA, or a corporation such as EA Sports. What this does is construct the athlete as what Martin Heidegger (1977) termed a standing reserve. A standing reserve is something or someone who is called upon at command and on demand when someone else wants to be entertained. The athlete has become an object to be manipulated for someone else's viewing pleasure and someone else's profit. Should amateur athletes not be compensated their efforts? If they are compensated, does this still not treat the athlete as a standing reserve who acts like a human money-generating machine?

In order to highlight the broader consequences of the athlete becoming a standing reserve, we want to highlight the Kobe Bryant sexual assault case. In 2003 a young woman in Colorado accused Bryant of sexual assault. Eventually the case was settled; Bryant did not admit to any guilt, and the accuser was not convicted of perjury. However, during the proceedings, which were conducted more in the media than in the courtroom, the debate within the sports world was not the severity of rape or the seriousness of perjury. Instead the debate was, If Kobe's image is tarnished too much in this case, who will replace him as the marquee player of the NBA? At the time the debate was between Melo

(Carmelo Anthony) and Bron (LeBron James). Not only was Bryant treated like an object corporations could discard if he became "defective," but Anthony and James were as well. They were temporary replacements for Bryant as the image of all that is great about the NBA until someone else comes along, and they can be constructed as a marketing image. All three athletes were treated as expendable raw material, and the woman in this whole matter was unimportant. She would not have been remembered as the woman Bryant assaulted. She would have been remembered as the woman who tore down an image and threatened the game of professional basketball. Treating individuals as images or using individuals to invent media images is demeaning to all involved, and it eventually diminishes the importance of all individuals as human beings. To be a human is not to be treated as an object or an avenue through which other people or corporate entities can make money.

FANTASY FOOTBALL LEAGUES

With forty-three seconds left in Super Bowl XLIII, the Steelers were at the six-yard line. They had trouble scoring touchdowns all game, and a field goal here would mean overtime and the flip of a coin. I, Daniel, am a Pittsburgh native, and like all men, women, and children who were born near the confluence of the three rivers in western Pennsylvania, I am a Steelers fan. So, of course, I wanted a touchdown in this situation. However, the Steelers' quarterback, Ben Roethlisberger, takes risks, and so an interception or a fumble was also possible. On this second-down play, Roethlisberger was dancing around looking for someone to throw it to. Stepping to the left, stepping to the right, pump faking, looking into the end zone . . . looking unsure and making me very nervous, as usual. He threw a high line drive to the back right corner of the end zone, and I instantaneously thought, Good, it's out of bounds, no interception, next play. But Santonio Holmes had another idea. He extended his entire body to reach this high ball yet kept both feet close to the ground, to make sure he landed in bounds. It was like he jumped five feet in the air, but his feet only jumped a few inches. This bullet of a throw didn't wobble one bit the moment it touched his hands, as though they were made of glue. Any shift of the ball, at this point, could have negated the play. He pulled the ball into his chest and protected it with his arm so that when he landed the ball would neither touch the ground nor shift in his grasp. Even after he hit the ground, a slight movement of the ball could have negated the play. All of this happened in an instant. It was a tremendous play at a tremendous moment. As I wrote this paragraph, I rewatched the play on YouTube and smiled at the sheer beauty of it.

The aesthetics of the players' skill level and talent, along with the excitement of the game, stood above the hype that went along with the 2009 Super Bowl. An amazing feat, actually, when you consider all of the money and effort that goes into creating the spectacle that is the Super Bowl. This includes the pyrotechnics beforehand, the flyover by military planes in formation, the buzz that surrounds the Super Bowl commercials, and even the halftime show, which featured Bruce Springsteen this particular year. At times, the game and the beauty of the players' talent and skill pierced through and the human elements of sport rose above the objectifying elements of sport. That is something to celebrate.

In recent years, a different kind of objectification of the players has grown into nearly a billion-dollar industry (FSTA, 2008). Rather than endless hype, personal tragedies, hero worship, smoke machines, and cheerleaders, fantasy football relies on NFL statistics. Fantasy football has fundamentally changed the way fans interact with the game and the players, and the media have responded to this shift. Some will say that fantasy football has been great for football, the fan, and its players because it increases fan participation. Broadcasters would agree with this assessment, as recent research shows that fantasy football players watch more football than do nonfantasy fans (FSTA, 2008). The NFL certainly applauds the increased viewership, since it can demand more money in television contracts. The broadcasters and the NFL (along with their sponsors) have a shared interest in increasing viewership. In the past, the best ideas were pyrotechnics, military flyovers, and big-name halftime entertainment. Today, an answer to increased viewership that no corporate executive planned on is fantasy football. However, it does not only increase the number of viewers; it changes the way the viewers interact with the game. As they watch the football game they are not appreciating the competition of the NFL game and the abilities of the athletes; rather, they are watching their own game unfold and responding emotionally to their personal choices and/or fortune.

I have played fantasy football for five years now. A brief tutorial will likely be helpful. Fantasy football runs concurrently with the NFL season. A league begins by gathering eight to twelve friends (or strangers who "meet" online), each of whom will be the "coach" of a team. Once the coaches have named their teams (usually something one would hear in a high school locker room), a draft takes place. For the draft, each coach selects players from the NFL based on position (quarterback, running back, wide receiver, etc.) and how well the coach believes they will perform throughout the season. Each week, the fantasy teams get points based on the performance of the selected players. Points are generally awarded for yards gained and touchdowns scored, although there are many variations from league to league. In some leagues, the fantasy teams rotate each week to play head to head, and in some leagues overall points are what matters. As the season goes on, the coach can choose which NFL players to play and which ones to bench on a week-to-week basis. Coaches can make trades and pick up undrafted players, as well.

The history of fantasy football goes back to Oakland, California, in 1962 (Dickey, 2004). In those days, and in the following three decades, it took a tremendous effort to compile all of the statistics and compute what each fantasy player scored each week. It was also necessary for the coaches to meet in person for the draft and to keep tabs on records throughout the season. The computer and the Internet, however, have changed these aspects drastically. Statistics are compiled automatically, and coaches can be online anywhere in the world to draft, trade, and even smack-talk. The growth of the Internet in the past decade has spurred on the growth of fantasy sports.

Impact on the Spectator

As I mentioned earlier, the game of fantasy football has increased the number of NFL viewers. The seasoned fantasy player knows players not only from their favorite team but from all around the league. The fantasy player is familiar with all of the tight ends in the NFL and can probably name many place kickers, as well. Here is another indicator that many use to show that the fantasy player is more engaged with the NFL game: They watch more and they familiarize themselves with more of the players around the league. However, we will still argue that the fantasy player is less engaged with the NFL game, even as they watch more and know more. The fantasy player does not always watch and enjoy the NFL games in order to appreciate the excitement and the skill of the game but to view the statistics as they are generated for the fantasy game. As a fantasy coach, one is not necessarily interested in whether an NFL team succeeds; rather, one is interested in the players' statistics.

Earlier we stated that sports are a cultural experience that connects fans with players in an aesthetic and communal manner. Fantasy football, I argue, is detrimental to both ends. It reduces players to statistics. On more than one occasion, I have watched an NFL team come close to scoring in a game where the running back is on my fantasy team and the wide receiver is on my competitor's team. In that moment, I could care less whether the NFL team scores, but I am very interested in the running back scoring and the wide receiver not scoring. The game is of little consequence to me. If the team scores with the running back I am elated, but if they score with the wide receiver I am despondent. If they score with a different player, I feel little excitement. This is a very different way to watch a sporting event. It can be said that I am not watching the NFL game but only watching the fantasy game unfold. I am not paying attention to the intensity of the game or to the skill level of the players, but only to the numbers they generate.

Indeed, I watch more football now than I did in the past. Before fantasy football, I would only watch the Steelers' games. But now just about any NFL game impacts my fantasy game and therefore is of interest to me. Watching the Steelers has become a layered and emotionally complicated event, where two identities—Steelers fan and fantasy coach—are sometimes in conflict. When a Steelers player on my fantasy opponent's team scores, I am joyful that the Steelers scored and upset that my fantasy opponent scored. And here is where we lose the communal role of sports.

Many fantasy players claim that they play in order to stay in touch with people and therefore it is good for community. And there is truth to this claim. The other coaches in my league tend to be friends strewn across the country whom I do not stay in touch with otherwise. It is nice to be able to use fantasy football to be able to communicate with them over the football season. This is the main reason I continue to play. Nonetheless, when I cheer for the Steelers I ride the emotional highs and lows with all of the men, women, and children who were born near the confluence of three rivers in western Pennsylvania. It is a part of my life I share with friends, family, and many strangers. However, when I cheer for my fantasy team, I am the only one who shares in the highs and lows. As I watch the NFL games as a fantasy coach, I am cheering for a team that only I care about. It is no longer a communal event but a solitary one.

Effects on the NFL Game

The way football is presented in the media has changed dramatically in response to the fantasy viewer. There are magazines, websites, and television shows dedicated to fantasy football. On Sundays, individual statistics throughout the league scroll at the bottom of any football broadcast. After a play, the individual statistics of the players involved will flash on the screen. The NFL website keeps real-time statistics for all players in every game. When a team scores or is close to scoring, an indicator light will highlight that game letting fantasy coaches know that someone's statistics may soon be impacted. Every major sports website hosts fantasy leagues, including Yahoo, ESPN, the NFL, and even the NFL Player's Association (NFLPA).

The NFLPA charges a licensing fee for other websites to use the players' statistics, images, and biographical information. In 2008, CBS Sports.com sued the NFLPA for charging these licensing fees, claiming that statistics are in the public domain and should be free to use. Again, we are confronted with the question of who owns whom? The NFLPA argued that the statistics are the intellectual property of the players, and thus the players should be compensated. Of course, players' statistics have always been considered free to view and use, but they have historically been used to bring attention to the game and the players. By doing so, they created excitement around the game and directly benefited the players. In this case, fantasy football uses players' statistics as an engine that drives their own game and creates excitement about their own game with little benefit to the players.

CBSSports.com won the case; the NFLPA appealed the ruling and eventually settled out of court. Many people believe that the players were being greedy and that this case was judged correctly. However, the questions raised by this case are still worth considering. If fantasy football is generating $1 billion a year, then who deserves that money? Those who run the websites, the magazines, and the television shows clearly deserve a share. But why not the players? They put their bodies on the line to generate the statistics. Without them, there would be no billion-dollar fantasy football industry. Again, we have to ask the question, Why do corporations always benefit from the hard work of individuals?

There is another effect on the game that is speculative only. It is well known that NFL players also play fantasy football. In fact, the NFLPA runs a fantasy game of its own and advertises that eight NFL players will play. It is safe to assume that, like non-NFL players, some play for money and some do not. Is this the same as an NFL player gambling on an NFL game itself? Is it possible that a player will shave points because of a financial investment in his fantasy game? In a 2006 *Washington Post* article, NFL spokesman Brian McCarthy said, "It's highly unlikely a player who participates in fantasy football would alter his performance on the field. We're certainly aware that some fans play for money—and on NFL.com there are prizes available like a trip to the Super Bowl—but fantasy football is a game of skill, and gambling is not" (Canfora, 2006). While McCarthy tries hard to distinguish fantasy football from gambling, the suspicion that fantasy interests could have an impact on how players play the game will remain.

In 2007, late in a game against their division rivals, the Dallas Cowboys, the Philadelphia Eagles were ahead by four points. Suddenly, Eagles' running back Brian Westbrook broke free and was running toward the end zone for a certain touchdown when he purposely fell at the one-yard line. Some fantasy coaches were furious. He robbed them of six points, and in some cases that cost them the game. Some accused Westbrook of not scoring because of his own fantasy interests. It turns out that Westbrook had a great reason to fall down at the one-yard line. He did not want to give the ball back to the Cowboys and give them even a slim hope of winning. It was a very good football decision. However, fantasy football introduces another level of doubt about the intentions of some players. Did that quarterback choose to throw rather than run based on his own fantasy interests? Did that ref make a blatantly bad call based on his fantasy interests? While there is no proof that fantasy football impacts the way the players play, the suspicion is there, and given the history of gambling and sports, it will only be a matter of time before someone is caught manipulating the NFL game for financial rewards in the fantasy game.

FANS AS CONSUMERS

If athletes are treated as entertainment objects in an exchange in which the fans enter an arena demanding to be entertained, what are we teaching the young through sports? Do the young emulate adults and view their favorite athlete or team as an object that better not let them down? Do adults and the young who paid for their tickets have a right to display their ire if they feel they were not given what they expected? We live in an age of entitlements in which middle- and upper-class people believe they are entitled to everything they demand. Sports are no different. If middle- and upper-class North Americans believe they can drive SUVs, Suburbans, Hummers, and Yukons because they can afford to and are not compelled to contemplate the broader environmental and social consequences on the lives of others, why wouldn't they believe that since they paid money for a ticket to a game they are entitled to be entertained?

If fans should not act as consumers, then how should they act toward athletes and sporting events? One thing we are not suggesting is to stop interacting emotionally with athletes and sports teams. Emotions are very much a part of the game. Take away emotions from sporting events and there is no real reason to enjoy sports. However, there are different ways to experience a sporting event emotionally. Athletic events are one of the major ways we connect with a community and build a sense of community, so if emotions were removed from the game experience, then a bond would be lost and meaningful experiences would be lost as well. When fans become consumers and athletes become objects to purchase, the emotional connection is different. The emotions in this scenario are not based on community building or bonding; they are based on economic exchanges that are always impersonal and ephemeral. Once the event is experienced the connection is over, the transaction has ended, the ticket can be discarded, and a new experience is immediately needed. Superficiality dominates the emotional experiences of the consumer.

Another way to experience an athletic competition with all its emotions is to view the athlete as part of the community. The Green Bay Packers, for example, are owned by the community. The history of the Packers, from Curly Lambeau to Vince Lombardi to Lynn Dickey to Brett Favre, is part of the community, and although Lambeau and Lombardi are dead and Favre calls southern Mississippi home, they are all part of the legend, lure, and memory of the Green Bay community. The same can be said about the Boston Red Sox. Any fan is part of the Red Sox nation; one does not have to live in Boston to be a part of this community.

Another example is personal. Daniel Cavicchi is a Bruce Springsteen fan who wrote a book called *Tramps Like Us*. In his study he interviewed Boss fans who felt true fans never drank or got high at a Springsteen event, because one could not experience the concert if one were drunk or stoned. When I, John, first read this I thought these fans were purists and were merely trying to prove they were better than other Springsteen fans. Then I thought about my own experiences as a fan and how I experience a Mountaineer football game. I have been going to WVU football games since 1987 with family and friends, but I have never had a drink before or during a game. It is an event to go to Mountaineer Field and join 60,000 other fans to cheer on the home team. I experienced the highs of the 1988 season, when WVU went undefeated and crushed almost every team, and I have expressed frustration and anger in games where the Mountaineers were losing or not playing well. My most memorable experience was when in 2003 WVU beat Maryland in overtime. It was a thrilling game, and afterward almost every fan stayed and spontaneously we started singing, "Almost heaven, West Virginia . . ." It was a bonding emotional experience like no other. The whole gamut of emotions is part of the experience, and to taint these with some mind-altering drug would ruin it. Anyone who knows me knows I am no prohibitionist. I love Baudelaire's poetry and, like him, I love wine. However, as a fan bonded to other people in a community called Mountaineer

Nation, I believe wine can wait till later when I relive memories of WVU games I have experienced.

When sporting events are experienced as community events, the athletes are not seen as objects and the fans are not consumers of a good. Instead athletes and fans come together to experience a moment in time that connects them as part of a unique experience never to be duplicated. Experienced this way the emotions and the mythology of athletes performing superhuman feats are no less intense than if they were treated as entertainers and objects presented to fans for consumption. But this way the bonds are tighter between athletes and fans, and the memories are deeper. There is a reason the Brooklyn Dodgers are still cemented into the minds of Brooklynites even though the team left the borough fifty-two years ago, and there is a reason Jerry West, Sam Huff, Major Harris, Darryl Talley, and Pat White are legends in West Virginia. They are all part of a community, not a consumer, experience.

References

Canfora, J. L. (2006). Beating Yourself Takes New Meaning. *Washington Post*, August 13.

Cavicchi, D. (1998). *Tramps Like Us: Music and Meaning Among Springsteen Fans*. Oxford: Oxford University Press.

Dickey, G. (2004). Fantasy Football: Craze's Roots Go Back to Oakland. *San Francisco Chronicle*, November 27.

FSTA (2008). 2008 Fantasy Sports Industry Research Overview. Retrieved through e-mail correspondence.

Fisher, E. (2008). CBS Sues NFLPA Over Fantasy Football. *The Sporting News*, September 5.

Gumbrecht, H. U. (2006). *In Praise of Athletic Beauty*. Cambridge, MA: Belknap Press of Harvard University Press.

Heidegger, M. (1977). *The Question Concerning Technology*. New York: Harper Row Publishers.

Chapter 10

HIP HOP AND CRITICAL PEDAGOGY: FROM TUPAC TO MASTER P TO 50 CENT AND BEYOND

Greg Dimitriadis

THE FIRST EDITION OF *Kinderculture* (1997) forwarded several groundbreaking ideas about the role and importance of popular culture and education. Perhaps most important, the editors and authors argued for the fundamentally important role of the popular culture industry in "educating" youth. Popular culture, the authors collectively maintained, has become a key site of "cultural pedagogy," where curricular "power is organized and deployed" (Steinberg and Kincheloe, 1997, 4). They go further, "The organizations that create this cultural curriculum are not educational agencies but rather commercial concerns that operate not for the social good but for individual gain" (4). The charge was severe, the implications far-reaching. Indeed, because popular culture has become an increasingly important pedagogical site, the volume maintained, the need for critical, liberatory education has become more pressing.

Yet traditional educative institutions have largely lost their claim to an exclusive hold on young people's lives. As Steinberg and Kincheloe wrote in the updated, second edition of this volume (2004), "By the middle of the first decade of the twenty-first century more and more people are understanding this historic change," though many "child professionals remain oblivious to these social and cultural alterations" (1)—giving the popular culture industry free rein to operate in this gap. We are, it seems, in the middle of several key tensions and paradoxes, ones that have become increasingly pressing since the publication of *Kinderculture*.

No cultural movement marks these various tensions as clearly as hip hop. Hip hop music has emerged as perhaps the pre-eminent cultural movement of our time, the profoundest statement of the complexities of this generation of youth and young adults. More than a quarter of a century after the release of the first hip hop single, "Rapper's Delight," the music is still at the epicenter of popular controversy and critique. Over the past thirty years, hip hop has reinvented itself again and again, pushing its creative parameters in important and always unpredictable ways.

Hip hop emerged in the late 1970s and early '80s in areas of New York City blighted by deindustrialization (Rose, 1994). The collective, party-oriented ethic of this moment spoke to the intense needs and desires of youth, the impulse to carve out space in increasingly hostile social and cultural terrain. In years hence, the music has morphed and grown in important ways. It has become a complex medium, reflecting a wide range of creative and substantive interests and impulses. Today, the aggressive "gangsterism" of 50 Cent, the entrepreneurism of Jay-Z, the pro-sex feminism of Foxy Brown, the problack sentiments of Mos Def, the ironic self-deprecation of Eminem, the reflective poetics of Common, the prolific, lyrical dexterity of Lil Wayne, all sit side by side. Hip hop is a genre of music that has again and again defied the impulse to contain and control it.

I argue here that taking up the challenges of hip hop means giving up our certainty and control over our understandings of young people and youth and entering into more thoughtful kinds of relationships with more and more unpredictable constituencies. Hip hop has collectively challenged those of us in education to wrestle with the specificity of our moment, in ways that force us beyond our ready-made pedagogical theories and models. Drawing together textual and ethnographic approaches, I highlight here the history and importance of several hip hop music and culture icons. This work, I argue, tries to take us beyond nostalgia for the civil rights movement, to new terrain. It takes seriously the ways that popular artists are self-reflexively theorizing what it means to live in what Mark Neal calls a "post soul" moment. This work, I conclude, provides us with models for rethinking our roles as pedagogues and intellectuals, a necessary gesture as this historical conjuncture.

TUPAC AND THE TRANSITION FROM SOUL TO POST SOUL

No artist reflects the contradictions and paradoxes of hip hop the way rapper Tupac Shakur did. Tupac began his career in hip hop in 1990, when he joined the rap group Digital Underground, where he danced and rapped. He released several albums over the next few years (e.g., *2Pacalypse Now*, 1990) and starred in several films (e.g., *Juice*, 1992). Perhaps his most well-known song, "Dear Mama," a tender ode to his mother, was released in 1995 on the album *Me Against the World*. At the time, Tupac was incarcerated for sexual assault. He would have numerous scuffles with the law. He was shot and nearly killed in 1995, an incident for which he blamed fellow rapper Notorious B.I.G. (a.k.a. Biggie Smalls). The two had a high-profile feud that escalated when Tupac signed to the record label Death Row Records, a company that cultivated an outlaw image. The conflict became known as the War of the Coasts—the "West Coast" (represented by Tupac and others on Death Row Records) verses the "East" (represented by Notorious B.I.G. and others on Bad Boy Records). Sadly, the conflict ended in death for both. Tupac was shot and killed in 1996 in Las Vegas. Six months later, B.I.G. was shot and killed in Los Angeles. Both homicides remain unsolved, but there has been speculation the murders were linked (see Nick Broomfield's 2002 film *Biggie and Tupac*).

In many respects, Tupac's life was an allegory for the transition from a civil rights to a "post soul" ethic. As is widely known, Tupac's mother was a Black Panther, one of the so-called New York 21, arrested for a series of suspected bombings. Intense government pressure and surveillance were an increasing challenge to her ideals, and she eventually became addicted to crack cocaine. Tupac was at the center of these tensions from a very young age, the idealistic impulses of the civil rights and problack movement side by side with the more immediate and individualistic kinds of physical gratifications that emerged as so compelling in the movement's wake. In fact, he "claimed" two fathers at point: one a Black Panther, the other a local gangster.

As Michael Eric Dyson (2002) made so clear in his brilliant book *Holler If You Hear Me: Searching for Tupac Shakur*, Tupac had to figure his own way through these various tensions and complexities. He was surrounded by activists as well as gangsters. From a young age, Tupac was also deeply interested and invested in the arts both in school (he attended Baltimore School for the Arts) and out of school (his very early interest in hip hop). Even though he dropped out of school, he never stopped pushing his own intellectual boundaries and limits. In perhaps the book's most moving and provocative chapter, Dyson looks at Tupac's collection of books, highlighting the eclectic nature of his reading practices, from Richard Wright to Friedrich Nietzsche to J. D. Salinger to Maya Angelou to Gabriel García Márquez to Henry Miller (94). Largely on his own and outside traditional school settings, Tupac wrestled with a complex set of ideas. Dyson writes, "Tupac's voracious reading continued throughout his career, a habit that allowed him to fill his raps with acute observations about the world around him. . . . Tupac's profound literacy rebutted the belief that hip-hop is an intellectual wasteland. . . . Tupac helped to combat anti-intellectualism in rap, a force, to be sure, that pervades the entire culture" (99–100).

Tupac's music reflects the paradoxes and conflicts he faced as a youth. His music ranged from tender odes to his mother (as in, noted above, "Dear Mama") to brutal invectives to his rivals (as in "Hit Em Up"). He looked toward a broad black-power agenda, just as he detailed his own intense conflicts with other black artists. These conflicts and paradoxes marked his high-profile career. He publicly presented himself as an "unfinished project," always struggling to make sense out of a broader social context while dealing with the pressing immediacies of the moment. He speaks from a context where he cannot fall back on notions of monolithic black community, just as he could not ignore the historical durability of those narratives.

In many respects, Tupac can be seen as signaling a transition from the relative certainties of narratives of racial uplift to more uncertain contemporary terrains. Tupac's life seems endemic of the landscape academics now face, a landscape that challenges our own certainties. His work forces us—intellectuals, pedagogues, and concerned adults alike—to decenter our ready-made intellectual and political paradigms. To understand Tupac, we cannot only look to the discourses that pervade academic life. As Tupac's own mother so eloquently said:

> I've heard enough of [our youth] to know that we ought to be holding them up and sharing with them what we know instead of standing on top of them telling them what they're not doing right. They're doing a lot right and some things wrong. We continue to fail these brilliant, very talented, very creative and courageous young people because they're not saying what our message was. But for Christ's sake . . . we're about to enter the 21st century. Something should be different. And they may be right about some things. (Kitwana, 2002, 3)

In giving up her own sense of certainty about racial politics, Afeni Shakur provides a model for what it means to reposition oneself as an intellectual.

For me, this repositioning was effected through four years of ethnographic work in the urban Midwest. In this study, I looked to understand the relationship a group of young black adolescents and teens had with hip hop. The study was conducted in a community center where I held weekly focus groups and also worked as a volunteer and staff member. In the book that resulted, *Performing Identity / Performing Culture: Hip Hop as Text, Pedagogy, and Lived Practice* (2001), I looked at how young people constructed notions of tradition, history, and self through talk about hip hop. In the follow-up book, *Friendship, Cliques, and Gangs: Young Black Men Coming of Age in Urban America* (2003), I looked more closely at the lives of two teens over a six-year period, as well as my evolving relationship with each. I discussed what it meant to decenter my own agenda on popular culture in time.

I found, throughout this all, that Tupac provided many of these young people with a certain kind of "equipment for living" (to evoke Kenneth Burke [1941]), discursive strategies for confronting and coping with specific day-to-day concerns. For example, one youth who had a history of both personal and familial confrontations with the police drew on Tupac to talk about these experiences: "Like when he's [Tupac's] talkin' about the police harassin' him all the time? . . . Every time the police see me, they got something to say to me, about my daddy, and my brothers . . . tellin' me I sell dope and all this." This young person's feelings toward the police and the life-stance he has had to take gelled together into a kind of philosophy of invulnerability and a kind of grim resignation to death. Drawing on the work of Tupac, he noted:

> To live in fear is not to live at all. . . . You can't run from every damn thing all the time. . . . You might as well not even live. . . . It's like you dead anyway, you keep thinking motherfuckers gonna kill you. . . . I ain't trying to say make yourself die. . . . [But] don't worry when it comes to you 'cause it's gonna happen anyway. . . . We live to die. You know what I'm saying? That's one thing we know for sure. Like, like you say you're gonna go to college when you get older? You might not make it to older. Like you say . . . I finna go down to the gas station and get some squares [cigarettes]? I might not make it to the gas station. . . . But I know I'ma die. I know I'ma die. We live to die. . . . Don't fear no man but God. . . . Just like Pac [Tupac] said.

This research gave me greater focus on young people's relationship to and with black popular culture, helping me expand my extant textual and historical work in important ways. I would come to see the role of rap in offering these young people (especially the young men) hyperreal, superinvulnerable figures, ones that helped to militate against a brutal and unforgiving social context. Clearly, Tupac was a mythic figure to this young man, one who allowed him to face the contingency of life with a steely resolve toward death. His relationship with Tupac speaks to the specificity of concerns and needs of the "post soul" generation.

POST CIVIL RIGHTS AND "SOUL"

In his controversial 2002 book *The New H.N.I.C. (Head Nigga in Charge): The Death of Civil Rights and the Reign of Hip Hop*, author Todd Boyd argues that we live in a post–civil rights moment, that the complexities and contradictions of hip hop music and culture have supplanted the transcendent claims of earlier generations. Above all else, Boyd stresses the dangers of nostalgia. Elsewhere, Cameron McCarthy and I have linked nostalgia to a broader set of "resentment" discourses, all of which have tried to contain the complexities of our contemporary moment (Dimitriadis and McCarthy, 2001). These include the certainties of race and nation, both of which were so critical to the civil rights movement of the 1960s. Yet as Boyd so powerfully implores us,

> We cannot live in the past forever. Civil rights had its day; now it's time to move out of the way. Civil rights was a struggle, and it remains an ongoing struggle for all disenfranchised people of color to pursue their civil rights. But many in the civil rights era have for too long gloated in a sanctimonious fashion, assuming that their day would never come to an end. This arrogant posture did little to inspire a new generation but went a long way toward alienating them. The posture of civil rights was such that it made future generations uncomfortable having to wear such restraints as they attempted to represent themselves. (152)

Boyd argues throughout his book that hip hop music and culture attempt "to navigate the world in a very different way." Boyd's comments clearly dovetail with Afeni Shakur's on the need not to lodge critiques from previous generations but perhaps to listen and learn as well.

Boyd points to the stress on material survival and wealth that marks this generation's needs, concerns, and desires. We see a desire to survive, to access the resources of capitalism, while still retaining a strong notion of blackness. We see these concerns instantiated in the critiques of black men who have attained some degree of wealth. Boyd documents the intense public criticism from older blacks as well as whites that many rap artists and record label owners face, many of whom are accused of "selling out" when they make some money. He cites Master P, Snoop Dogg, and Puff Daddy, among others. In part, such changes reflect an ambivalence about African Americans entering mainstream American life. Boyd notes, "What in an earlier generation might have been called 'showing off' has now grown into an integral part of self-expression in hip hop circles. The idea of the 'come up' represents social mobility in spite of overwhelming obstacles and the politics of this move are deeply embedded in hip hop's master narrative. The expression of this upward mobility by these lower-class individuals, flossin' on one's cars, homes, clothes, money, and lifestyle, have become commonplace" (77).

Boyd is not uncritical of these tendencies. But he stresses that their whole-cloth condemnation is often about earlier and nostalgic notions of blackness. He writes, "Change in status, be it financial, cultural, or political, is not always the worst thing in the world, nor should it be. Actually, it represents progression. Change is at the heart of creativity, and that should be embraced while one maintains a solid understanding of the history that precedes it" (101). According to Boyd, charges of "selling out" sometimes impede the organic creativity and unpredictable social impacts of rap music. Such charges work mostly to maintain center/periphery or, better yet, mainstream/underground dichotomies that no longer strictly hold.

Others have wrestled with the specificity of this moment and this generation in similarly powerful ways. For example, Mark Anthony Neal's *Soul Babies: Black Popular Culture and the Post-Soul Aesthetic* describes what he calls a "post soul" moment, the moment when the transcendent certainties of the civil rights and Black Power Movements have largely been elided. According to Neal, "soul" was the most powerful expression of modernity for African Americans of previous generations (3). For the next generation of African Americans, however, these claims to certainty have been called into question. This new generation "came to maturity in the age of Reaganomics and experienced the change from urban industrialization to deindustrialism, from segregation to desegregation, from essential notions of blackness to metanarratives on blackness, without any nostalgic allegiance to the past (back in the days of Harlem, or the thirteenth-century motherland, for that matter), but firmly in grasp of the existential concerns of this brave new world" (3).

For this next generation, hip hop music and culture have emerged as the defining cultural statement. The music and culture are filled with complex and often contradictory narratives. Yet, according to Neal, these need to be met with an expansive set of explanatory criteria. He writes, "We cannot simply reject these narratives on a moral basis that is itself the product of a profoundly different world; we must at least critically engage them with the same energy and passion that many of these artists themselves inject into their creative efforts" (11). Neal spends a great deal of his book attempting to unravel the work of hip hop artists and their whole cultural surround.

In the book's final chapter, Neal discusses how hip hop provides the cultural soundtrack to his own life and the lives of his students. He discusses, as well, the ways both try to unravel some of its complexities and contradictions. For example, many of his students have middle-class aspirations that are cross-cut by some strident and at times impossible ideals about "keeping it real" and "being black." He writes,

> The radical transformation of hip-hop over time, especially its crossing over into the market of white youth, has complicated its ability to proclaim black identity. It has come to symbolize the utter ambivalence of the black situation; on the one hand, serving up versions of a richly "black" identity, on the other showing an eagerness to join the American dream. (189)

He continues, "The challenge to 'keep it real' and 'still get paid' may seem crass to older generations, but it is the dominant ethos of Generation Hip Hop" (194). Navigating these waters is quite complicated, the desire to "succeed in the mainstream and survive in the margins" (194). Neal, like Boyd, shows a willingness to take on the specificity of this generation without falling into the trap of nostalgia.

As the above indicates, it seems, our moment necessitates moving beyond the kinds of liberation narratives so often associated with modernist movements. These narratives often rely on stable notions of identity and clear notions of ideology critique. I argue here that we need to perhaps give up our ideological certainties if we are to meet young people "where they're at" today. More and more, we need to "work the hyphen" between these different roles, responsibilities, and positions (Dimitriadis, 2003).

MASTER P AND MATERIAL IMPERATIVES OF THE POST-SOUL GENERATION

I would like to focus now on an artist who emerged in the wake of the Tupac–Notorious B.I.G. conflict—Master P. P himself acknowledged as much on his 1997 album *Da Last Don*, released months after B.I.G.'s murder. Here, he said that Biggie and Tupac "took the kiss of death" so he could be "The Last Don." P was part of an emerging group of southern rap artists who seemed to look beyond and transcend the "East vs. West" controversy that ended so tragically. His work marks many contemporary existential anxieties around racial identities, offering educators a key lens for grappling with the realities of race today.

Like Tupac's biography, Master P's is part of his public claim to authority and authenticity. Part of his mythos is his former life as a drug dealer in Louisiana, his brother's violent death, and his effort to "get out of the drug game" and go legitimate with music, specifically his label No Limit Records. The label's symbol and moniker is a tank (known as "*the* tank"), and all of its artists wear diamond-studded tank medallions and frequently reference it on record and in film. All this is part of the group, familial ethic, which P stresses on all No Limit recordings. He often, in fact, deploys Mafia-like imagery on his label's releases, as underscored by album titles including *Da Last Don* (1997), *Made Man* (1999), and *Goodfellas* (2000).

Master P's story was documented, in rough autobiographical fashion, in his straight-to-video film, *I'm Bout It* (1997), filmed on location in the Calliope projects, in New Orleans, where he grew up. The film also features other members of P's No Limit Family, including his brothers Silk and C-Murder, as well as Mystical, Mia X, and Fiend. The film opens with Master P and his crew sitting around a table, crowded with money, guns, and drugs. The members of the group, as the scene unfolds, put their fists together and say in unison, "True," a sign of solidarity and unity. Master P then rises, taking center stage, and informs the group about a stolen "kilo" of cocaine, a betrayal that prompts him to say, "This shit is crazy . . . think motherfuckers are your friends" before confronting and shooting a suspect. We thus see the complexities of trust and betrayal play out here, the notion that one's crew is one's family, cross-cut by the idea that one can only really trust oneself in the end. *I'm Bout It* details these concerns throughout P's efforts to leave the drug game and invest in the music business, his confrontations with crooked cops, the multiple betrayals of his own "crew," and his own sense of personal triumph and invulnerability.

Similar such anxieties and themes play out in *I Got the Hook Up* (1998), P's follow-up effort, though they are more closely linked here to material survival. This film stars Master P and A. J. Johnson as Blue and Black, friends who run a large, open-air pawn shop/flea market down South. The duo, by chance, get hold of some cellphones and conspire to steal air time. Though they make a great deal of money, the phones prove faulty, and both, along with various and sundry others, wind up on the run from some local thugs. *I Got the Hook Up* is about "making a dollar out of fifteen cents," the everyday hustle often necessitated by life in the ghetto. We see P evoke here the day-to-day concerns that propel the lives of many young people today, the reality of having to scheme to survive, the necessity of having friends and family to look out for you at all times. In such a world, racial affiliation is not given a priori but is a function of moment-to-moment and day-to-day survival.

These films, like Master P's work generally, are part of a broad structure of feeling among young people today, who have similar desires for, and anxieties about, trust, friendship, and survival. Hence, we see fierce notions of individual autonomy, notions that one can in the end only rely on oneself, juxtaposed and cross-cut by the necessity of local allegiances, of the social networks that often make life in poor and dangerous communities livable. These twin imperatives are embodied in gang life and imagery, in the fiercely individual and independent gang member whose sense of personal respect and autonomy is paradoxically linked to his or her crew. This image reached its apex in mid-'90s rap, as noted, in the public personas of Tupac Shakur and Biggie Smalls as well as the conflict that ensued between these men and their record labels.

In many ways, such images have taken center stage in rap today. They are the "myths" that help define this particular social and cultural moment for contemporary youth. Artists like Master P foreground complex personal biographies that young people articulate with and against, often fatalistic narratives that register unique tensions around trust and betrayal, vulnerability and invulnerability. On a telling track, "Would You Hesitate," from the soundtrack to *I Got the Hook Up*, Master P's brother C-Murder spells out some of these anxieties, simultaneously affirming and questioning the loyalty of label mates including Kane and Abel, Fiend, Mac, and Big Ed. One senses intense anxiety here, the anxiety of having to give yourself over to the group as well as the uncertainty of doing so. One cannot ultimately trust anyone, a theme evidenced by the constant anxiety of C-Murder, who asks plaintively, "Would you die for me?" "Would you kill for me?" and "Would you hesitate?" throughout. These are existential demands, demands that inform much of the fatalism and anxiety so pervasive in the popular imagination today, demands necessitated by the stark material reality many young people face.

We thus see a complex set of tensions registering in contemporary black film and music, as fundamental questions of distrust versus trust and autonomy versus collectivity proliferate. Racial identity is not given in the popular cultural forms but is radically contingent and dependent upon moment-to-moment and day-to-day survival. These narratives are crucial for disenfranchised youth today, who have watched such spectacles unfold and draw upon them in their own intensely fraught lives. These resources, these stories and myths, are the ones that young people gravitate toward while making sense out of their lives, in the unfortunate absence of other models and in the face of day-to-day struggle. They exceed the explanatory frameworks offered in traditional approaches to multiculturalism and take us to the terrain of everyday struggle, a terrain that does not privilege nostalgia and transcendence but the very real and the very immediate. This work signals a set of concerns that cannot be explained away in a civil rights–era discourse of racial uplift, of "good" and "bad" role models.

I would now like to explore a telling set of interactions around Master P from my ethnographic study of young people and hip hop noted earlier, highlighting some of the complexities around generation and generational identity (Dimitriadis, 2001; 2003). Master P was a big favorite early in 1998, particularly after the deaths of Tupac and Biggie. P was not a "studio rapper," according to these youth; he "wasn't fake." Clearly, he embodied many of the dualities that are so much a part of the so-called hip hop generation. In a key example, he talked about his wealth but also kept in touch with his roots. This was a precarious balance. I recall one focus group discussion in which a young person commented, "I hate rappers who talk about how all they got this and they got that." Such rappers, it seems, aligned themselves too closely and uncritically with the mainstream. I asked if Master P talked about his wealth, this kind of conspicuous consumption. The youth responded, "He in between, he talk about both. He talk about how much money he had, and . . . " Struggling for the correct phrase, another youth finished his thought—"where he came from." Master P, it seems, occupies the kind of "in between" space Neal evokes above.

Yet older community members didn't quite see the same balance being struck. I recall another focus group discussion with older teens, which the education director, Bill, walked in on. While Bill was supportive of young people and felt the work I was doing was important, he was distrustful of some of the tendencies within hip hop. When he walked in, we had been talking about the history of rap and hip hop. As an older staff member, he might, it seemed, have something to say. One teen said that we were talking about how "things were easier in the '80s." Bill responded:

> It was easier back in the '80s than it is now . . . I done heard too much "murder murder" [a popular song]. That's what I think. Think teenagers done lost it. . . . They feel comfortable picking up a gun. It don't prove nothing. . . . In the '80s people had fun. I don't think people have fun these days. I think people out to see how macho they can be. How many women they can call "bitches" and "hoes" and all that. It's all about dissing somebody. Soon as somebody hit you, you ready to do something. . . . I mean, they was starting in the later '80s, but early '80s [it wasn't like that]. And all because of, what's this stuff called? Rap music.

After his rhetorical question, Bill continued, "Snoop Dogg, Ice Cube, Tupac—I was never really into that," to which another teen responded, "That was old school." Bill then said, "That's old school? So what's new school? Master P? He 'bout it bout it,' huh? . . . I don't know, fellas. I heard he's a millionaire. He got a lot of money. Isn't he putting some money back in his neighborhood?" Another youth said immediately that he did. Bill didn't seem convinced.

We can see some important distinctions between older and younger people around Master P. Clearly, there was a strong investment in P from those younger. He was "real" to these youth, and his life was evidence of this on multiple levels, wrapped up in his efforts at day-to-day survival. For Bill, a staff member in his fifties, the issue was whether or not P "gave back" to his community. As I noted elsewhere, rap music has provided youth with super-invulnerable figures, resources for survival for dealing with a profoundly hostile social, cultural, and material reality. The conflict between Tupac and Biggie, and the rise of Master P, evidences much of this, in ways that often escape the purview of those older.

Indeed, these young people explicitly compared Master P to Tupac. One youth said of Tupac, "He was a true mug, right there. He got shot in the balls, shot in the chest," to which another responded, "I think he got shot in the head too." Another said, "Master P gonna end up dying. He gonna be the next one to go," to which another responded, "'cause he right after Tupac." The first youth continued, "What he say in his songs? . . . 'Keep an eye on your enemies.' . . . He already been shot in the back." Both Master P and Tupac talked about dying in their songs, these youth said. Specifically, in the wake of Tupac's death, these youth combed P's songs for similar references.

Master P and Tupac both offered new models for "blackness," for what it means to engage with the American Dream on new contentious and dangerous terrain. Both embody the gangster archetype, standing inside and outside the American mainstream at the same time. On the title track to his popular album *Da Last Don*, Master P evokes much of this ambivalence from the very first line, addressing "America" and its seeming hypocrisy: "Good Day America this is Mr. No Limit!" He continues, "You always point the finger at the bad guy / But what if the bad guy points the finger at you? / Fuck the politicians the media and the government / The fucking world was built on corruption." P then says he "made millions from raps," but is still tied to his "No Limit niggas," "strapped thug niggas [who] bust caps," or fire guns. It is here that he ties himself most explicitly to Tupac Shakur and his legacy—Tupac "took the kiss of death" so he could be "The Last Don."

We see this thread continue to this day in rap. While Master P's career seemed somewhat in decline by 2003, a "new school" has risen. In particular, the work of 50 Cent picks up on many of these themes detailed throughout. Material struggle, for example, is evidenced by 50's album title *Get Rich or Die Trying* (2003), while songs like "Many Men

(Wish Death Upon Me)" highlight the dangerous terrain he walks—a theme he does not shy away from in discussions of his life. 50 Cent has pointed out again and again how he survived an attempt on his life and has hinted of his own retaliation. He elaborates on his near-fatal shooting, "Sneaky motherfucker, man . . . He [the gunman] did it right. He just didn't finish. He like Allen Iverson shakin' a nigga, go to the basket and miss . . . You don't actually feel each one hit you . . . The adrenaline is pumping. You movin' and tryin' to get out of the way" (quoted in Touré, 2003). He raps about the shooting in the song "Many Men," hinting at the retaliation he has also denied, "In the Bible it says, 'What goes around, comes around' / Hommo shot me, three weeks later he got shot down / Now it's clear that I'm here for a real reason / 'Cause he got hit like I got hit, but he ain't fucking breathing."

The comparisons to Tupac were perhaps inevitable. Popular rapper Eminem notes, "One of the things that excited me about Tupac . . . was even if he was rhymin' the simplest words in the world, you felt like he meant it and it came from his heart. That's the thing with 50. That same aura. That's been missing since we lost Pac and Biggie. The authenticity, the realness behind it" (quoted in Touré, 2003). On the 50 Cent song "Patiently Waiting," guest star Eminem raps about the deaths of Tupac and Biggie: "It's like a fight to the top, just to see who'll die for the spot / You put your life in this / Nothing like surviving a shot." The sense of existential angst and danger has remained a constant theme in the music, underscored by a profound ambivalence around the "American Dream" and "crossing over."

Yet hip hop is not static—and the unfolding careers of these artists tell us much about the post-soul condition. Indeed, a recent confrontation between these two now financially successful artists and businessmen is telling. According to *Forbes* magazine, Master P and 50 Cent are among the two richest rappers of all time—with conservative estimates of their net worths in the tens of millions. Yet they have taken different paths. Since the release of his first album, 50 Cent has largely stayed grounded in the themes that marked his earliest efforts—including violence, money, sex, and the relationship among all three. He has engaged in a series of high-profile feuds with other rap artists, including Game, Young Buck, Lil Wayne, Rick Ross, and others. One need only look at the titles of the first songs of his last album, *Curtis* (2007)—"My Gun Go Off," "Man Down," "I Still Kill," and "I Get Money"—to see this continuity. On the other hand, Master P has stepped out of the rap limelight to devote himself to various community causes, including projects to educate youth about entrepreneurship and financial independence. Perhaps most symbolically, he replaced Bill Clinton as the NAACP's keynote speaker on the "State of Young Black America" in 2007. He has spoken out against "negativity" in rap and has reintegrated himself into traditional black institutions and leadership structures.

We see here a key fault line in discussions around the role of hip hop in understanding what Neal calls our "post-soul" moment. When asked during a BET news conference about Master P's call for more "positive" rap, 50 Cent dismissed him, simply stating—"Master P doesn't sell records anymore." Master P responded in an open letter, writing that "there are a lot of immature people in the world," then noting, "Oprah Winfrey is absolutely right, we need to grow up and be responsible for our actions." He continued, "It's simply disappointing to see black people that are in a position to help make a change just sit back and entertain the negativity" (www.xxlmag.com/online/?p=10281). One gets the sense that these concerns are secondary for 50 Cent, whose interest in "selling records"—and, by extension, staying relevant in hip hop culture—is paramount. This discussion highlights the ways hip hop itself has become a sphere in which the issues Neal, Boyd, and others have raised can be entertained.

POPULAR CULTURE, PEDAGOGY, AND NEW ROLES FOR THE INTELLECTUAL

Throughout this chapter, I have tried to access some of the specificity of the "hip hop generation" and its needs and concerns. These texts articulate much of the specificity of this moment, what Boyd has called a "post–civil rights" and Neal has called a "post-soul" moment. I have highlighted some efforts to stand "side by side" with hip hop and not "above" it. This work, I think, can go some way in helping us rethink the nature of intellectual work today. More and more, we need to rethink the ways we position ourselves as cultural studies of education scholars and activists. We need to understand and engage with contemporary youth in ways that look past modernist notions of emancipation and liberation. Moreover, this work needs to be ever mindful of the dangers of "post-race" thinking. Barack Obama's recent U.S. presidential victory marked for many a broad transformation in American culture and history—a "breakthrough," to use the term coined by journalist Gwen Ifill. Some even said it signaled "The End of White America," as a recent cover story in *The Atlantic* declared. The persistence of race and racism needs to be center stage, alongside efforts to understand their unique, contemporary inflections.

I would join, as well, a growing group of scholars who are attempting to articulate a kind of specific politics "from the ground up" in hip hop. While not the focus of this essay strictly speaking, this work is worth highlighting. For example, according to Bakari Kitwana (2002), young people who came of age in the 1980s and '90s "share a specific set of values and attitudes." He continues, "At the core are our thoughts about family, relationships, child rearing, career, racial identity, race relations, and politics. Collectively, these views make up a complex worldview that has not been concretely defined" (4). The specific concerns of this generation are not so clearly linked to an overarching political movement like the civil rights movement, but they are no less pressing. In particular, he discusses: the continuing rise of stark economic disparities; police brutality; gangs and drugs; new generation gaps within black communities; exploding racial tensions; and finally the continued deferment of the American dream (37–44). He writes, "The older generation can't entirely identify with the mode of oppression facing our generation. Oppression for us is not simply a line in the sand with white supremacists blocking access—us over here and them over there" (41).

For Kitwana, this emerging worldview, with its specific needs, concerns, and desires, first emerged in rap in the mid- to late '80s in the "sociopolitical critiques of artists like NWA, KRS-One, Poor Righteous Teachers, Queen Latifah, and others" (4–5). Since then, hip hop music has emerged as a uniquely relevant landscape for this generation of youth sorting out these issues and concerns, as evidenced by figures such as Tupac, Biggie, Master P, and 50 Cent. To echo Neal (2002) again, "We cannot simply reject these narratives on a moral basis that is itself the product of a profoundly different world; we must at least critically engage them with the same energy and passion that many of these artists themselves inject into their creative efforts" (11). We must face them head-on, I argue, without recourse to nostalgia. At stake is a new, truly relevant critical pedagogy for urban youth.

References

Boyd, T. (2002). *The New H.N.I.C. (Head Nigga in Charge): The Death of Civil Rights and the Reign of Hip Hop*. New York: NYU Press.

Burke, K. (1941). *The Philosophy of Literary Form: Studies in Symbolic Action*. Berkeley: University of California Press.

Dimitriadis, G. (2003). *Friendship, Cliques, and Gangs: Young Black Men Coming of Age in Urban America*. New York: Teachers College Press.

———. (2001). *Performing Identity/Performing Culture: Hip Hop as Text, Pedagogy, and Lived Practice*. New York: Peter Lang.

Dimitriadis, G., & McCarthy, C. (2001). *Reading and Teaching the Postcolonial: From Baldwin to Basquiat and Beyond*. New York: Teachers College Press.

Dyson, M. (2002). *Holler If You Hear Me: Searching for Tupac Shakur*. New York: Basic Books.

Kitwana, B. (2002). *The Hip Hop Generation: Young Blacks and the Crisis in African American Culture*. New York: Basic Books.

Neal, M. (2002). *Soul Babies: Black Popular Culture and the Post-soul Aesthetic*. New York: Routledge.

Rose, T. (1994). *Black Noise*. Hanover, NH: Wesleyan University Press.

Steinberg, S., & Kincheloe, J. (Eds.) (1997). *Kinderculture: The Corporate Construction of Childhood*. Boulder, CO: Westview.

———. (2005). *Kinderculture: The Corporate Construction of Childhood* (2nd Edition). Boulder, CO: Westview.

Touré. (2004). The Life of a Hunted Man. *Rolling Stone*, 919, April 3.

Chapter 11

McDONALD'S, POWER, AND CHILDREN: RONALD McDONALD/ RAY KROC DOES IT ALL FOR YOU

Joe L. Kincheloe

In his book *The Hawkline Monster: A Gothic Western*, the late Richard Brautigan develops the character of Cameron:

> Cameron was a counter. He vomited nineteen times on his way to San Francisco. He liked to count everything that he did. This had made Greer a little nervous when he first met up with Cameron years ago, but he'd gotten used to it by now.
>
> People would sometimes wonder what Cameron was doing and Greer would say, "He's counting something," and people would ask, "What's he counting?" and Greer would say, "What difference does it make?" and the people would say, "Oh."
>
> People usually wouldn't go into it any further because Greer and Cameron were very self-assured in that big relaxed casual kind of way that makes people nervous now. (Brautigan 1974, 11)

I can relate to Cameron, for I too am a counter. McDonald's is also a counter—and like the people who noticed Cameron's peculiar proclivity, most Americans don't go very far in analyzing McDonald's propensity for counting or, for that matter, anything else about the fast food behemoth. Like Greer and Cameron, McDonald's self-assurance (i.e., power) must make people a little nervous.

I was destined to write about McDonald's, for my life has always intersected with the golden arches. As part of my undergraduate comedy shtick, I told my listeners (truthfully) that I had consumed 6,000 McDonald's hamburgers before graduating from high school. In junior high and high school we were allowed to go off campus to eat. My friends and I (before we had driver's licenses) would tromp through the Tennessee woods rain or shine to McDonaldland; in high school we drove. After six years of three-hamburger lunches, not to mention three more on Wednesday nights with my parents and several on weekend nights after cruising with friends, the count began to mount. A secondary bonus for my fifteen-cent burgermania involved the opportunity to count my cholesterol numbers as they crept higher and higher. Ray Kroc, the man who made McDonald's a household name, would have been proud.

Somewhere in my small-town-Tennessee adolescent consciousness, I understood that McDonald's was the future. I couldn't name it, but the standardized hamburger was a symbol of some vague social phenomenon. Like Italian or Polish immigrants of another place and time, I was ethnic (hillbilly). And like all children of traditional ethnic parents, I struggled for an American identity free from the taint of ethnicity. Though it hadn't yet assumed the mantle of All-American symbol around the world, I knew that McDonald's of the early 1960s was mainstream American through and through. As such, my participation in the burger–fries ritual was an act of shedding my ethnic identity. Understanding McDonald's regulation of customer behavior, I complied readily, knowing the menu in advance and placing my order quickly and accurately. My parents, on the other hand, raised in the rural South of the early twentieth century, were lost at the ordering counter—lost in the Hamburger Patch. Never understanding the menu, always unsure of the expected behavior, they frustrated the effort to shape their customer conduct.

On a very different level, however, my parents were seduced by McDonald's. Students of media have come to understand that individuals' readings of film, TV, and TV commercials is idiosyncratic, differing significantly from individual to individual. So it was in my home. As victims of the Great Depression in southern Appalachia (a double economic whammy), my mother and father came to see excessive spending as a moral weakness. Eating out, when it was possible to prepare food at home, was especially depraved. My father would darken the door of McDonald's only if he was convinced of its economic "good sense." Indeed, advertisers struck an emotional chord when they pitted McDonald's fifteen-cent hamburgers and twelve-cent french fries as an alternative to the extravagant cost of eating out. To my self-identified working-class father, eating McDonald's was an act of class resistance. He never really cared much for the food—he would rather eat my mother's country ham and cornbread. But as we McDined, he spoke with great enthusiasm about how McDonald's beat the price of other burgers around town by fifty or sixty cents. Such statistics made him very happy.

Like others in peculiar social spaces around the world, my father consumed a democratic egalitarian ethos. French teenagers accustomed to the bourgeois stuffiness of French restaurants could have identified with my father's class-resistant consumption, as they revel in the informality and freedom of McDonald's "American atmosphere." The inexpensive fare, the informal dress, the loud talk are class signifiers (Leidner 1993). Such coding is ironic in light of McDonald's right-wing political history, its manipulations of labor, and its cutthroat competition with other fast food enterprises. That McDonald's continues to maintain an egalitarian image is testimony to the power and expertise of its public relations strategists. And here we find the major questions raised by this chapter: What is the nature of these PR strategies? What do they tell us about McDonald's? And how do they affect American culture—particularly its kinderculture?

SHAPING CULTURE, SHAPING CONSCIOUSNESS

Few Americans think about efforts by powerful interests in the larger society to regulate populations to bring about desired behaviors. In America and other Western societies political domination shifted decades ago from police or military force to cultural messages. Such communications are designed to win the approval or consent of citizens for actions taken by power elites (Giroux 1988). The contributors to this book in their own ways are involved in efforts to expose the specifics of this process of cultural domination (often labeled hegemony). The process takes place in the everyday experience of our lives. The messages are not sent by a clandestine group of conspirators or devised by some secret ministry of propaganda; neither are they read by everyone in the same way. But some people understand their manipulative intent and rebel against their authority (Goldman 1992). The company's role in these power dynamics illustrates the larger process. If any organization has the power to help shape the lives of children, it is McDonald's.

The construction of who we are and what we believe cannot be separated from the workings of power. Americans don't talk much about power; American politicians don't even talk about power. When power is broached in mainstream sociology, the conversation revolves around either the macro level, the political relations of governments, or the micro level, the personal relations between two people (Abercrombie 1994). Power, as the term is used in this essay, is neither macro nor micro, nor does it rely on legality or coercion. Power, as it has evolved in the first decade of the twenty-first century, maintains its legitimacy in subtle and effective ways.

Consider the power generated by McDonald's use of the media to define itself not simply as an American institution but as America itself. As the "land we love" writ small, McDonald's attaches itself to American patriotism and the cultural dynamics it involves. Ray Kroc understood from the beginning that he was not simply selling hamburgers—he was selling America a vision of itself (Luxenberg 1985). From the All-American marching band to the All-American basketball and football teams to the All-American meal served by All-American boys and girls, the All-American of the Year, Ray Kroc, labored to connect the American signifier to McDonald's. The American flag will fly twenty-four hours a day at McDonald's, he demanded. Using the flag as a backdrop for the hamburger count, Kroc watched the burger numbers supplant the Dow Jones closing average as the symbolic statistical index for America's economic health. In the late 1960s and early 1970s, Kroc saw the perpetually flying flag as a statement to the war protesters and civil rights "kooks" that McDonald's (America) would not stand for anyone criticizing or attempting to undermine "our" country (Kroc 1977).

One of the reasons Americans don't talk much about power is that it works in a subtle, hard-to-define manner. Ask Americans how McDonald's has shaped them or constructed their consciousness, and you'll draw blank stares. What does it mean to argue that power involves the ability to ascribe meanings to various features of our lives? Return to the McDonald's All-American ad campaign. Kroc and the McDonald's management sanctioned the costliest, most ambitious ad campaign in American corporate history (Boas and Chain 1976). All this money and effort were expended to imbue the hamburger—the McDonald's variety in particular—with a star-spangled signification. And it worked in the sense that Americans and individuals around the world began to make the desired connection. Described as the "ultimate icon of Americana," a "cathedral of consumption" where Americans practice their "consumer religion," McDonald's, like Disneyland, transcends status as mere business establishment (Ritzer 1993). When McDonald's or Disney speak, they speak for all of us. How could the Big Mac or Pirates of the Caribbean mislead us? They are us.

Just as Americans saw mystical implications in Thomas Jefferson and John Adams both dying on July 4, 1826—the fiftieth anniversary of the Declaration of Independence—contemporary Americans may see mystical ramifications in the fact that Ray Kroc and Walt Disney were in the same company in the U.S. Army. Having lied about their age, the two prophets of free enterprise–grounded utopian Americana fought the good fight for the American way. It takes nothing away from the mystery to know that Kroc described Disney as a "strange duck" (Donald? Uncle Scrooge? Daisy?) because he wouldn't chase girls (Kroc 1977).

No expenses were spared, no signifiers were left floating freely in the grand effort to transfer reverence for America to McDonald's. The middle-class cathedral was decorated as a shrine with the obligatory plastic eagle replete with powerful wings and glazed, piercing eyes. A banner held in the bald eagle's beak reads "McDonald's: The American Way" (Boas and Chain 1976). These legitimation signifiers work best when they go unnoticed, as they effectively connect an organization's economic power to acquire property, lobby Congress, hire lawyers, and so on to its power to ascribe meaning and persuade. In the process the legitimated organization gains the power to create and transmit a view of reality that is consonant with its larger interests—American economic superiority as the direct result of an unbridled free enterprise system.

A recent ad campaign paints a nostalgic, sentimentalized, conflict-free American family pictorial history. The purpose of the ad is to forge an even deeper connection between McDonald's and America by creating an American historical role for McDonald's where none ever existed. You can almost hear the male voice-over: "Though we didn't yet exist, we were there to do it all for you—McDonald's then, McDonald's now." We're all one big, happy family with the same (European?) roots. "We" becomes McDonald's and America—"our" family (Goldman 1992). The only thing left to buttress the All-American image would be a Santa Claus connection. Kroc's PR men quickly made their move, inducing Kroc himself to distribute hamburgers to Chicago's street corner Santa Clauses and Salvation Army workers. Newspapers noticed the event and, to Kroc's delight, linked Santa Claus to a chauffeur named McDonald's. The legend grew when the PR men circulated a story about a child who was asked where Santa had met Mrs. Santa. "At McDonald's," the child reportedly said. Wire services picked up the anecdote, sending it to every town in the country (Boas and Chain 1976). Big ad campaigns or bogus anecdotes, McDonald's has used the media to create an American mythology.

Like other giant international corporations of the contemporary era, McDonald's has used the media to invade the most private spheres of our everyday lives. Our national identifications, desires, and human needs have been commodified—appropriated for the purposes of commerce (Giroux 1994; Kellner 1992). Such media usage grants producers a level of access to human consciousness never imagined by the most powerful dictator. Such power is illustrated in the resistance McDonald's elicits as signifier for America. Time and time again in McDonald's brief history, neighborhood organizers have reacted to the firm's efforts to enter their communities. Seeing McDonald's as a form of cultural colonization that overwhelms locally owned businesses and devours local culture, individuals have fought to keep McDonald's out. In the 1970s opposition became so intense in New York City that Kroc ordered high walls built around construction sites to keep them hidden from local residents. At the same time in Sweden, radicals bombed two restaurants in hopes of thwarting "creeping American cultural imperialism" (Boas and Chain 1976). In various demonstrations against the World Trade Organization in the early years of the twenty-first century demonstrators smashed McDonald's windows and vandalized stores (Kincheloe 2002). For better and for worse, McDonald's has succeeded in positioning itself as America.

MCDONALD'S, GLOBALIZATION, AND HEGEMONY: CONSTRUCTING KINDERCULTURE

Ironically, as McDonald's became America it outgrew U.S. borders. By the last quarter of the twentieth century the golden arches represented a global enterprise. In this transnational process, the company became the symbol of Western economic development. Often McDonald's was the first foreign corporation to penetrate a particular nation's market. Indian social critic Vandana Shiva (1997) found dark humor in the symbolism of the golden arches. They induce the feeling that when you walk into McDonald's, you are entering heaven. The corporate marketers want children around the world to view the "McDonald's experience" as an immersion in celestial *jouissance*—while they are actually eating junk. In terms reminiscent of the outlook of the Pentagon in the second Iraq war, McDonald's executives refer to their movement into foreign markets as the company's "global realization" (Schlosser 2001). When statues of Lenin came down in East Germany after reunification, giant statues of Ronald McDonald took their place almost overnight. Driving through that country in the late 1990s and the first decade of the twenty-first century, I imagined cartoon bubbles coming out of each Ronald's mouth as the clown proclaimed: "No Nikita, we buried you— the West has won."

In the city of Santos, Brazil, several schoolteachers told me that they worried about the impact of McDonald's on their pupils. One teacher contended: "The danger of McDonald's imperialism is that it teaches children to devalue Brazilian things and to believe that the U.S. is superior to all of us poor South Americans." The anger these women directed at McDonald's and the company's ideological impact on Brazilian children was inscribed on each word they spoke. Western societies and the United States in particular have set up this corporate colonialism via the construction of corporatized governments (Kincheloe 1999) over the past twenty-five years. Particular types of consciousness are needed for such political economic reforms to work. Individuals in Brazil, Mexico, Malaysia, and the United States need to dismiss from their consciousness questions of social justice, egalitarianism, and environmentalism. Corporatized, globalized governments and their corporate allies need well-managed, socially regulated, consumption-oriented children and adults who understand that economic growth demands "good business climates," antiunion perspectives, and low wages for those lower in the hierarchy.

To gain the ability to introduce these ideas to children in the United States and around the world, corporations such as McDonald's continue to refine their appeal to the affective dimension. Their ability to produce entertainment for children that adults deem inappropriate is central to this enterprise. After decades of marketing research including, over the years, Ugly Stickers, Wacky Packs, Toxic High stickers, Garbage Pail Kids, Mass Murderer cards, and McDonald's cuisine, producers of kinderculture understand that part of the appeal of children's consumer products lies in vociferous parental disapprove of them. Indeed, the more subversive the kinderculture, the better. Schools not only ignore the power of such influences on children but have allowed McDonald's and other marketers into their hallways and classrooms (Molnar 1996; Kenway and Bullen 2001).

In addition to selling its products in schools, McDonald's has almost unlimited ideological access to elementary and secondary students by way of such ploys as, for example, "job interview seminars." Analysis of such seminars reveals that they are less about the interviewing process and more about inculcating particular beliefs about the social benefits of McDonald's and the unregulated free enterprise system. Creating a positive affective valence with the subversive kinderculture, McDonald's goes in for the knockout punch with its ideological treatises. In my research I found that students who were savvy enough to recognize the covert ideological dimensions of McDonald's seminars and brave enough to expose them to the school community were often punished for such "misbehavior" by school officials (see Kincheloe 2002 for an expansion of this theme).

A critical pedagogy of childhood cannot ignore these political, economic, social, and ideological dynamics. It is important for children around the world to understand the ways commercially produced children's culture (Kenway and Bullen 2001) in general and the subversive kinderculture in particular wins their consent to positions that serve the interests of multinational corporations and their allies, not young people or anybody else. Children are directly affected by corporate hegemonization and globalization—forces that are central players in the social construction of childhood in hyperreality (Jans 2002). As always in discussions of these hegemonic dynamics, it is important to outline the complex issues of the production and reception of ideology. Daniel Cook (2004) offers valuable insights in this context that are important in the reading of McDonald's impact on children. Arguing that we must reject the dichotomy of the exploited child and the empowered child, Cook maintains that children are inevitably positioned in market relations and are always empowered to make decisions in this context.

Such a point resonates with what Shirley Steinberg and I argue in the introduction to this volume: Researchers of childhood must always maintain a delicate balance between structure and agency. We cannot understand contemporary childhood(s) outside of their relation to the market, and children always make decisions in this context. Importantly, they are not free to make any consumption or ideological decision they want—they must make decisions based on their social, political, economic, and cultural terrain. In the twenty-first century, that terrain cannot be understood outside of the commodification of children's culture. The market does not snatch children from the innocent garden of childhood and transform them into crazed consumers. Concurrently it does not simply have to do with providing empowerment for self-sufficient agential children. Corporate producers and marketers must be exerting economic and ideological effects by their efforts, since they keep pouring billions of dollars into advertising directed at children from New

Orleans to Nigeria, from Jacksonville to Jakarta. While children construct their own meanings, the corporate culture of power does exploit them—the corporate effort to ideologically construct children's consciousness is a cold reality.

Social scholars who do not value the importance of studying the effects of dominant power on the lived world often slam more critical takes on the effects of political economic structures on the lives of children. They often interpret critical charges of ideological exploitation with the assertion that the dominant power of McDonald's, for example, produces standardized and homogenized "corporate children." (See Kincheloe 2002 for examples of this dynamic in anticritical scholarship from various disciplines.) This is not what McDonald's and other producers of kinderculture do. Producers of commercial children's culture reshape everyday places and activities in ways that resonate with corporate economic and ideological interests. In this context, as parents of young children often describe, the relationship of children to, say, eating is reconfigured as children cry out for McDonald's hamburgers. For example, as I sat in the waiting room of a doctor's office I observed a young mother of a restless, frightened six-year-old boy struggle to contain him as they waited to see a pediatrician.

MOTHER: Would you please sit still and stop crying. Stop it! Now! I'm not going to take you to McDonald's if you don't stop it.

CHILD: (screaming) I want to go to McDonald's. Let's go, Mommy. Please . . . let's go now. (crying) I want to go to McDonald's.

MOTHER: I'm going to brain you. Now you just stop it.

CHILD: I want a coke and a cheeseburger. Please (screaming) McDonald's, McDonald's, McDonald's. Cheeseburger!

MOTHER: (slapping child's face) You're not going to McDonald's, young man.

CHILD: (louder screams and hysterical crying) McDonald's, McDonald's, McDonald's.

McDonald's advertisers have tapped into this child's affect at a level that transcends rational understanding. In his time of stress in the pediatrician's office the little boy seeks the comfort of his provider of pleasure. I can recall a similar moment at a similar age in my own pre-McDonald's early childhood. In seeking the comfort of food from the stresses of the doctor's office, I begged my mother to take me home for some of her southern fried chicken and pinto beans. But this little boy doesn't want to go home; he wants to visit the golden arches. Reading her child's reactions, the mother appeals to the most severe threat she can formulate in the situation—the threat of not going to McDonald's. As the child breaks free from the mother's restraint, he runs around the waiting room screaming, crying, and flailing his arms. She chases him for several moments, finding it difficult to corral him. Finally catching him, she carries him back screaming, crying, and flailing to her seat. Panting for breath, she reassesses her strategy in her attempt to get control of the situation:

MOTHER: I'm going to buy you two cheeseburgers and one of them hot apple pies.
CHILD: (immediately calmed by the prospect of consumption at McDonald's) You are?!
MOTHER: Yes, and I'm going to get you some of those animal cookies you like. Hippo-hippo-hippopotamus.
CHILD: I love those cookies. I LOVE THEM! Cheeseburgers and cheeseburgers.

Everyday places and activities have been reshaped by McDonald's kinderculture. There are no standardization and homogenization processes at work here. A new relationship has emerged that will be acted on in diverse ways by differing children and parents. The complexity of the relationship between corporate producer and child consumer is so powerful that I cannot produce a final interpretation of what this vignette means. Though meaning here is loose and slippery, it does not mean that my readings are irrelevant. I stand ready to argue their contribution to the effort to understand McDonald's social power and resulting impact on contemporary childhood. It could be argued that the vignette is a micropolitical reflection of a new knowledge order that decenters parents' roles as the primary providers of aid and comfort to their children. It may tell us that a new set of material realities, ideological assumptions, and configurations of power have made an impact on contemporary childhood. The little boy in the doctor's office possessed a detailed, if not expert, knowledge of McDonald's product line that he had learned via TV. Such knowledge shaped his behavior and his relationship to his mother. Undoubtedly the child's cultural identifications and affect had been rerouted by corporate marketers.

Consumption and pleasure are intimately connected in the life of this young boy and millions of other children. Corporate power has entered domains of life once free from market influences. Without their conscious awareness such children may eventually find that this power and the connections it forges exert a significant impact on their life choices. Young boys in China, for example, fantasize about opening chains of McDonald's restaurants in Beijing (Yan 1997). In a communist country such dreams are ideologically significant and alter the relationship between the young boy and Chinese politics. Like the U.S. military in Vietnam and Iraq, corporations work to win the hearts and minds of young consumers; the only difference is that corporate methods are more sophisticated and work much better than the military strategies. Subtle kinderculture is amazingly intrusive, working twenty-four hours a day to colonize all dimensions of lived experience (Kenway and Bullen 2001; Cook 2004).

MCDONALD'S IS A KIDS' KIND OF PLACE: E-I-E-I-O

Contrary to the prevailing positivist wisdom, we begin to understand in more detail that childhood is not and never has been an unchanging developmental stage of humanness. Rather, it is a social and economic construction tied to prevailing perceptions of what constitutes the "natural order" (Polakow 1992). Forces such as urbanization and industrialization have exerted significant influences on the nature of childhood—as have the development of media and the techno power it produces. By "techno power" I mean the expansion of corporate influence via the use of recent technological innovation (Kellner 1989; Harvey 1989). Using techno power, corporations like McDonald's have increased their ability to maximize capital accumulation, influence social and cultural life, and even help mold children's consciousness. Since childhood is a cultural construction shaped in the contemporary era by the forces of this media-catalyzed techno power, the need for parents, teachers, and community members to study it is dramatic. Let us turn now to McDonald's and the construction of childhood in contemporary globalized society.

Even the name, "McDonald's," is kid-friendly, with its evocation of Old MacDonald and his farm—E-I-E-I-O. The safety of McDonald's provides asylum, if not utopian refuge, from the kid-unfriendly contemporary world of child abuse, broken homes, and child-napping. Offering something better to escape into, McDonald's TV depiction of itself to children as a happy place where "what you want is what you get" is very appealing (Garfield 1992). By the time children reach elementary school, they are often zealous devotees of McDonald's who insist on McDonaldland birthday celebrations and surprise dinners. Obviously McDonald's advertisers are doing something right, as they induce phenomenal numbers of kids to pester their parents for Big Macs and fries.

McDonald's and other fast food advertisers have discovered an enormous, previously overlooked children's market. Children aged five to twelve annually spend almost $5 billion of their own money. They influence household spending of an additional $140 billion each year, more than half of which goes to soft drinks and fast food. Every month nineteen out of every twenty kids aged six to eleven visit a fast food restaurant. In a typical McDonald's promotion, where toys like Hot Wheels or Barbies accompany kids' meals, company officials can expect to sell 30 million to child customers. By the time they reach the age of three, over four out of five children know that McDonald's sells hamburgers. As if this level of child consciousness colonization were not enough, McDonald's, along with scores of other companies, has targeted the public schools as a new venue for child marketing and consumption. In addition to hamburgers for A's programs and advertising-based learning packets for science, foreign language, and other subjects, McDonald's and other fast food firms have gained control of school cafeterias, much to the consternation of many advocates of child health (Hume 1993; Ritzer 1993; Giroux 1994; Kincheloe 2002).

Make no mistake about it, McDonald's and its advertisers want to transform children into consumers; indeed, they see children as consumers in training (Fisher et al. 1991). Ellen Seiter (1993), however, warns against drawing simplistic conclusions about the relationship between advertisers and children, as have, she says, many well-intentioned liberal children's advocacy groups. The leading voice against corporate advertising for children, ACT (Action for Children's Television), fails to capture the subtle aspects of techno power and its colonization of childhood, the complicated interactions of structure and agency. Seeing children as naive innocents who should watch only "good" TV, meaning educational programs that portray middle-class values, the ACT has little appreciation of the complexity of children's TV watching. As argued in this chapter and in the introduction, children are not passive, naive TV viewers. As advertising professionals have learned, children are active, analytical viewers who often make their own meanings of both commercials and the products they sell. These social and psychological dynamics between advertiser and child deserve further analysis.

One important dynamic is advertisers' recognition that children feel oppressed by the middle-class view of children as naive entities in need of constant protection. By drawing on the child's discomfort with middle-class protectionism and the accompanying attempt to "adjust" children to a positivist "developmentally appropriate" norm, advertisers hit on a marketing bonanza. If we address kids as kids—a dash of anarchism and a pinch of hyperactivity—they will love our commercials even though parents (especially middle-class parents) will hate them. By the end of the 1960s, commercial children's TV and advertising were grounded on this premise. Such video throws off restraint, discipline, and old views that children should be seen but not heard. Everything, for example, that educational TV embraces—earnestness, child as an incomplete adult, child in need of correction—commercial TV rejects. In effect, commercial TV sets up an oppositional culture for kids.

One doesn't have to look far (try any middle-class home) to find that children's enthusiasm for certain TV shows, toys, and foods often isolates them from their parents. Drawing on this isolation, children turn it into a form of power—they finally know something that Dad doesn't. How many dads or moms understand the relationship between Mayor

McCheese and the French Fry Guys? Battle lines begin to be drawn between children and parents, as kids want to purchase McDonald's hamburgers or action toys. Conflicts in lower-middle-class homes may revolve around family finances; strife in upper-middle-class homes may concern aesthetic or ideological concerns. Questions of taste, cultural capital, or self-improvement permeate child–adult interactions in such families. The child's ability to negotiate the restrictions of adult values is central to the development of an independent self. A common aspect of this developing independence involves the experience of contradiction with the adult world. Children of upwardly mobile, ambitious parents may find it more difficult to negotiate this experience of contradiction because of the parents' strict views of the inappropriateness of TV-based children's culture. Thus the potential for parent–child conflict and alienation may be greater in this familial context.

PLAY IN HYPERREALITY: MCDONALD'S COLONIZATION OF FUN

In this context play is placed in cultural conflict. Over the past several decades psychologists and educators have come to recognize the importance of play in childhood and child development. With this in mind, our examination of McDonald's opens a window into what can happen when the culture and political economy of play begins to change. With a changing culture of play, we begin to discern different effects of play on the construction of children's identities and with their cognitive development. New forms of play may accelerate particular forms of intellectual development while concurrently limiting the imagination—a dynamic that holds interesting implications for universalist perspectives on child development. With the corporate colonization of play in hyperreality, play begins to lose its imaginative dimensions. Contemporary children's play occurs in the same public spaces as adult labor, as children enter into cyberspace using the same hardware and software that their parents use in their professional lives.

McDonald's is, of course, just one producer in an expanding children's commercial culture. Again, it is important to note that children in their interactions with McDonald's and other manifestations of this commercial kinderculture use its symbolic and material dimensions in often unique and idiosyncratic ways. McDonald's and other corporations worry about this idiosyncratic agential dynamic of childhood play. Like other marketers McDonald's wants children to engage its products and company-produced meanings in an "appropriate" manner. Such engagement would not include "playing" with environmental and health concerns by developing cyber communities of like-minded children calling for corporate responsibility. McDonald's and other corporations do not want power-savvy children engaging in socially conscious use of their products—such as the ones who formed the organization Children Against McDonald's. Corporate marketers and other protectors of the status quo fear the agential, empowered child. Media corporations and companies like McDonald's work hard to control and structure the way consumers interact with their products. Indeed, child consumers do not experience the freedom and empowerment some advocates of the agential childhood claim for them. Play as political resistance must be opposed at all costs (DuBois-Reymond, Sunker, and Kruger 2001; Hengst 2001; Nations 2001; Cassell and Jenkins 2002; Mouritsen 2003; Jenkins 2003).

A covert children's culture has always existed on playgrounds and in schools. The children's culture of the past, however, was produced by children and propagated through child-to-child contact. The postmodern children's culture of today is increasingly created by adults and dispersed via television for the purpose of inducing children to consume. (Children's use of the Internet may provide a countervailing trend in this context.) As they carefully subvert middle-class parents' obsession with achievement, play as a serious enterprise, and self-improvement oriented "quality time" (a subversion that in my opinion probably contributes to the public good), advertisers connect children's culture to their products. McDonald's commercials reflect these themes, although less blatantly than many advertisers.

Attempting to walk a tightrope between tapping the power of children's subversive culture and offending the middle-class guardians of propriety—a walk that has become increasingly difficult in the first decade of the twenty-first century—McDonald's developed a core of so-called "slice-of-life" children's ads. Casting no adults in the commercials, advertisers depict a group of preteens engaged in "authentic" conversations around a McDonald's table covered with burgers, fries, and shakes. Using children's slang ("radical," "dude," "we're into Barbie") to describe toys in various McDonald's promotions, children discuss the travails of childhood with one another.

In many commercials children make adults the butt of their jokes or share jokes that adults don't get (Seiter 1993; Goldman 1992). McDonald's subtly attempts to draw some of the power of children's subversive culture onto their products without anyone but the kids knowing. Such slice-of-life ads are opaque to the degree that adults watching them don't get it—they don't see the advertiser's effort to connect McDonald's with the subversive kinderculture. The notion of oppositionality has fueled numerous aspects of children's commercial culture (e.g., several Nickelodeon shows, Paul Reubens's transgressive Pee-wee's Playhouse, many video games, etc.) that play on children's differences from adults. It is a key weapon in the corporate construction of childhood.

THE BLOODY FIGHT FOR CONFORMITY, COURTESY, AND ESTABLISHED VIRTUE: MCDONALDLAND, RONALD, AND RAY

TV ads often serve as postmodern myths, as they resolve cultural contradictions, portray models of identity, and glorify the status quo. While all McDonald's ads accomplish these mythic functions to some degree, none do it better than ads and promotions involving McDonaldland. To understand the mythic dynamics of McDonaldland, one must appreciate the psychological complexity of Ray Kroc. Born in 1902 in a West Side Chicago working-class neighborhood into what Kroc called a "Bohunk" (Bohemian) family, Kroc was obsessed throughout his life with proving his worth as both a human being and a businessman. Having failed in several business ventures in his twenties and thirties, Kroc had much to prove by the time the McDonald's opportunity confronted him at the age of fifty-two (Boas and Chain 1976). Kroc defined McDonaldland the same way he defined himself—through consumption. Driven by an ambition to own nice things, Kroc's autobiography is peppered with references to consumption: "I used to comb through the advertisements in the local newspaper for notices of house sales in the wealthier suburbs . . . I haunted these sales and picked up pieces of elegant furniture . . . " (Kroc 1977, 27). Watched over by the messianic Ronald McDonald, McDonaldland is a place (your kind of place) where consumption functioned as the means through which its inhabitants gained their identities.

McDonaldland is a kid's text fused with Kroc's psyche that emerges as an effort to sell the system, to justify consumption as a way of life. As the central figure in McDonaldland, Ronald McDonald emerges as a multidimensional clown deity, virgin-born son of Adam Smith, press secretary for free enterprise capitalism. He is also Ray Kroc's projection of himself, his ego creation of the most loved prophet of utopian consumption in the McWorld. Ronald's life history begins in Washington, D.C., with *Today Show* weatherman Willard Scott. Struggling to make it as a junior announcer at WRC-TV in D.C. in the early 1960s, Scott agreed to play Bozo the Clown on the station's kid show. When Scott donned the clown suit, he was transformed from Clark Kent to Superman, bumbling Willard to superclown. The local McDonald's franchisees recognized Scott's talent and employed Bozo as a spokesperson for McDonald's. When the Bozo show was canceled by WRC, McDonald's lost a very effective advertiser. The local D.C. McDonald's owners worked with Scott to create Ronald McDonald (Scott's idea), debuting him in October 1963. Ronald created traffic jams every time he appeared in public, and local operators suggested to the Chicago headquarters that Ronald go national (Love 1986).

After a lengthy debate over whether they should employ Ronald McDonald as a clown, a cowboy, or a spaceman, corporate leaders and advertisers settled on the clown Ronald. Dumping Scott because he was deemed too fat for the image they wanted to promote, the company in 1965 hired Coco, an internationally known clown with the Ringling Bros. and Barnum & Bailey Circus. Beginning with his first national appearance in the Macy's Thanksgiving Day parade on November 25, 1966, the deification of Ronald began. The press releases on Ronald issued by the McDonald's Customers Relations Center are sanctification documents cross-pollinated with frontier tall-tale boasting. "Since 1963,

Ronald McDonald has become a household name, more famous than Lassie or the Easter Bunny, and second only to Santa Claus" (McDonald's Customer Relations Center 1994).

The other characters in McDonaldland, the company's promotional literature reports, revere Ronald (a.k.a. Kroc). He is "intelligent and sensitive . . . he can do nearly anything . . . Ronald McDonald is the star." If children are sick, the promos contend, Ronald is there. Even though he has become an "international hero and celebrity," Ronald is the same friend of children he was in 1963. Ninety-six percent of all children, claimed a bogus "Ronald McDonald Awareness Study" fed to the press, can identify this heroic figure (Boas and Chain 1976). Ronald was everything Kroc wanted to be: a beloved humanitarian, an international celebrity, a philanthropist, a musician (Kroc made his living for a while as a piano player; Ronald has cut children's records). Even the sophisticates loved Ronald, Kroc wrote in his autobiography—a group whose affection Kroc sought throughout his life. Unfortunately he had to settle for it vicariously through Ronald. Abe Lincoln too was rejected by the sophisticates of his day; as a twentieth-century Lincoln, Kroc prominently displayed the bust of Ronald adjacent to the bust of Lincoln on a table behind his desk at the Chicago headquarters (McCormick 1993; Kroc 1977).

According to the promotional literature designed for elementary schools, Ronald "became a citizen of [the McDonald's] International Division" in 1969 and soon began to appear on TV around the world. Kroc was propelled to a new level of celebrity as the corporation "penetrated" the global market. Now known everywhere on earth, Kroc/Ronald became the grand salesman, the successful postindustrial Willie Loman— they love me in Moscow, Belgrade, and New York. Stung by a plethora of critics, Kroc was obsessed with being perceived as a moral man with a moral company that exerted a wholesome influence on children around the world. Kroc wrote and spoke of his noble calling, establishing his "missions" with the golden arches as part of his neo–white man's burden. I provide a humanitarian service, Kroc proclaimed: "I go out and check out a piece of property [that's] not producing a damned thing for anybody," he wrote in his epistles from California. The new franchise provides a better life for scores of people: "out of that bare ground comes a store that does, say, a million dollars a year in business. Let me tell you, it's great satisfaction to see that happen." Kroc/Ronald personified the great success story of twentieth-century capitalism. The fortunes that were made by Kroc and his franchisees came to represent what happens when one works hard in the free enterprise system. McDonaldland and the McWorld—signifiers for the McDonaldization of the planet.

The convergence of the growth of international mega-corporations with the expanding technological sophistication of the media has prompted a new era of consumption. Some analysts argue that the central feature of the postmodern lifestyle revolves around the act of consuming. In McDonaldland Ronald McDonald serves as CEO/archduke over his fiefdom of consumer junkies. The Hamburglar is "cute" in his addiction to hamburgers. According to the literature provided to schools about McDonaldland the Hamburglar's "main purpose in life is the acquisition of McDonald's hamburgers." Grimace is described as "generous and affectionate . . . [his] primary personality attribute is his love for McDonald's shakes." The most important passion of Captain Crook is his love of McDonald's Filet-O-Fish sandwiches.

As a free enterprise utopia, McDonaldland erases all differences, all conflicts; social inequities are overcome through acts of consumption. As such messages justify existing power relations, conformity emerges as the logical path to self-production. The only hint of difference in McDonaldland involves Uncle O'Grimacey, the annual Irish visitor who speaks with a brogue and is defined by his obsession with Shamrock shakes. The emphasis on standardization and "sameness" is so intense that all Ronald McDonalds go to school to learn a uniform image. The training system is so rationalized that students are tracked into one of two groups; throughout pre-service and in-service experiences the clowns are either "greeting Ronalds" or "performing Ronalds." The most compelling manifestation of conformity in McDonaldland involves the portrayal of the French Fry Guys. As the only group of citizens depicted in the Hamburger Patch, these faceless commoners are numerous but seldom seen:

They tend to look, act, and think pretty much alike. Parent French Fry Guys are indistinguishable from children, and vice versa. They are so much alike that, so far, no individual French Fry Guy has emerged as a personality identifiable from the others. They resemble little mops with legs and eyes and speak in squeaky, high-pitched voices, usually in unison. They always move quickly, scurrying around in fits and starts, much like the birds one sees on sandy beaches. (McDonald's Customer Relations Center 1994)

As inhabitants of a McDonalidized McWorld, the French Fry Guys are content to remove themselves from the public space, emerging only for brief and frenetic acts of standardized consumption—their only act of personal assertion.

Life in McDonaldland is free of conflict—the Hamburger Patch is a privatized utopia. It is contemporary America writ small, corporate-directed and consumer-oriented. Questions such as distribution of income among classes, regulation of corporate interests, free trade, minimum wage, and collective bargaining traditionally elicited passion and commitment—now they hardly raise an eyebrow. The political sphere where decisions are made concerning who gets what and who voted for what is managed by a small group. Their work and the issues they confront are followed by a shrinking audience of news watchers tuned to CNN and C-SPAN. Politics, Americans have concluded, is not only useless but, far worse in the mediascape, boring. It can't be too important; it gets such low Nielsens. The political structure of McDonaldland reflects this larger depoliticization with its depiction of the inept, superfluous Mayor McCheese. The school promotional literature describes him as a "silly" character not "to be taken seriously." As a "confused and bumbling" politician, the mayor would rather spend his time in the privatized space of McDonald's eating cheeseburgers. The lesson is clear to children—politics doesn't matter; leave McDonald's alone; let these businessmen run their business the way they see fit.

The benign nature of capitalist production with its freedom from serious conflict of any type portrayed by McDonaldland and Kroc/Ronald is a cover for a savage reality. Business analysts, for example, liken McDonald's operations to the Marine Corps. When a recruit graduates from basic training (Hamburger University), he believes that he can conquer anybody (Love 1986). Motivated by an econo-tribal allegiance to the

McFamily, store operators express faith in McDonald's as if it were a religion. Kroc openly spoke of the Holy Trinity—McDonald's, family, and God in that order (Kroc 1977). Released from boot camp on a jihad for a success theology, these faceless French Fry Guys have forced thousands of independent restaurant owners out of business (Luxenberg 1985). Competing fast food franchisees tell of their introduction to recent Hamburger University graduates and other McDonald's managers with amazement. "We will run you out of business and bury you," these Khrushchevs of fast food proclaim.

No matter how ruthless business might become, there is no room for criticism or dissent in McDonaldland. "I feel sorry for people who have such a small and wretched view of the system that made this country great," Kroc (1977) wrote in his autobiography. The "academic snobs" who criticized McDonald's tapped a sensitivity in Kroc's psyche that motivated counterattacks until the day he died. This love-it-or-leave-it anti-intellectualism finds its McDonaldland expression in the Professor. Described as the proud possessor of various degrees, the Professor is a bumbling fool with a high-pitched, effeminate voice. As none of his theories or inventions ever work, he meets Kroc's definition of an overeducated man: someone who worries about inconsequential affairs to the degree that he is distracted from the normal problems of business. Kroc never liked books or school and saw little use for advanced degrees: "One thing I flatly refuse to give money to is the support of any college" (Kroc 1977, 199). Intellectuals don't fit into the culture of the Hamburger Patch.

As much as the Professor is effeminate, Big Mac, McDonaldland's policeman, is manly. The promotional literature describes him as "the strong, silent type. His voice is deep and super-masculine; his manner is gruff but affectionate . . . his walk is a strut. His stance is chest out, stomach in." The gender curriculum of McDonaldland is quite explicit: Big Mac as the manly man; Birdie, the Early Bird, as the pert, nurturing female. As the only female in McDonaldland, Birdie is faced with a significant task. She is the cheerleader who encourages the male residents to jump into the activities of the new day. "Her enthusiasm and energy are infectious . . . her positive attitude is emphasized by her bright, perky, cheerful voice" (McDonald's Customer Relations Center

1994). Once the McDonaldlanders have gobbled down their Egg Mc-Muffins and are off to their respective occupations, Birdie retires to the sidelines as a passive observer.

The Kroc influence is alive and well in the gender dynamics of the corporation. Referring to himself in the third person as Big Daddy, Kroc expressed a sometimes disturbing misogyny in his handling of company affairs. Ray's personality, one colleague observed, would never allow a woman to gain power (Love 1986). To Kroc women were to take care of frills, leaving the important work to men:

> Clark told me I should hire a secretary. "I suppose you're right," I [Kroc] said. "But I want a male secretary . . . I want a man. He might cost a little more at first, but if he's any good at all, I'll have him doing sales work in addition to administrative things. I have nothing against having a pretty girl around, but the job I have in mind would be much better handled by a man. . . . My decision to hire a male secretary paid off when I was hospitalized for a gall bladder operation and later for a goiter operation. [The male secretary] worked between our office and my hospital room, and we kept things humming as briskly as when I was in the office every morning. (Kroc 1977, 48–49)

June Martino was a very talented woman who had been with Kroc from the earliest days of his involvement with McDonald's. Corporate insiders described her as a gifted businesswoman whose expertise often kept the company going during difficult times. Kroc's view of her reflected his view of women in general:

> I thought it was good to have a lucky person around, maybe some of it would rub off on me. Maybe it did. After we got McDonald's going and built a larger staff, they called her "Mother Martino." She kept track of everyone's family fortunes, whose wife was having a baby, who was having marital difficulties, or whose birthday it was. She helped make the office a happy place. (Kroc 1977, 84)

Such attitudes at the top permeated all levels of the organization, expressing themselves in a variety of pathological ways. Management's sensitivity to sexual harassment was virtually nonexistent well into the 1980s. Interviews with women managers reveal patterns of sexual misconduct involving eighteen- and nineteen-year-old women employees being pressured to date older male managers. Reports of sexual harassment were suppressed by the company bureaucracy; women who complained were sometimes punished or forced to resign. One successful manager confided that after she reported harassment, company higher-ups stalked her both on and off the job. She was eventually forced to leave the company. Not surprisingly, such an organization was not overly concerned with women's complaints about the exaggerated gender roles depicted in McDonald's commercials and promotions. From Birdie as cheerleader to Happy Meals with Barbies for girls and Hot Wheels for boys, McDonald's has never escaped Kroc's gender assumptions (Hume 1993).

McDonald's perpetuates what Allen Shelton (1993) refers to as a hegemonic logic—a way of doing business that privileges conformity, zealously defends the middle-class norm, fights to the death for established virtue, and resists social change at all costs. As a passionate force for a Warren G. Harding "normalcy," McDonald's is the corporation that invites the children of prominent civic, military, and business leaders to the opening of its first McDonaldland Park—but leaves the daughters and sons of the not so rich and famous off the list. This hegemonic logic holds little regard for concepts such as justice or morality—McDonald's morality is contingent on what sells. This concept is well illustrated in McDonald's emphasis on the primacy of home and family values in its advertising.

WE'VE GOT OURSELVES A FAMILY UNIT: HOME IS WHEREVER RONALD MCDONALD GOES

Kroc and his corporate leaders unequivocally understood their most important marketing priority—to portray McDonald's as a "family kind of place." As they focused on connecting McDonald's to America and the family, they modified the red and white ceramic take-out restaurants to look more like the suburban homes that sprang up throughout Amer-

ica in the late 1950s and 1960s. Ad campaigns proclaimed that Mc-
Donald's was home, and that anywhere Ronald goes "he is at home."
Like many other ads in American hyperreality, McDonald's home and
family ads privilege the private sphere, not the public sphere, as the important space where life is lived. As an intrinsically self-contained unit,
the family is removed from the public realm of society; such a depiction, however, conceals the ways that politics and economics shape everyday family life. The greatest irony of these ads is that even as they isolate
the family from any economic connections, they promote the commodification of family life. A form of doublespeak is discernible in this
situation: The family is an end in itself; the family is an instrumental
consumption unit whose ultimate purpose is to benefit corporate profits and growth.

McDonald's ads deploy home and family as paleosymbols that position McDonald's as the defender of "the American way of life." Kroc
(1977) never knew what paleosymbols were, but he understood that
McDonald's public image should be, in his words, a "combination
YMCA, Girl Scouts, and Sunday School." Devised to tap into the right-
wing depiction of the traditional family under attack from feminists,
homosexuals, and other "screwballs," these so-called legitimation ads
don't sell hamburgers—they sell social relations. Amid social upheaval
and instability, McDonald's endures as a rock of ages, a refuge in a world
gone mad. McDonald's brings us together, provides a safe haven for our
children. The needs the legitimation ads tap are real, but the consumption panacea they provide is false (Goldman 1992). After its phenomenal growth in the 1960s, McDonald's realized that it was no
longer the "cute little company" of the 1950s (Love 1986). The anti-
war, civil rights, and other social movements of the late 1960s were re-
pugnant to Kroc's American values. Such views, when combined with
the marketing need for McDonald's to legitimate itself now that it was
an American "big business," made home and family the obvious bat-
tlefield in the legitimation campaign. As the public faith in corporations declined, McDonald's used the paleosymbols to create an
environment of confidence. Going against the grain of a social context,
perceived to be hostile to big business, the ads worked. The lyrics of
accompanying music read:

You, you're the one.
So loving, strong, and patient.
Families like yours
made all the states a nation.
Our families are our past,
our future and our pride.
Whatever roots we come from,
we're growing side by side.
                (quoted in Goldman 1992, 95)

The world of home and family portrayed by the McDonald's legitimation ads is a terrain without conflict or tension. In an ad produced in the early 1980s as the Reagan family values agenda was being established, a typical white, middle-class family is returning to the small town of Dad's childhood. Excited to show his preteen son and daughter his childhood world, Dad tells the family that his old house is just up the street. As the "Greek chorus" sings "things have changed a bit since you've been around" as background music, Dad is shocked to discover new condominiums have replaced the old house. Dismayed but undaunted, Dad tells the family that his old friend Shorty's house is just around the corner. Shorty's house is also gone, replaced by a car wash. From the backseat the daughter tells her disappointed father that she hopes the place he used to eat at is still standing because she's hungry. Dad immediately begins to look for the unnamed eating place; the background chorus sings: "In the night, the welcome sight of an old friend." The camera focuses on Dad as his eyes brighten and a smile explodes across his face. Camera cuts to car pulling into McDonald's. The chorus sings: "Feels so right here tonight at McDonald's again."

Once again consumption at McDonald's solves the problem of change. The consumptive act in this case serves to affirm family values in a world where the larger society threatens them. Nothing has changed at McDonald's, as Dad tells the perky counter girl that he had his first Big Mac at this McDonald's. The camera focuses across the dining room to a short man expressing surprise and disbelief. Of course, it is Shorty. As Shorty embraces Dad, we find out that Dad's childhood name was

Curly—ironic in the fact that he is now bald. The camera retreats to frame the old friends embracing in the light cast by the golden arches. Dad is at McDonald's; he is home with old friends and family. McDonald's made it all possible (Goldman 1992). The turbulent 1960s are finally over. We (America) have "come home" to the traditional family values that made us great. The chorus has already reminded us that it "feels so right . . . at McDonald's again," the key word being "again." Reagan, whose candidacy Kroc and the McDonald's management fervently supported, has brought back traditional values—McDonald's wants viewers to know that McDonald's is an important aspect of the traditional family values package.

In the final scene of this "Home Again" commercial, the camera shoots a close-up of the son and daughter. Having just watched the embrace between Dad and Shorty, the daughter turns to her brother and says with ironic inflection, "Curly?" Her brother shrugs and rolls his eyes in recognition of the generational rift between Dad's understanding of the scene as compared to their own. The reunion is irrelevant to the son and daughter, the camera tells us as it focuses on the attention they pay to the hamburgers sitting in front of them—the only time McDonald's food is displayed in the ad. McDonald's wants it both ways: the adult identification with Reagan, America, and the return to traditional family values, as well as child identification with the subversive kinderculture described previously. The subversive kindercultural subtext of this ad involves the children's shared recognition of the father's fatuous pursuit of a long dead past and his embarrassing public display of emotion. Dad blows his "cool pose." The "Curly irony" is the overt signifier for these deeper generational divisions—differentiations described by advertisers as market segments.

The grand irony of this and many other subversive kindercultural ads is that under the flag of traditional family values McDonald's actually undermines the very qualities it claims to promote. The McDonald's experience depicted does not involve a family sharing a common experience—each market segment experiences it in a different, potentially conflicting way. The family depicted here, like so many American middle-class families, is an isolated unit divided against itself. In terms of everyday life McDonald's does not encourage long, leisurely, interactive family meals. The seats and tables are designed to be uncomfortable to the point that customers will eat quickly and leave. In the larger scheme of things, family values, America, and home are nothing more than cynical marketing tools designed to legitimate McDonald's to different market segments. Kroc made his feeling about family very clear—work comes first, he told his managers. "My total commitment to business had long since been established in my home" (Kroc 1977, 89). The cynicism embedded in ads by McDonald's and scores of other companies undermines the social fabric, making the culture our children inhabit a colder and more malicious place. Such cynicism leads corporations to develop new forms of techno power that can be used to subvert democracy and justice in the quest for new markets. Such cynicism holds up Ronald McDonald/Ray Kroc as heroes, while ignoring authentic heroes—men and women who struggle daily to lead good lives, be good parents, and extend social justice.

References

Abercrombie, N. 1994. "Authority and Consumer Society." In R. Keat, N. Whiteley, and N. Abercrombie, eds., *The Authority of the Consumer*. New York: Routledge.

Boas, M., and S. Chain. 1976. *Big Mac: The Unauthorized Story of McDonald's*. New York: Dutton.

Brautigan, R. 1974. *The Hawkline Monster: A Gothic Western*. New York: Pocket Books.

Cassell, J., and H. Jenkins. 2002. "Proper Playthings: The Politics of Play in Children." web.media.mit.edu/~andrew_s/andrew_sempere_2002_politics_of_play.pdf.

Cook, D. 2004. *The Commodification of Childhood: The Children's Clothing Industry and the Rise of the Child-Consumer*. Durham, N.C.: Duke University Press.

DuBois-Reymond, M., H. Sunker, and H. Kruger, eds. 2001. *Childhood in Europe*. New York: Peter Lang.

Fischer, P., et al. 1991. "Brand Logo Recognition by Children Aged 3 to 6 Years." *Journal of the American Medical Association* 266, no. 22: 3145–3148.

Garfield, B. 1992. "Nice Ads, But That Theme Is Not What You Want." *Advertising Age* 63, no. 8: 53.

Giroux, H. 1994. *Disturbing Pleasures: Learning Popular Culture*. New York: Routledge.

———. 1988. *Teachers as Intellectuals: Toward a Critical Pedagogy of Learning*. Granby, Mass.: Bergin & Garvey.

Goldman, R. 1992. *Reading Ads Socially*. New York: Routledge.

Harvey, D. 1989. *The Condition of Postmodernity*. Cambridge, Mass.: Basil Blackwell.

Hengst, H. 2001. "Rethinking the Liquidation of Childhood." In M. du Bois-Reymond, H. Sunker, and H. Kruger, eds., *Childhood in Europe*. New York: Peter Lang.

Hume, S. 1993. "Fast Food Caught in the Middle." *Advertising Age* 64, no. 6: 12–15.

Jans, M. 2002. "Children and Active Citizenship." www.surrey.ac.uk/education/etgace/brussels-papers/march-paper-jans.doc.

Jenkins, H. 2003. "The Poachers and the Stormtroopers: Cultural Convergence in the Digital Age." web.mit.edu/21fms/www/faculty/henry3/pub/stormtroopers.htm.

Keat, R., N. Whiteley, and N. Abercrombie. 1994. Introduction to R. Keat, N. Whiteley, and N. Abercrombie, eds., *The Authority of the Consumer*. New York: Routledge.

Kellner, D. 1989. *Critical Theory, Marxism, and Modernity*. Baltimore: Johns Hopkins University Press.

———. 1992. "Popular Culture and the Construction of Postmodern Identities." In S. Lash and J. Friedman, eds., *Modernity and Identity*. Cambridge, Mass.: Blackwell.

Kenway, J., and E. Bullen. 2001. *Consuming Children: Entertainment, Advertising, and Education*. Philadelphia: Open University Press.

Kincheloe, J. 1999. *How Do We Tell the Workers? The Socio-Economic Foundations of Work and Vocational Education*. Boulder: Westview.

———. 2002. *The Sign of the Burger: McDonald's and the Culture of Power*. Philadelphia, PA: Temple University Press.

Kroc, R. 1977. *Grinding It Out: The Making of McDonald's*. New York: St. Martin's Paperbacks.

Leidner, R. 1993. *Fast Food, Fast Talk: Service Work and the Routinization of Everyday Life*. Berkeley: University of California Press.

Love, J. 1986. *McDonald's: Behind the Arches*. New York: Bantam.

Luxenberg, S. 1985. *Roadside Empires: How the Chains Franchised*. New York: Viking Penguin.

McCormick, M. 1993. "Kid Rhino and McDonald's Enter Licensing Agreement." *Billboard* 105, no. 8: 10–11.

McDonald's Customer Relations Center. 1994. Handout to Schools.

Molnar, A. 1996. *Giving Kids the Business: The Commercialization of America's Schools*. Boulder: Westview.

Mouritsen, F. 2003. *Project Demolition: Children's Play-Culture and the Concept of Development*. www.hum.sdu.dk/projekter/ipfu.dk/online-artikler/mouritsen-demolition.pdf.

Nations, C. 2001. "How Long Do Our Children Have to Wait? Understanding the Children of the Twenty-first Century." pt3.nmsu.edu/edu621/cynthia2001.html.

Polakow, V. 1992. *The Erosion of Childhood*. Chicago: University of Chicago Press.

Ritzer, G. 1993. *The McDonaldization of Society*. Thousand Oaks, Calif.: Pine Forge.

Schlosser, E. 2001. *Fast Food Nation: The Dark Side of the All-American Meal*. Boston: Houghton Mifflin.

Seiter, E. 1993. *Sold Separately: Parents and Children in Consumer Culture*. New Brunswick, N.J.: Rutgers University Press.

Shelton, A. 1993. "Writing McDonald's, Eating the Past: McDonald's as a Postmodern Space." *Studies in Symbolic Interaction* 15: 103–118.

Shiva, V. 1997. "Vandana Shiva on McDonald's Exploitation and the Global Economy." www.mcspotlight.org/people/interviews/vandanatranscripts.html.

Yan, Y. 1997. "McDonald's in Beijing: The Localization of Americana." In J. Watson, ed., *Golden Arches East: McDonald's in East Asia*. Stanford: Stanford University Press.

Chapter 12

THE BOOK OF BARBIE: AFTER HALF A CENTURY, THE BITCH CONTINUES TO HAVE EVERYTHING

Shirley R. Steinberg

In the beginning . . .

1:1 This is the book of the generations of Barbie. 1:2 Ruth Handler created her, the third day of March in nineteen hundred and fifty-nine—in the likeness of Ruth's daughter and Lily, a German whore, she made her. 1:3 Female first she created, and blessed her and called her name Barbie after her firstborn. Ruth saw that it was good and there was much money to be made. 1:4 And Barbie lived three years and Ruth created Ken, male and female she created them both. 1:5 Then Ruth said, Let there be baby sister Skipper, by the year of our Lord nineteen hundred and sixty-four, they were three. 1:6 In later years, ten friends were created for Skipper, and Midge was created to be Barbie's best friend. 1:7 And in the year nineteen hundred and sixty-eight, Christie was created. Christie was unlike any other creation; verily, her skin was black. She was to be known as the black Barbie. And it was so, Barbie was diverse. 1:8 And these are the years and days of Barbie, the days of Barbie and the Rockers; the days of Barbie and her pets, including puppy Sachi and horse Rosebud; and the years of Barbie's family, cousins Francie and Jazzie; siblings Tutti, Todd, and Stacie, and Spice Girl Barbie.

1:9 And through Stacie, friends were born, Whitney and Janet. 1:10 And through Ken, multiple male friends were born, and like Ken, none of them ever married, and verily their manhood was always in question, as it was never visible. 1:11 However, Barbie was most plentiful with friends, by the year two thousand and nine, having multitudes of girlfriends with whom to shop. Among them were Cara, who was also black; Teresa, who was made Hispanic; and Kira, who was Asian. 1:12 Hence Barbie was known through the land as multicultural and virtual—having become cyber-connected. 1:13 No one in the Land ever spoke of Barbie's origin as a German working girl, her occupations were truly varied and she was a nurse and a doctor; a pilot and a stewardess; and Scully and Mulder. 1:14 Barbie was blessed with the gift of shopping, and yea verily, she had a Bloomingdale's credit card, a Mercedes Benz, a pink condo, corvette, and yacht. 1:15 Chosen ones were picked by Ruth and Mattel to design for Barbie: Dior, Channel, Mackie, Nicole Miller, and Versace, they created for her all. 1:16 Little girls knew throughout the Land that they, too, could be Barbie, yea, they were told that "we girls can do anything." 1:17 Nonbelievers questioned Barbie, for she was created without a brain, nipples, or conscience. 1:18 In later years, Barbie and her name were sold to the highest bidders: McDonald's, Pizza Hut, NASCAR, and Disney, her name was bought by all. 1:19 In the year of our Lord two thousand and four, Barbie and Ken announced their breakup; it was known throughout the Land that Ken was not manly, but all were relieved that they would remain friends. 1:20 By the fiftieth year, those who sold Barbie found revelation that they must reinvent the plastic girl in order to replenish the coffers. 1:21 And so it came to be that these were the days of Barbie; and it came to pass, when Barbie and her friends began to multiply on the face of the earth, little girls began to buy, as verily, one doll was never enough. And Barbie lived fifty years until this record.

TWENTIETH TO TWENTY-FIRST CENTURY FOX

Playing Barbies in the fifth grade consisted of lugging plastic cases laden with "outfits" to the playground and constructing scenarios around Barbie and "getting" Ken. I knew at this early age that Barbie (as a female) must have an "outfit" for every occasion and that wearing the same thing within some unspoken frame of time was just not done.

When I was twelve or thirteen I began meticulously recording what I wore each day on a calendar. I made sure that at least a month went by before I wore an outfit again. When I was a high school teacher, my students called attention to my idiosyncrasy by applauding the first day that I duplicated an outfit in the classroom. Did Barbie construct this behavior, or do I just love clothes? Cultural scholars have written in detail on the feminist readings of Barbie, the cultural text of Barbie, and the place of Barbie in childhood. In this chapter, I will discuss the cultural and the consumptive aspects of the now-fifty-year-old Barbie.

Where does the text of Barbie begin? Fifty years ago, Mattel invested in the production of a slim, blonde doll who (that?) wore a variety of coordinated "outfits." While on vacation in Europe, Mattel co-founder Ruth Handler discovered Lily. Lily was a prominent star of comics—a sexy blonde with loose morals who adorned dashboards throughout Germany and Switzerland. Her origin is not well documented, although her lineage has been traced back to a Lily comic strip. Handler decided to take the model of Lily back to the States and create a doll that could wear multiple outfits. She named her Barbie, after her daughter, Barbara. The promotional "hook" that Handler cited was the possibility that the doll could have multiple outfits and girls could just own one doll. Ironically, the first Barbie was designed to be the only Barbie for each little girl, and the marketing goal was to tap into the supposed innate female desire to own as many clothes as possible. As we all know, the intent changed drastically within fifteen years, and the goal became to own as many Barbies as possible. Indeed, you cannot buy individual outfits any longer; if you want your doll to change clothes, you buy another doll.

Physiologically, Barbie had perky breasts, a tiny waist and long, slender legs. Much has been written in a feminist framework about the doll, discussing the unrealistic body shape and so on. I won't "go there." Barbie was made slim so that layers of designer fabric would flow nicely and realistically on her body. She was, first and foremost, a model—fabric by Dior, designs by Mackie. Nothing was beyond reach for her. I am not offended by her figure; I do wonder, however, about her poorly constructed private part—or lack thereof. Barbie is a plastic formation of non-genitalia. Having neither anything "down there," a belly button, or nipples, Barbie has reached half a century in age without having sexual organs.

Speaking of private parts, in 1964, Barbie was given a boyfriend, Ken—a boy minus genitals. Ken's crotch was (and is) as flat and smooth as Barbie's. I remember specifically my disappointment in disrobing my first Ken—nothing to see. Possibly that physical defect is in line with the personality that Ken has displayed throughout the years (although Earring Ken had a certain flair). Ken and Barbie have gotten as far as their wedding but never past it. The couple never had a wedding night, and Barbie is always seen pushing a stroller of cousins, younger siblings, or friends. Only Ken's friends of color, Derek and Steve, radiate any machismo sexuality, though they are still crotchless. Finally, after forty-five years of never getting it on, Barbie and Ken "announced" they were breaking up—at the time of this writing, they are still "close friends."

Within months of her creation, Barbie was a sensation. Mattel had transformed toys, especially dolls, and Barbie became "us." Little girls were frenzied to own a Barbie, each one coming in her own long, thin box, wearing a black-and-white striped swimsuit. Barbie had a blonde ponytail and earrings. She was a teen model. Girls moved from cradling baby dolls to demanding the latest in haute couture à la Mattel. Barbie was sexy, although most of her owners were not even aware of the genre of sexiness—they just loved their Barbies.

WILL SHOP FOR RESEARCH

I take my work seriously. I am an active researcher. I love the challenge of finding strange and wonderful factoids of trivia in little-known academic nooks and crannies. However, Barbie caused financial havoc in my life. About fifteen years ago, I became fascinated with Barbie's effect on little girls. I started to pick up Barbies, Barbie furniture, Barbie comics, Barbie books, Barbie jewelry, and Barbie toys wherever I went. I even found the Benetton Barbie in the Istanbul airport (under a sign featuring the Marlboro man).

In order to do thorough textual analyses of Barbie and Barbie ac-coutrements, I needed to purchase my artifacts. I sit now, with great em-barrassment, in an office with scores of Barbies, Kens, Skippers, and a plethora of "ethnic" and "special edition" Barbies. I have Barbie watches, a $300 Barbie jacket from F.A.O. Schwartz, a Barbie McDonald's play set, Christmas play set, and bakery set. I bought my husband a Nicole Miller Barbie tie and silk Barbie boxers (which he immediately regifted to me). I have Barbie board games, computer games—Barbie Goes Shopping—and a floppy disk game, Barbie Design Studio. I have Bar-bie books, purses, records, CDs, DVDs, socks, jewelry, and T-shirts. Bar-bie shopping can be out of control. When children come to visit, they plow through my Barbies in an hour and then inquire, "Do you have anything else?" Obviously I don't have enough. What kid law was writ-ten that expressed the need to have multiples of any and every toy and object? Even the cyber-conscious Webkins fanatics are not happy with one, or two, or three . . . they must have every one made. Barbies are that way: you can never have enough.

My ownership of Barbies and Barbie paraphernalia qualifies me as an expert. I am a consumer and a scholar; there is no better combination. Historically, I come by the expertise naturally: I have had Barbies since she was invented. However, as I trace my Barbie autobiography, I am only able to single out my fetish for outfits as a permanent influence à la Barbie. I remain untouched from other taint . . . unless one looks at my research.

IS THERE ANYTHING BARBIE DOESN'T HAVE?

Discussing what Barbie doesn't have is easier than discussing what she does have. The list is much shorter. Barbie doesn't have a locomotive, a battleship (although she is a sailor), a rocket (although she is an astro-naut), or an Uzi (although she is a soldier). Thematically Mattel still has not invented the Homeless Barbie, the Abortion Barbie, the Alcoholic Barbie, or the S&M Bondage Barbie. As far as special editions, Barbie still has not come out as a criminal—she has, however, come out in spe-cial editions of fairy tales (never a witch), "true" history, careers, and in different ethnicities—different from white, that is. There is no North-ern Barbie, but the Southern Beauty Barbie features "today's Southern belle with charm and style!"

Barbie doesn't have holes in her clothes (unless placed there by Bob Mackie); she doesn't ever walk because she has a plane, boat, Corvette, bicycle, horse, roller blades, and Ken. Barbie doesn't have a favorite color other than hot pink; she has one logo and no last name. Actually, I once heard her last name is Roberts; so, where are her people from? Barbie does not have holiday sets for Chanukah or Ramadan, although she does have them for Easter and Christmas. Kmart does not have a Kmart Bar-bie, but there are Barbies for Walmart, Saks Fifth Avenue, Gap, Bloom-ingdale's, Avon, and Nicole Miller.

It is also easier to look at what Barbie isn't. Barbie is never sad, she is always available, and she "saves the day" in every story written about her. Barbie is timeless; she existed in the days of the Mayflower, she was in Oz as Dorothy, and she ran for president in several U.S. elections. She has never been a cook but has been a chef; she has never been a con-struction worker but has been a fashion designer. She has been a soloist, a rock star, and the mythical tooth fairy. Barbie is exclusively thematic; Ken, Christie, and the rest are occasionally given professions.

THE BITCH WHO BUYS EVERYTHING

She does. From the pink condo, to the swimming pool, to the RV, to the recording stage, to more friends than anyone. Everyone loves Bar-bie, and Barbie loves everyone. Barbie proves to us that if we try hard enough, we can own anything and everything. Barbie always succeeds. She becomes whatever she sets her mind to—she influences generations of children and adults and is a perpetual reminder of all that is good, wholesome, and pink in our lives. Barbie is a true American. She stands for the family values that our country holds dear. She is strictly hetero-sexual, self-providing, philanthropic, and moral. She is also ready to bring "other" people into her life, no matter what color or ethnicity.

Barbie moves in and out of social circles with ease. Her plate is al-ways filled with charity organizations and doing "good." The "Love to

Read" Barbie comes with two children (one black and one white) and a book; for every LTR Barbie sold, Mattel donates a dollar to the Reading Is Fundamental organization. As consumers, we are able to support reading by purchasing this doll. That makes all the difference.

BARBIE AND CORPORATE LOVERS

As much as Barbie is a virgin in sexual relationships, she is a whore in the corporate world. Barbie has "been in bed" with more Fortune 500 members than anyone. She has worked in and owned her own Pizza Hut and McDonald's; she is a special Walmart edition; she is also the star of *Baywatch* and a perennial guest in Happy Meals. Disney's Epcot Center features a "Magical World of Barbie" show, complete with dancers, singers, and fireworks. Avon regularly offers a special-edition Barbie, and Hallmark has Barbie Christmas ornaments, a new one issued each year. I already mentioned the Benetton Barbie, my unlikely find in a broken-down Turkish airport. The online auction site eBay is filled with bidding searchers for the rare Holiday Barbie each year. Barbie wanders in and out of corporate headquarters with ease. Companies know that if they tap into her resources, it is a quick ride to higher profits. No one really wants the tiny hamburger in the child's meal; they are all looking for the Barbie: Which one is she? The Kenyan? The Ballerina? Or the Wedding Barbie? As a professional, Barbie chooses from her cellphone, her video camera, and numerous pink briefcases, searching for "just the right thing" to break that glass ceiling. Many of the Barbies with store tie-ins come complete with a store credit card and branded shopping bags.

As a professional, Barbie has set records for changing vocations. In the early days, she was featured as a nurse, a baby-sitter, and a secretary. Within months of the emergence of political correctness, she became a doctor, a pilot, and a businesswoman. Naturally, many of her careers still smack of nurturing; how can one avoid it with a perpetual pink motif? One of my favorite fashion sets is the Caring Careers Fashion Gift Set. These "play pieces for Barbie at work" include a firefighter suit with pink trim, a teacher set, and a veterinarian's smock. Dr. Barbie is a pediatrician with a little black child and a little white child, all adorned in pink and blue.

Astronaut Barbie came out in the 1980s and reappeared in the late '90s. As part of the Career Collection, this Barbie first appeared as a space pioneer. A newer version highlights Space Week and NASA and "encourages children of all ages to discover the past and future of the exploration in space." All of the boxes featuring careers have the slogan "We Girls Can Do Anything!" ribboned across the front. Police Officer Barbie is a "friend to all in the community! In her glittery evening dress, Police Officer Barbie shines with pride at the Police Awards Ball. Everyone applauds as she receives the Best Police Officer Award for her courageous acts in the community." Police Officer Barbie comes with a badge and a short formal gown for the ball. And there is also a NASCAR Barbie.

No group of careers could be complete without acknowledging our armed forces. As sergeants and majors, these booted girls march to the beat of proud, patriotic America. Choosing a favorite would be hard, but, well, okay, I guess mine was the Desert Storm Barbie. "Wearing authentic desert battle dress uniforms" of camouflage material—"Sergeant Barbie is a medic, and she's ready for duty! Staff Sergeant Ken is ready too! Their berets bear the distinctive 101st Airborne unit insignia with the motto Rendezvous with Destiny. Both are proud, patriotic Americans serving their country wherever they are needed."

Rounding up the professions, 1992 ushered in the Barbie for President gift set. This was a Toys"R"Us limited edition. "Barbie hits the campaign trail in spectacular style! Dressed in her winning red and gold suit she's the picture perfect candidate to get out the vote. Then, at her inaugural ball, the festive crowd cheers as Barbie enters in a sensational sparkling gown sprinkled with silver stars!" We girls can do anything. How about the $75 Statue of Liberty Barbie? Holding the torch of freedom, this golden-haired doll stands perched on a plastic island, adorned with a shimmery crown, beckoning all who will listen to join her in liberty and justice for all.

ETHNIC BARBIES MAKE FOR GOOD SALES

Barbie's other identities lie in ethnic and historical roots. Not satisfied with the existential Barbie, Mattel allowed Barbie to revisit—ergo, rewrite—the past through a series of historical dolls. Each doll belongs to a collector's set, usually priced from $5 to $100 more than a regular Barbie. A collector's doll should be kept in her box, appreciating in value as the years tick by.

One must take a little boat down the It's a Small World ride in Disneyland or Disney World to understand how ethnicity is defined by a corporation. Sailing down that channel, listening to hundreds of little dolls sing—constantly—we see different peoples grouped together on their continents. Northern countries show a preponderance of buildings and clothing—countries from south of the equator seem to exhibit dolls wearing scant clothing, selling vegetables, taking a siesta, or climbing trees. No buildings are evident in Africa, and only huts appear in the South American countries. Taking the ride seriously as a metaphor for "the world," we are able to understand the consciousness that constructed Mattel's line of ethnic Barbies.

Imagine we are sailing through our own small world and meeting these diverse Barbies; we hear their words describing their heritage. Each Barbie is distinct in native dress and manner. The Jamaican Barbie comes with large hoop earrings and a red bandanna. Many exclaim how much she looks like Aunt Jemima or a slave. Jamaican Barbie claims that her people speak patois, "a kind of Jamaica talk" filled with English and African words. She also insists Jamaicans are a very "happy" people and are "filled with boonoonoonoos, much happiness." Culturally, this Barbie teaches us that her country is filled with higglers (women merchants) who sell their food in open markets. Along with pictures of Bob Marley, sugarcane, and palm trees, the Jamaican Barbie is prettily packed in hot pink.

In keeping with the island theme, we move to the Polynesian Barbie. The box never mentions which island she is from—somewhere within the thirteen groups of tropical islands. We are told that people live closely together and are kind to one another. Polynesians enjoy luaus and like to eat.

Another Barbie "of color" is the Indian Barbie. Unlike the boxes that her island cousins come in, hers shows a picture of a building, the Taj Mahal. We are reminded that India is a very old country and that most people eat only vegetables and rice "with their fingers." It is not mentioned whether or not Indians are happy or kind. None of these Barbies discuss their skin color or hair texture, and there is no mention of physical attributes. Naturally, they are all standing on tiptoe. Puerto Rican Barbie is dressed all in white as she readies herself for—dare I say?—her confirmation. No self-respecting Puerto Rican girlfriend of mine has ever done anything but shriek in horror at this plastic sista.

As we visit Northern Europe, we do not meet amalgamated Barbies. For instance, there are no British Isles Barbies or Scandinavian Barbies. Each has her own country. The German Barbie looks splendid in her milkmaid's outfit, with long blonde braids. We are welcomed to a country that is known for its "breathtaking beauty and hard-working people." Evidently the Barbies south of the equator do not work, or at least not hard. Mentioned on the box are modern cities, museums, art galleries, and industries. The Norwegian Barbie tells us of her mythological tradition and describes her people as "tall, sturdy, fair-skinned, blonde and blue eyed." Food is not mentioned nearly as often on Northern Barbies as on their Southern counterparts. Evidently the farther north one moves, the less people talk or think about food.

There is no specifically American Barbie. However, there is a Native American Barbie in the Dolls of the World Collection. She is part of a "proud Indian heritage, rich in culture and tradition." Long ago her people belonged to a tribe. Her dress is that of a Plains Indian, yet she describes homes like those constructed by East Coast Indians. Three times she mentions her pride in her people.

What's going on here? Mattel has defined ethnicity as other than white. Regular blonde Barbie is the standard from which the "others" come. As it emulates the dominant culture, the norm is Barbie, without a title. All other Barbies are qualified by their language, foods, and "native" dances. Attempting to be multicultural, parents buy these dolls for their children to teach them about "other" people. No "regular" Barbie ever talks about her regular diet, the personality of "her" people, or her customs. Only the designated "ethnic" dolls have those qualifications. Much like the sign in the local Kmart that designates the location of ethnic hair products, Barbie has otherized dolls into dominant and marginal cultures. Barbie's whiteness privileges her to not be questioned; she is the standard against which all others are measured.

CORPORATE WRITING OF HISTORY

A couple of years after introducing the ethnic Barbie line, Mattel introduced the American Stories Collection, which featured a Civil War Nurse Barbie, a Pilgrim Barbie, a Pioneer Barbie, and an American Indian Barbie (there she is again). Each doll comes with a storybook that places Barbie in the middle of essential historical action. Each book ends with Barbie "saving the day" and changing history for the better.

As you have probably guessed, the Pilgrim Barbie meets Squanto, who teaches her how to plant corn: "he wasn't savage at all." She grows a successful crop of corn and decides to share it with her neighbors; hence, the first Thanksgiving. And Barbie was there. Conveniently neglected are the Pilgrims' grave robbing, confiscation of Indian lands, and, yes, the sticky matter of genocide.

Since Betsy Ross already made the flag in 1776, Colonial Barbie decides to make a quilt to celebrate the thirteen colonies. The quilt was embroidered "Happy Birthday America," and Barbie and her female helpers were congratulated for it and treated "with great respect." Western Barbie cleverly brings dried apples on the long journey during the westward expansion. When her friends get hungry, the apples are produced to make a delicious apple pie. American Indian Barbie takes care of a papoose, parentage unknown, and tells stories to the little Indian villagers. I will stop here, fearing an overload of saccharine.

Each book is signed on the back with a personal note from the author. History becomes firm in the eyes of the reader as it is legitimized by the author. Here are a few excerpts:

> During my research for Western Promise, I learned a lot about pioneers. The more I read, the more I admired these courageous, self-reliant people.
> Even though it's fun to read books, I still love to hear someone tell a good story! In the early days of the American Indians, there were no books or schools like there are today.
> In writing this story for you, I have learned so much! What I noticed most about the story of the Pilgrims and Thanksgiving is how the

Native Americans became their friends and helped these strangers in a new land.

I hope you enjoyed imagining Barbie as a colonial girl. Perhaps you will think of her on the next 4th of July and what it must have been like during the early days when America was first "born."

Consumers are told that history is being taught in a friendly way through Mattel. Children now place Barbie within historical contexts in order to understand what really happened.

Fairy tales and fiction are not immune from Mattel's rewriting. The Children's Collection Series features heroines from different stories. "Childhood favorites 'come to life' with Barbie. Play out the story of Rapunzel." Barbie as Scarlett O'Hara promises to be one of the most successful dolls of the decade. Promoted in a thirty-minute infomercial by Kathie Lee Gifford (a TV Barbie), the doll is sold as essential for anyone who was affected by the novel or movie version of *Gone with the Wind*: "See Barbie as your favorite character, Scarlett," Kathie Lee advises us. She recalls that when she was a little girl, Barbie was her favorite doll and there is nothing more special than having her best friend become Scarlett. The line between reality and fantasy is blurred. Barbie acting as a character?

BUYING BARBIE WILL TEACH US TO READ

In its merchandising Mattel recognizes the importance of reading and education, creating hundreds of types of reading materials that feature Barbie. Not satisfied with the toy market, the company has branched out to themes in magazines, books, newspapers, and film.

The "Adventures with Barbie" book series features a set of paperback books in which "Barbie stars in her own series of fabulous adventures that tie inspiring messages in with action, suspense and fun with friends—and set an example of independence, responsibility and kindness for young girls everywhere." *Barbie*, the magazine for girls, gives fashion tips, promotes new Barbie themes, teaches fun crafts, and gives beauty advice. The comics market promotes *Barbie Fashion* and *Barbie*. Both comics are monthly and tell "stylish stories" and give "trend-setting tips." Little Golden Books for toddlers include several Barbie titles, including *Very Busy Barbie* (Barbie as a model who gives up her career), *A Picnic Surprise* (Barbie finding an old lady's puppy instead of having fun), and *Barbie, the Big Splash* (Barbie's photo shoot is spoiled, but she is able to take disappointment). We are constantly bombarded by the altruistic blonde (in the books she is usually mono-colored) giving up something sensational for the good of all humankind. Little girls are taught at an early age that it is more important to give up one's own goal than to disappoint someone else. Disney did it well with *The Little Mermaid* and *Beauty and the Beast*. It is a female's place to sacrifice for the good of others. What about Pocahontas? Esmeralda? You get the point.

Not to be outdone by three-foot-tall competitors, adults have their own Barbie literature: *Barbie Collector's Magazine* and several weekly and monthly newspapers, the most circulated paper being *Miller's Market Report: News, Advice and Collecting Tips for Barbie Doll Investors*. The tabloid features Barbie events; in an April issue, nineteen "don't miss" gatherings were advertised, including the Great Barbie Show of Southern California, Barbie Comes to Bloomingdale's, Seventh Annual Barbie Grants-A-Wish, and many regional conventions. Barbie clubs adorn the United States from sea to sequined shining sea. There is an annual Barbie world convention, classes on Barbie, and, a couple of years ago, a Barbie summit in New York. To emulate a global consciousness, Mattel organized this summit for women and girls to caucus about their needs and desires from Mattel for the twenty-first century. Always the educator, Barbie proves to us that reading and schooling cannot be left behind. Math becomes essential in order to add up the values of vintage dolls and collectors' items. Barbie, for many, is a full-time occupation. Barbie is the only nonhuman figure in the famed wax museum of Hollywood. Naturally, she had her own Barbie Boutique on Fifth Avenue adjoining F.A.O. Schwartz, a store that provided myriad books, magazines, videos, and objects devoted to Barbie. The market flourishes.

WHAT COULD POSSIBLY BE NEXT?

Are Barbies good for children? Should our girls play with them? How many Barbies should a child own? Do the dolls teach us what true beauty is? Can a child have self-esteem and not look like Barbie? Should we bend to peer pressure and allow our children to reside in pink-trimmed junior condos, dreaming of faraway places and exotic men? Does Barbie assist in constructing childhood consciousness? Do Barbie-centered websites increase the obsession with pink consumerism and girlishness?

Of course she does—just like any other feature of kinderculture. The effect of the Barbie curriculum is idiosyncratic—for some it facilitates conformity; for others, it inspires resistance. Multiple readings aside, Barbie does operate within the boundaries of particular cultural logics. She does celebrate whiteness, blonde whiteness in particular, as a standard for feminine beauty; she does reify anorexic figures coupled with large breasts as objects of male desire. She does support unbridled consumerism as a reason for being. She never questions American virtue and supports the erasure of the colonial genocide in America's past. Make no mistake: she is a Christian, not a Jew, and certainly not a Muslim; mainstream and not countercultural. No poor girl is Barbie, as she repeatedly displays her upper-middle-class credentials. Again, the curriculum may not take, no effect is guaranteed, but we must be aware of the terrain on which Barbie operates.

Barbie enthusiasts feel great anticipation about the next line of Barbies. Having featured professions, movie stars, stories, sports, and fashion, could Barbie ever run out of themes? By maintaining authenticity, Mattel is able to continue rewriting history and life. Reinvention of Barbie is a constant in Mattel world. As Barbie adapts to current lifestyles and girl-fads, cross-marketing with Disney and Hollywood gives her extra earning power.

I'd like to see Barbie a bit more realistic: in keeping with real-life professions, wouldn't we be wise to wait for Factory Worker Barbie, Prostitute Barbie, Drug Pusher Barbie—can a Pimp Ken be far behind? What about more politically active Barbies? Protest Barbie, chained to her dream house; Bisexual Barbie, complete with both Ken and Midge (or Steve and Christie)? Green Barbie? Bo-ho Barbie? Neo-Marxist Barbie?

MORE THAN HALF A CENTURY OLD

As the fiftieth anniversary of Barbie's birth approached, marketing and publicity for the birthday was unparalleled. Enormous websites were developed to herald the birth of the modern-day princess of consumerism. Sponsors like Mercedez Benz, Bloomingdale's, Sephora, and a few plebeian corporations were the embedded links that took us directly to corporate sites. Imagine a ten-year-old linking onto the "Barbie's Fiftieth" website and being taken directly to the showroom of the new Benz.

The unattainable (at least, for us) ticket to New York Fashion Week 2009 was given to Barbie, as designers Rachel Roy, Michael Kors, Diane von Furstenberg, and Tommy Hilfiger dressed models as retro-Barbies for the new millennium. Creating a postmodern collection of original Barbie styles with the new millennial look, the show premiered on Valentine's Day. Mothers, not daughters, attended the runway show, replete with their own Barbie memories, emulations, and lots of pink . . . I mean *lots* of it. Karl Lagerfeld created an entire "art" installation celebrating the plastic blonde's half century. When Barbie is treated as a fashion idol, a heroine, she becomes reality, as flesh and blood beings retreat into becoming simulacra . . . Is this marketing at its best? Lines blurred between toy and reality have created an industry that marketing has turned into art, culture, memory, and history. One can only wait until the Ken Fiftieth, when he finally comes out, does a full three-snap at society, legally marries Steve, and drives off to his honeymoon in a company-supplied Mercedes.

Portions of this chapter appeared previously in earlier editions of Kinderculture: The Corporate Construction of Childhood, *and various articles and writings.*

Chapter 13

HOME ALONE AND BAD TO THE BONE: THE ADVENT OF A POSTMODERN CHILDHOOD

Joe L. Kincheloe

HOME ALONE (1990) and *Home Alone 2: Lost in New York* (1992) revolve around Kevin McAlister's (Macaulay Culkin) attempts to find his family after (1) being left behind on a family Christmas trip to Paris and (2) being separated from his family on a Christmas trip to Miami. Wildly successful, the two movies portray the trials and tribulations of Kevin's attempts to take care of himself while his parents try to rejoin him. In the process of using these plots to set up a variety of comedic stunts and sight gags, the movies inadvertently allude to a sea of troubles relating to children and family life in the late twentieth century. As we watch the films, an entire set of conflicts and contradictions revolving around the lives of contemporary children begin to emerge. In this way *Home Alone* and *Home Alone 2* take on a social importance unimagined by producers, directors, and screenplay writers. In this chapter I use the family dynamics of the *Home Alone* movies to expose the social forces that have altered Western childhood over the past couple of decades. In all three films a central but unspoken theme involves the hurt and pain that accompany children and their families in postmodern America. The *Home Alone* films are modern classics.

A GENERATION OF KIDS LEFT HOME ALONE

Child rearing is a victim of the past fifty years of cultural change. Divorce and both parents working mean that fathers and mothers are around their children less each day. As parents are still at work in the afternoon when children get home from school, children are given latchkeys and expected to take care of themselves. "Home aloners" are kids who in large part raise themselves. We have witnessed a change in family structure that must be taken seriously by parents, educators, and cultural workers of all stripes. Since the early 1960s the divorce rate as well as the percentage of children living with one parent has tripled. Only one-half of today's children have parents who are married to each other. In the twenty-first century only one-third of U.S. children will have such parents. Among children under six, one in four lives in poverty. The stress that comes from the economic changes of the past twenty years has undermined the stability of the family. Family incomes have stagnated, as costs of middle-class existence (home ownership, health care, and higher education) have skyrocketed. Since the late 1960s the amount of time parents spend with their children has dropped from an average of thirty hours per week to seventeen (Lipsky and Abrams 1994; Galston 1991). Increasingly left to fend for themselves, contemporary children have turned to TV, video games, and the Internet to help pass their time alone.

Any study of contemporary children must analyze the social conditions that shape family life. Rarely do mainstream social commentators point out that the American standard of living peaked in 1973, followed by a declining economic climate that forced mothers to work. While the effects of international competition, declining productivity, and the corporate reluctance to reinvent the workplace all contributed to a depressed economy, not all recent family problems can be ascribed to the declining post-Fordist economy. The decline of the public space and the growth of cynicism have undermined the nation's ability to formulate creative solutions to family dysfunction. The 1970s and 1980s, for example, while witnessing the birth and growth of a family values movement, also represented an era that consistently privileged individual gratification over the needs of the community (Paul 1994; Coontz

1992). Such an impulse justified the privatistic retreat from public social involvement that was institutionalized in the 1990s as part of a larger right-wing celebration of self-reliance and efficient government. Unfortunately, it is often our children who must foot the cost of this perverse abrogation of democratic citizenship.

One scene in *Home Alone* highlights the decline of the public space in postmodern America. While Kevin's parents attempt to arrange a flight from Paris to their home in Chicago, the rest of the family watches *It's a Wonderful Life* dubbed into French on TV. This positioning of movie within a movie confronts viewers with the distance between the America of Jimmy Stewart's George Bailey and Macaulay Culkin's Kevin McAlister. Kevin has no community, no neighbors to call for help—he is on his own in his "private space." George Bailey had a score of neighbors to bail him out of his financial plight and help him fight the capitalists' efforts to destroy the community. Kevin is not just home alone—he is socially alone as well. But such realizations are not present in the conscious mind of the moviemakers. On the surface the McAlisters live in a desirable community and are a perfect family. Like millions of other late-twentieth-century families, they are physically together but culturally and emotionally fragmented. Plugged into their various "market segments" of entertainment media, they retreat into their "virtual isolation booths."

Like millions of other kids, Kevin feels isolated in such an existence, and isolation leads to powerlessness, hopelessness, and boredom. How could kids with everything handed to them, adults ask, become so alienated from their parents, schools, and communities? The answer to this question involves on some level the pervasive violation of childhood innocence. Popular culture via TV promised our children a *Brady Bunch* family circus, but they had to settle for alienated, isolated homes. The continuing popularity of *The Brady Bunch* testifies to the mind-set of American children. *The Brady Bunch,* with its family values and two engaged parents, seemed to provide what children found lacking in their own homes. This melancholy nostalgia for suburban family bliss indicates a yearning for a less lonely childhood. All those hours home alone have taken their toll (James 1990; Rapping 1994; Ferguson 1994).

THE UNWANTED

Although *Home Alone* and *Home Alone 2* work hard to deny it, they are about an unwanted child, as are many other films of the 1980s and early 1990s. The comedic form supposedly renders the unwanted theme harmless, in the process revealing contemporary views of parenting and the abandonment of children. In one particular scene in *Home Alone* Kevin's mother (Catherine O'Hara) pays for abandoning her son by riding home to Chicago through midwestern snowstorms in a truck carrying a polka leader (John Candy) and his band. In one dialogue mother and band leader engage in a confessional on bad parenting and child abandonment:

> MOTHER: I'm a bad parent.
> BAND LEADER: No, you're not. You're beating yourself up. . . . You want to see bad parents. We're [band] on the road 48 to 49 weeks out of the year. We hardly see our families. Joe over there, gosh, he forgets his kids' names half the time. Ziggy over there hasn't even met his kid. Eddie, let's just hope none of them [his children] write a book about him.
> MOTHER: Have you ever gone on vacation and left your child home?
> BAND LEADER: No, but I did leave one at a funeral parlor once. Yeah, it was terrible. I was all distraught and everything. The wife and I, we left the little tike there in the funeral parlor all day, *all day.* We went back at night when we came to our senses and there he was. Apparently, he was there alone all day with the corpse. He was okay. You know, after six or seven weeks he came around and started talking again. But he's okay. They get over it. Kids are resilient like that.
> MOTHER: Maybe we shouldn't talk about it.
> BAND LEADER: You brought it up.

So comfortable are marketers with the theme of abandonment that promos on the home video of *Home Alone 2: Lost in New York* pitch a *Home Alone Christmas Album.* Commodifying child abandonment, promoters urge viewers to "begin a tradition in your house." Something is happening in these movies and the promotions that surround them that is not generally understood by the larger society. By the early 1990s social neglect of children had become so commonplace that it could be presented as a comedic motif without raising too many eyebrows. There was a time when childhood accorded protected status, but now safety nets are disintegrating and child supports are crumbling. As children are left to fend for themselves, few public institutions exist to address their needs.

In *Home Alone* and *Home Alone 2* not only is Kevin left to take care of himself, but his parents and family treat him with disdain and cruelty. In one scene Kevin's uncle unjustifiably calls him a "little jerk." After understandably asking why he always gets "treated like scum," Kevin is banished to the attic, where he proclaims on behalf of his generation, "Families suck." These early experiences set up the comedic bread and butter of *Home Alone*: Kevin transfers his anger for his family to burglars Marv (Daniel Stern) and Harry (Joe Pesci) and subsequently tortures them. These two films are not the only movies of the era that address child abandonment and child revenge. In horror-thrillers *Halloween* and *Friday the 13th* the only individuals spared from violence are those who give time to and care for children. Those who neglect children ultimately pay with their lives. As neglected social rejects, children are relegated to the margins of society. It is not surprising, therefore, that in *Home Alone 2* Kevin forges an alliance with a homeless pigeon lady who lives in Central Park—they are both social castoffs. Together they learn to deal with their cultural status.

THE AMERICAN AMBIVALENCE TOWARD CHILDREN

After World War II Americans began to realize that childhood was becoming a phase of life distinctly separate from adulthood. This distinction was most evident in the youth culture beginning to take shape in the 1950s; this youth culture convinced parents that they were losing the ability to shape their children's lives. This fear has informed the academic study of youth in the last half of the twentieth century, often focusing attention on children as "the problem." Too often refusing to question the dominant culture and values of the adult world and the tacit assumptions of the field of childhood studies itself, mainstream scholars have often viewed conflict between children and parents as dysfunctional. Childhood "experts" and the mainstream education establishment have often insisted in this academic context that children need to be instructed to follow directions. This functionalist orientation assumes that the order and stability of environments must be maintained (Paul 1994; Lewis 1992; Griffin 1993; Polakow 1992). This, of course, ensures that institutions such as schools become unable to accommodate change, as they regress into a state of "equilibrium" (i.e., rigidity).

The virtual ubiquity of parent–child alienation and conflict is rarely perceived at the individual level of human interaction as a social phenomenon. When such conflicting dynamics occur in almost all parent–child relations, it is not likely that fault rests solely with individual parents and individual children. As already noted, something larger is happening here. Individual children cannot help but judge parents for their inconsistencies and shortcomings. On the other hand, parents cannot help but resent being judged and strike back with equal venom (Ventura 1994). Adults must understand the social nature of this familial phenomenon and, based on this recognition, attempt to transcend the demand for order inscribed into their consciousness by the larger culture. Americans don't understand their children or the dynamics of children's culture. Kids understand that adults just don't get it, as they listen and watch adults express and act on their misunderstandings of the differences between generational experiences and mindsets. Schools are perceived by children as virtually hopeless; indeed, they are institutionally grounded on a dismissal of these differences. Little has changed since the 1960s, when Kenneth Keniston wrote that adult misunderstanding of youth contributed to a conclusion reached by many children: American mainstream culture offers us little to live for (Lewis 1992).

Understanding this adult–child alienation, children slowly begin to withdraw into their own culture. Culkin's Kevin has absolutely no need for adults, as he shops (with newspaper coupons even), takes care of the house, and defends himself against robbers. This is quite typical for the films of John Hughes. Children and teenagers rule in a world where youth culture is the only one that matters. Parents in these films are notoriously absent, either at work or on vacation; their advice is antiquated, consisting generally of pompous pronouncements about subjects they obviously know nothing about. Typical of the genre is *The Breakfast Club,* which revolves around the stupidity of parents and adult authority. While it is a flagrant attempt by Hughes to commodify and exploit youth culture, the film does point out the width and depth of the chasm that separates kids and adults (Rapping 1994). Children's culture, of course, takes shape in shadows away from the adult gaze—as well it should. Consequently it behooves parents, teachers, social workers, and other cultural workers who are interested in the welfare of children to understand the social dynamics that shape children and their culture in the early years of the twenty-first century. When parents intensify their anxiety about the threat of postmodern kinderculture and strike out against it, they simply widen the chasm between themselves and their children. In this situation, the assertion of parental control becomes simply an end in itself, having little to do with the needs of children.

As adults in the 1950s and early 1960s began to understand the power of children's culture and the separations between childhood and adulthood it represented, parental and educator anxiety levels reached new highs. Adult fears that the kids were out of control expressed themselves in a variety of ways, none more interesting than in two British films of the early 1960s, *Village of the Damned* and its sequel, *Children of the Damned*. *Village of the Damned* is based on an invasion by an intergalactic sperm that impregnates earth women to produce a new race of mutant children who mature quickly and are capable of reading adult minds. Reflecting adult anxieties of the era concerning the growing partition between childhood and adulthood, the movie offers a "solution" to the youth problem. Adults in *Children of the Damned* reluctantly decide that they must kill their children. Understanding that child murder is suicidal in that it involves killing a part of oneself, parents sacrifice themselves in order to eradicate the iniquity their children embody. The youth rebellions of the mid- and late 1960s that followed *Children of the Damned* served to raise the emotional ante expressed in the movie's fantasized infanticide.

The adult hostility toward children is omnipresent in *Home Alone* and its sequel, but such issues are consistently hidden from overt recognition.

Previous films—*The Other, The Exorcist, The Bad Seed, Firestarter, It's Alive*—recognized adult hostility but projected it onto evil children as a means of concealing it. The abundance of these evil children films points to a social tendency of parents to view their children as alien intruders. This child-based xenophobia positions children as foreigners whose presence marks the end of the family's configuration as a couple (Paul 1994). Old routines are undermined and new demands must be met, as harried adults experience the child's power as manipulator. Such familial dynamics set the scene for the postmodern child custody case, where lawyers, judges, and parents decide who takes the kids.

Commercial children's culture understands what parents and educators don't—children and adolescents are wracked by desire that demands stimulation and often gets out of hand. We see its manifestation in children and children's culture with the constant struggle to escape boredom. Of course, most adults view this childhood desire as a monstrous quality to be squashed by any means necessary even if it requires the stupidification of young people in the process. In the *Home Alone* movies Kevin constantly feels as if he has done something terribly wrong, as if he were a bad kid. In *Home Alone 2: Lost in New York* Kevin prays to the Rockefeller Square Christmas tree: "I need to see my mother, I need to tell her I'm sorry." Exactly for what he should be sorry, no one is quite sure. One can only conclude that he is sorry for being a child, for intruding on the smooth operation of the family, of being goaded by his monstrous desire.

If we equate children with monstrousness, it is not a long jump to the position that the manipulative aliens are evil. In *The Bad Seed*, a successful novel, play, and movie of the mid-1950s, Rhoda is an eight-year-old murderess endowed with a greed for material things—childhood desire run amuck. As the first work that explored this homicidal dimension of childhood, *The Bad Seed* equates youth with absolute malignancy—concealed at first in an innocent package. As Rhoda's landlady says of her: "She never gets anything dirty. She is a good child, a perfect child. She saves her money and keeps her room clean." The appearance of evil so close to goodness and innocence made the child monster that much more horrible. Children who are so evil (or at least so capable of it) in a perverted sense justify child abuse. This image of the bad child was used for comic effect in *Problem Child* (1990) and *Problem Child 2* (1991). The way adults in the *Problem Child* movie reacted to the problem child is revealing:

> SCHOOL PRINCIPAL: Being a principal's great 'cause I hate kids. I have to deal with the weenies.
>
> SCHOOL TEACHER to principal after he brings problem child to her class as a new student: O God, another one. How many kids are they going to make me teach?
>
> LAWANDA, the owner of the bank: What's this thing [referring to problem child]? This kid's a nightmare. . . . Kids are like bum legs. You don't shoot the patient, you cut off the leg.
>
> PROBLEM CHILD'S GRANDFATHER to father: You little psycho—you're an evil boy. You got to learn to respect your elders.
>
> LAWANDA: Listen, you little monster. I'm going to marry your father and send you to boarding school in Baghdad.
>
> SCHOOL PRINCIPAL: You rotten kids should be locked in cages.
>
> LAWANDA: I hate children. They ruin everything. If I had enough power, I'd wipe them off the face of the earth.

Child murderer Sharon Smith never stated it this clearly and unambiguously.

Whenever the problem child seeks to subvert the status quo, viewers are alerted to what is coming by George Thorogood's blues guitar riff from "Bad to the Bone." Such innate "badness" cannot be indulged. As with the neofolk wisdom in contemporary America that criminals cannot be rehabilitated, there is no hope for the growth and development of the problem child. *Home Alone*'s Kevin, who is capable of "badness" and sadistic torture, is still struggling with parental forgiveness; the problem child is beyond all that. Parental and educational authority is concerned simply with control; the issue is naked power—there is no need for ameliorative window dressing in this realpolitik for children. In this context kindness becomes the cause of juvenile delinquency, child advocacy the response of dupes and bleeding heart fools. Movie audiences want to see the problem child punished, if not physically attacked. Child abuse lurks not far from such sentiments.

In John Carpenter's *Halloween* the camera shows the audience the point of view of an unidentified murderer who approaches a middle American suburban house occupied by two teenagers making love in an upstairs bedroom. As we watch through the murderer's eyes, he picks up a carving knife in the kitchen, observes the teenage boy leave the house, and walks back up the stairs to the bedroom where the teenage girl is now in bed alone. Looking directly into the camera, the girl expresses her annoyance with an obviously familiar character wielding the knife. At this point the hand carrying the knife stabs the girl to death, principally focusing the attack on her bare breasts. It is only after the murder that we are granted a reverse angle shot of the killer—a six-year-old boy. By 1978, when *Halloween* was made, movie commentators made little of the age of the murderer (Paul 1994). So accustomed was the American audience to children's "innate" potential for evil that moviemakers perceived no need to explain the etymology of the child's violent behavior. The end of the 1970s saw headlines such as "Killer Kids" and newspaper copy such as "Who are our children? One day they are innocent. The next, they may try to blow your head off." No more assumptions of innocence, no surprises. A new era had emerged.

THE BLAME GAME

Clusters of issues come together as we consider the role of mothers and fathers in the family wars of the late twentieth century. The battle to ascribe blame for family dysfunction in general, and childhood pathology in particular, plays out on a variety of landscapes: politics, religion, and popular culture. The political terrain of the 1990s included the Dan Quayle–Murphy Brown showdown over single mothers as parents, while on the religious battleground right-wing Christian fundamentalists fingered feminism as the catalyst for maternal child neglect. The analysis of this blame game as expressed in popular culture offers some unique insights.

In *Home Alone* and its sequel Kevin's mother has internalized the blaming of women for the neglect (abandonment) of Kevin in particu-

lar and for family pathology in general. There is no doubt about who is
to blame. Banished to the attic because he has been perceived as a nui-
sance, Kevin is (justifiably) hurt and angry.

> KEVIN: Everyone in this family hates me.
> MOTHER: Then maybe you should ask Santa for a new family.
> KEVIN: I don't want a new family. I don't want any family. Families suck.
> MOTHER: Just stay up there. I don't want to see you again for the rest
> of the night.
> KEVIN: I don't want to see you again for the rest of my whole life. And
> I don't want to see anyone else, either.
> MOTHER: I hope you don't mean that. You'd be pretty sad if you woke
> up tomorrow morning and you didn't have a family.
> KEVIN: No, I wouldn't.
> MOTHER: Then say it again. Maybe it'll happen.
> KEVIN: I hope I never see any of you again.

The mother is the provocateur, the one who plants the ideas that
emerge as Kevin's wishes. Insensitive to his emotional hurt, she induces
him to request a new family; she is the first to speak of not wanting to
see him; she is the one who dares Kevin to tempt fate by wishing away
his family (Paul 1994). In the *Home Alone* movies child care is the
mother's responsibility. John Heard's father character is virtually a nonen-
tity. He is uninterested in, condescending toward, and hostile to Kevin.
He knows (along with the audience) that he is not responsible for Kevin's
abandonment even though he was present during the entire episode.
He has no reason to gnash his teeth or rend his garment in displays of
penitence—this is the domain of the mother. And pay she does with her
polka band trip in the first *Home Alone* and her frenzied night run
through the streets of New York calling for her son in *Home Alone 2*. In
an era when child abuse and child murder by mothers occupy national
headlines, this mother's quest for forgiveness may signify a greater guilt.
The blame that the right-wing male places on women for the ills of the
family, however, is grotesquely perverse, implying that battalions of
strong but tender men are struggling with their wives to let them take
charge of child rearing—not hardly (Rapping 1994).

Feminist research and analysis of child abuse and domestic violence have subverted the happy depiction of family life as a safe haven far removed from pathologies emanating from internal power inequities. As scholarship documented how family life oppressed women and children, pro-family conservative groups responded by calling for a reassertion of patriarchal control in the home. Women, they argued, should return to child rearing. Some conservatives even maintain that women who don't adequately perform these "maternal" chores should have their children taken away and placed in orphanages. The most optimistic estimates place the number of children who would be institutionalized under this plan at over 1 million; the cost of such care would run over $36 billion (Griffin 1993; Morganthau et al. 1994). The male backlash to the assertive feminist critique has only begun with its depiction of women's political organization as the rise of a dangerous special interest group. Protectors of male power are waging an effective public relations battle. Any campaign that deflects blame for family failure from absent, often abusive fathers to mothers possesses a superior penchant for persuasion and little concern for truth.

Home Alone displays these gender dynamics in refusing to implicate the father in the abandonment. On learning that Kevin is not in Paris with the family, his mother exclaims, "What kind of mother am I?" The lack of affect on the part of the adult males of the family, Kevin's father and his uncle, is perplexing. The careful viewer can only conclude that they neither like nor care about the eight-year-old. The father's dismissiveness is never explained. All the viewer can discern is that the father and the uncle seem to be fighting for their manhood, expressing perhaps their resistance to the "breadwinner-loser" male character who forfeits his "male energy" in his domestication and subsequent acceptance of fidelity in marriage, dedication to job, and devotion to children (Lewis 1992). Such a male figure was ridiculed by beatniks as square, by Playboy devotees as sexually timid, and by hippies as tediously straight. The search for a hip male identity along with a healthy dose of irresponsibility has undermined the family as a stable and loving environment. Doing the right thing in regard to one's family as a man means losing status among one's fellow men.

An examination of adult male behavior in families indicates that many men are desperately concerned with peer group status. For exam-

ple, men on average pay pitifully inadequate child support to their former spouses, if they pay it at all. Only half of women awarded child support ever receive what they are owed, a quarter receive partial payments,
and the remaining quarter get nothing at all (Galston 1991). This ambiguous role of the father in the family highlighted by the indifferent
father of *Home Alone* is addressed in a more overtly oedipal manner in
other movies of the last couple of decades (Paul 1994). *The Shining,* for
example, retrieves a father's hostility toward his own son, which has always been repressed in Western culture, and builds an entire plot around
it. Danny, the child protagonist in *The Shining,* develops the psychic
power to see beyond the limits of time and space after his father (Jack
Nicholson) broke Danny's arm in an alcoholic stupor. Danny's power,
his shining, is expressed through his imaginary friend, Tony, who lives
in Danny's mouth. Tony exists to help Danny cope with his violent, abu-
sive father. Danny's presence and growth remind his father of his emas-
culation, his stultification by the family. The father's solution to his
problem—an attempt to murder his wife and child with an ax—allows
for none of the *Home Alone* ambiguity; the movie jumps headfirst into
the maelstrom of the conflict between virile masculinity and the demands of domesticity.

As the screen image of the crazed, ax-wielding Jack Nicholson fades
into a blurred image of *Jurassic Park* (1993), the continuity of the child-
hating adult male remains intact. Even in this "child-friendly" Spielberg-
produced dino drama, the paleontologist (Sam Neill) hates children and
refuses to ride in the same car with them. In response to a prepubescent
boy's sarcastic question about the power of dinosaurs, Neill evokes the
image of the violent Nicholson, circling and threatening the child with
the ominous claw of a velociraptor. The difference between *Jurassic Park*
and *The Shining,* however, involves Neill's moment of epiphany; when
the children are endangered by the dinosaurs, Neill sheds his hatred and
like a good father risks mutilation and death to save their lives. As in the
Home Alone movies, the issue of the father's hatred is buried in a happy
ending: the safe children celebrating with the "reformed" Neill and the
happy McAlister family celebrating Christmas in a frenetic present-open-
ing ritual. The demand for family values in the 1980s and 1990s
changed the cultural landscape: Family values must triumph, adult men

must be depicted as ultimately devoted to their children, the feminist portrayal of the "bad father" must not be reinforced.

AND AS IF THE AMBIGUITY WEREN'T BAD ENOUGH, SOME KIDS MATTER MORE THAN OTHERS

In class dynamics of the American childhood, poor children don't matter as much as upper-middle-class children (i.e., privileged children like the ones portrayed in the *Home Alone* movies). The frequent assertion that America is not a class society, uttered so confidently by mainstream politicians and educators, holds profound psychological and political consequences. This class silence undermines the understanding among the well-to-do that they were granted a head start, while paralyzing the less successful with a feeling of personal inferiority. On the political level, as it sustains the fiction, the belief that reifies the status quo: When the poor are convinced that their plight is self-produced, the larger society is released from any responsibility (Rubin 1994).

An overt class silence pervades *Home Alone* and its sequel. Even newspaper reviewers referred to the upper-middle-class, white, Protestant "bleached and sanitized" microcosm of the two movies (Koch 1990). The McAlisters are very wealthy, living in an enormous brick colonial in a generic Chicago suburb filled with extravagant furnishings and conveniences. Indeed, they are an obnoxious and loathsome crew; being privileged, they believe they can act any way they want. The filmmakers go out of their way to make sure viewers know that the family deserves its money—as father McAlister (John Heard) drinks from crystal in first class on the plane to Paris, he alludes to his hard work and humble origins. The message is clear—the American Dream is attainable for those willing to put in the effort. The McAlisters deserve their good fortune.

Into this restricted world of affluent WASPs Harry and Marv (two small-time robbers with an attitude) make their appearance as the only poor people and the only non-WASPs in the two movies. Harry (Joe Pesci) and Marv (Daniel Stern) are quickly positioned as "the other." They speak in lower-class accents; obviously ethnic, Pesci exaggerates his

working-class Italian accent, and just so we are not confused Stern sig-
nifies his Jewishness with a curiously gratuitous "Happy Hanukkah" reference as he steals money from a toy store. They are ignorant and
uneducated—Pesci refers to the fact that he never completed the sixth
grade; they hold an irrational hatred of the affluent; their "crime signature" involves flooding affluent homes after each robbery (they are
known as the "wet bandits"). These class- and ethnic-specific traits set
Marv and Harry apart to such a degree that the audience can unambiguously enjoy their torture at Kevin's hands.

Home Alone and its sequel pull their weight in the larger social effort to erase class as a dynamic in American life. Under interrogation
the movies confess their class complicity, as evidenced through the "oth-
erization" of Marv and Harry. Compare Marv and Harry with Mr. Duncan, the toy store owner who appears in *Home Alone 2*. Imbued with the
sweetness and generosity of Joseph the angel in *It's a Wonderful Life*,
Duncan is the most charming character in the *Home Alone* movies. After
the McAlister's reunification in *Home Alone 2*, he showers them with
scores of presents. His only motivation for being in business is that he
loves children and wants to see their happy faces when they open presents from his store. His loving smiles prove that capitalism cares and the
status quo is just. He deserves every penny of his profits just as much as
Marv and Harry deserve their torment. Such characterization gently
dovetails with the dominant political impulses of the moment, marked
by a callous acceptance of poverty, child poverty in particular, in the
midst of plenty.

Over 12.6 million children live below the poverty line, making one
out of every five American children poor. Too often unaware of such
class realities, Americans and their institutions are far removed from
the insidious effects of such poverty. Poor children too infrequently escape the effects of living with parents scarred by their sense of short-
coming, of having to negotiate movie and TV images of the poor and
the working class as dangerous and oafish caricatures (as in *Home Alone*
and its sequel), and of confronting teachers and social workers who hold
lower expectations for them than their middle- and upper-middle-class
peers. A key feature of the class dynamic in *Home Alone* and its sequel
involves the public reaction to the McAlisters' child abandonment

episodes as "good fun," as opposed to the real-life home alone cases that surfaced in the 1990s. When Kevin's parents report that he was left alone in New York to the police after they reach their vacation destination in Miami, it's no big deal. Even when they admit that abandoning the child has become "a family tradition," no one is excited—after all, the McAlisters are upper-class, well-to-do people. Almost daily, parents (especially single mothers) who leave their young children home alone for sometimes just a few hours are arrested and forced to relinquish their children to foster care. With child care often costing $200–400 a month, poor mothers are trapped in virtually impossible circumstances (Seligman, August 1, 1993). Society's refusal to address poor and single mothers' need for child care has contributed to the feminization of poverty (Polakow 1992). The first two *Home Alone* films indicate the double standard that dominates the American view of the rich and the poor and the mean-spirited class bias of some expressions of popular culture in this conservative age.

POSTMODERN CHILDHOOD

In *Home Alone* and its sequel—amid the bizarre mix of child abandonment and child–parent alienation, children caught in the crossfire of gender wars, crass class bias, and comedy—resides something profound about the role of children in contemporary American culture. The movies could have been made only in a culture experiencing a profound shift in the social role of children. For all individuals who have a stake in understanding childhood—parents, teachers, social workers, family counselors, and so on—knowledge of these changing conditions becomes a necessity. A no-growth economy has mandated that all adults in the family must work outside the home; subsequently children find themselves saddled with daily duties ranging from housecleaning, babysitting, and grocery shopping to cooking, laundry, and organizing carpools. With the "family values" agenda of right-wing movements threatening to eviscerate governmental support of poor and middle-class families, the economic problems of children look to get worse before they get better.

The new era of childhood, the postmodern childhood, cannot escape the influence of the postmodern condition with its electronic media saturation. Such a media omnipresence produces a hyperreality that repositions the real as something no longer simply given but artificially reproduced as real. Thus media-produced models replace the real—simulated TV kids on sit-coms replace real-life children as models of childhood. In this same media-driven postmodern condition a cultural implosion takes place, ripping apart boundaries between information and entertainment as well as images and politics. As media pushes the infinite proliferation of meaning, boundaries between childhood and adulthood fade as children and adults negotiate the same mediascape and struggle with the same impediments to meaning making. Children become "adultified" and adults become "childified" (Aronowitz and Giroux 1991; Best and Kellner 1991). Boundaries between adulthood and childhood blur to the point that a clearly defined, "traditional," innocent childhood becomes an object of nostalgia—a sure sign that it no longer exists in any unproblematic form (Lipsky and Abrams 1994; Postman 1994).

There is nothing childlike about a daily routine of child care, cooking, and shopping. In *Home Alone* and *Home Alone 2* Kevin is almost completely adultlike in meeting the demands of survival on his own. He checks into hotels, uses credit cards, orders pizzas, and grocery shops, all as a part of a day's work. He needs no adult figure; he can take complete care of himself. In the postmodern childhood being home alone is an everyday reality. Children now know what only adults used to know. Postmodern children are sexually knowledgeable and often sexually experienced; they understand (and many have experimented with) drugs and alcohol. New studies show they often experience the same pressures as single working mothers, as they strive to manage school attendance, work at home, and interpersonal family dynamics. When the cultural dynamics of hyperreality collide with post–baby boom demographics and the economic decline of the early 1970s, 1980s, and 1990s, the world changes (Lipsky and Abrams 1994). The daily life of media-produced family models such as the Cleavers from *Leave It to Beaver* is convulsed. June must get a job and Wally and Beaver must take care of the house. No longer can Beaver and his friends Larry and Whitey play on the streets of Mayfield after school. Anyway, it's dangerous—Mayfield is not as safe as it used to be.

Children under twelve belong to a generation only half the size of the baby boomers. As a result, children as a group garner less attention now than forty years ago and have a correspondingly diminished voice in the society's social and political conversation. In such a context, youth issues are not as important as they once were. Add to this a declining economy complicated by rising expectations. As American manufacturing jobs have disappeared and dead-end service jobs have proliferated, advertising continues to stimulate consumer desire. Frustration levels among children and teenagers rise as a direct result of this socioeconomic contradiction. Given the centrality of TV in the lives of this postmodern home-alone generation, the awareness of the desirability of children's consumer goods becomes a central aspect of their lived reality. Consumer desire, however, is only one aspect of the effect of TV and other electronic media on American children. TV introduces children to American culture. It doesn't take a movie critic to see how often Hollywood has drawn on the TV-taught-me-all-I-know theme. In *The Man Who Fell to Earth*, David Bowie as an alien learns all about earth culture from TV; in *Being There* Peter Sellers as idiot savant Chauncey Gardner knows nothing about the world but what he saw on TV. The movie ends with Chauncey on his way to a possible presidential candidacy—life imitates art? The robot in *Short Circuit*, the mermaid in *Splash*, the aliens in *Explorers,* and the Neanderthal in *Encino Man* all are socialized by TV (Lipsky and Abrams 1994).

What does the repeated invocation of this theme say to observers of childhood? With the evolution of TV as a medium that attempts to more or less represent reality, children have gained an adultlike (not necessarily informed) view of the world in only a few years of TV watching. Traditional notions of childhood as a time of sequential learning about the world don't work in a hyperreality saturated with sophisticated but power-driven views of reality. When a hotel porter asks Kevin in *Home Alone 2* if he knows how the TV in his hotel room works, Kevin replies, "I'm ten years old; TV's my life." The point is well taken, and as a consciousness-dominating, full-disclosure medium, TV provides everyone—sixty-year-old adults to eight-year-old children—with the same data. As postmodern children gain unrestricted knowledge about things once kept secret from nonadults, the mystique of adults as revered keepers of secrets about the world begins to disintegrate. No longer do elders know more than children about the experience of youth; often they know less, for example, about video games, computers, TV programs, and so on. Thus the authority of adulthood is undermined as kids' generational experience takes on a character of its own.

The social impact of such a phenomenon is profound on many levels. As I discuss in more detail in Chapter 11 on McDonald's in this book, a subversive kinderculture is created, in which kids through their attention to child-targeted programming and commercials know something that mom and dad don't. This corporate-directed kinderculture provides kids with a body of knowledge adults don't possess, while their access to adult themes, on TV at least, makes them conversant with marital, sexual, business-related, criminal, violent, and other traditionally restricted issues. When combined with observations of families collapsing, single mothers struggling to support their families, parents involved in the "singles" scene, and postdivorce imposition of adult chores, children's TV experience provides a full-scale immersion into grown-up culture.

In the context of childhood education the postmodern experience of being a kid represents a cultural earthquake. The curriculum of the third grade is determined not only by what vocabulary and concepts are "developmentally appropriate" but by what content is judged to be commensurate with third grade experience in the lived world (Lipsky and Abrams 1994; Postman 1994). Hyperreality explodes traditional notions of curriculum development—third graders can discuss the relationship between women's self-image and the nature of their sexual behavior. While parent groups debate the value of sex education in the public schools, their children are at home watching a TV docudrama depicting a gang rape of a new inmate in a federal penitentiary. When teachers and the school culture treat children as if they know nothing of the adult world, the kids come to find school hopelessly archaic, out of touch with the times. This is why the postmodern subversive kinderculture always views school with a knowing wink and a smirk—how quaint school must look to our postmodern children.

There is nothing easy about the new childhood. Many teenagers and young adults speak of stress and fatigue originating in childhood. If a teenager has juggled the responsibilities of adulthood since the age of seven, physical and psychological manifestations of stress and fatigue in adolescence should surprise no one. Adolescent suicide did not exist as a category during the "old childhood, " but by 1980 it was second only to accidents as the leading cause of death among teenagers. By the 1990s, 400,000 young people were attempting suicide yearly, and youth suicide was being described in the academic literature as an epidemic (Gaines 1990). The covenant between children and adults has been broken by parental and clerical child abuse and the pathological behavior of other caretakers. Too often children of the late twentieth and early twenty-first centuries have been shunted into inadequate child care institutions administered on the basis of cost-efficiency concerns instead of a larger commitment to the welfare of children. The tendency to segregate by age is well established, and unless steps are taken to reverse the trend more generational alienation and antagonism will result (Gaines 1994; Polakow 1992).

In the context of this child segregation, cultural pathologies manifest themselves. Excluded from active participation in the social order, children find themselves both segregated and overregulated by institutional forms of social control. The overregulators pose as experts on child raising, child development, child morality, and early childhood education with their psychodiscourse on the rigid phases of child development and the strict parameters of normality. In the name of "proper child-rearing techniques" experts tap into a larger ideology of personnel management that adjusts individuals to the demands of an orderly society. Like all strategies of personnel management, mainstream child psychology masks its emphasis on control. Intimidated by the scientific language of the experts, parents lose faith in their own instincts and surrender control to the authority figure on Sally Jesse. Play gives way to skill development, as structure permeates all aspects of the child's life. While middle- and upper-middle-class children suffer from the hyperstructure of skill development, poor children labeled "at risk" are medicated and drilled in a misguided effort to reduce chaos and disorder in their lives. In the name of order the experience of poor children is further bureaucratized (Seiter 1993; Polakow 1992).

THE WORLDLINESS OF POSTMODERN CHILDHOOD: THE WISEASS AS PROTOTYPE

The *Home Alone* movies can be understood only in the context of the postmodern childhood. Kevin McAlister is a worldly child; light-years separate Kevin from Chip, Ernie, and Robbie Douglas on *My Three Sons* of the late 1950s and early 1960s. As a black comedy for children, *Home Alone* struck an emotional chord with movie watchers that made it one of the most popular and profitable films of all time. Kevin, as kiddie-noir hero, is a smart kid with an attitude; Macaulay Culkin's ability to portray that character turned him into an overnight celebrity—a role model for the prepubescent wiseass.

Kevin as postmodern wiseass could not tolerate children from the 1940s and 1950s with their simpleminded "the policeman is our friend" view of the world. Bizarre in their innocence, such children are viewed by postmodern kids as antimatter reflections of themselves without responsibilities or cynicism. "What would we talk about?" Kevin might ask of a meeting with such kids. Unless Kevin had watched old movies or lived near a separatist group such as the Amish, he would have never seen such unworldly children. Almost every child depicted on TV in the contemporary era—Alex Keaton on *Family Ties*, Michele in *Full House*, Lisa and Bart Simpson on *The Simpsons*, Malcolm from *Malcolm in the Middle*, Cartman from *South Park*—is worldly and wise. Bart Simpson and Cartman may be underachievers, but only in school—a place that is boring, confining, and based on a childhood that no longer exists. Bart and Cartman are not childish; the school is. The Culkin-style smart-ass child (e.g., Bart and Cartman) is the symbol for contemporary childhood. Imagine their reaction to a "Yes, Virginia, there is a Santa Claus" adult monologue: "Right, dude, now eat me."

The wiseass is the hero of the subversive kinderculture. The appeal of *Home Alone* and its sequel is connected to this insurgent response to middle-class propriety with its assumption of child helplessness and its worship of achievement. Child and adult are pitted against each other with the child as the sympathetic character. In these two films no one could feel much sympathy for Kevin's parents with their lack of empathy for Kevin's position in the family and their lack of attention to his needs. Kevin's behavior is an act of righteous resistance to this unjust status quo. Like his kindred spirits, Bart Simpson, Cartman, and Malcolm, Kevin thrives on disorder—a chaos that undermines the social order constructed around bourgeois stability. As Cartman might put it, order "sucks," disorder is "cool." The subversive kinderculture of the postmodern childhood thrives on this disorder.

One of the subtexts running through both *Home Alone* movies involves the humorous juxtapositioning of comments of family members concerning poor, helpless little Kevin with the visual depiction of Kevin happy and in control of the disorder of his solitude. The appeal of the film revolves around Kevin's ability to tell his parents: "Even in the middle of all this exciting chaos, I don't need you." The self-sufficient boy hero of the postmodern era—what a movie-marketing bonanza. He shows no remorse on learning that his parents have left him home alone: (with eyebrows raised Kevin speaks to the audience) "I made my family disappear." Compare this postmodern reaction to parent–child separation to Dorothy's in *The Wizard of Oz*—Judy Garland's raison d'être is getting back home to Kansas. Kevin is self-actualized, living out the childhood fantasy of life without parental encumberment. Since he "can't trust anybody in this family," Kevin decides he would rather vacation alone than with "such a group of creeps." As a bellman scoops ice cream for him in his posh New York hotel room, it is obvious that Kevin's intuitions are correct. "This is a vacation," he sighs.

CONFRONTING THE INTENSITY OF YOUTH IN A POSTMODERN CHILDHOOD

As parties interested in the status of contemporary childhood, we ask, what does the popularity of the *Home Alone* movies tell us about the inner lives of children and their attempt to understand their relationship with the adult world? For a generation of home-aloners, Culkin's

Kevin is a character with whom they can identify, as he negotiates the cultural obstacles they also confront. He offers them a sense of hope, a feeling that there is something heroic in their daily struggle. Once again, the corporate marketers are one step ahead of the rest of us, as they recognize the changing nature of childhood and colonize the psychological ramifications such changes produce. In retrospect it seems so easy: to canonize a child who is left home alone for Christmas is to flatter every postmodern child in the audience. Kevin's predicament validates a generation's lived experience, transforming them from unwanted children into preteen ninja warriors. If nothing else, *Home Alone* is a rite of passage story about a boy home alone, endangered, besieged who emerges victorious and transformed (Koch 1990). "I'm no wimp," he proclaims as he marches off to battle, "I'm the man of the house." Ironically, as a postscript, the real-life character of Macaulay Culkin has become a replicated Kevin, with parental separation, parental litigation, and a troubled youth and young adulthood.

The *Home Alone* films have ushered in a plethora of smartass, parent-eschewing, bored, self-sufficient media icons. In a postmodern era where children have already seen everything, have watched the media sell laundry detergent by exploiting a mother's love for her children, it is no surprise that contemporary kids experience difficulty with emotional investment. As a result the interpersonal affect of postmodern children tends to be minimal—everything is kept at a distance and treated ironically (Grossberg 1994). Kevin offers such children something in which to invest and a sense that their desire for real experience is not pathological. This childhood and adolescent desire for intense sensation is typically viewed by the adult world as dangerous and misguided. Indeed, the very purpose of certain forms of traditional schooling and child rearing has been to tame such feelings. This visceral energy of the young—so central to Kevin in *Home Alone* and so enticing to young moviegoers—lays the foundation for a progressive postmodern child rearing and childhood education. Too often adults who are "in charge" of children forget the nature and power of this visceral energy/life force of young people. In their adult amnesia they fail to connect with the force and, as a result, relinquish the possibility of guiding it or being replenished by it. They have often blamed rock music, hip hop, MTV videos, video games, communists, or Satanists for creating the energy, forgetting that historically mediated forms of it have expressed themselves from ancient hunter-gatherer societies to modern and postmodern ones (Ventura 1994; Rodriguez 1994).

Suppressing this energy in the postmodern North American culture at the beginning of the twentieth-first century undermines our civic, psychological, and intellectual growth. The very qualities adults fear most in children—their passion, visceral energy, and life force—can be used as the basis for a postmodern childhood education. In a sense the genie is out of the bottle and is not going back in. As the communication revolution has opened adult esoterica to children, we find there is no turning back. The endless debates over movie and record ratings are futile exercises; the question now revolves around how we provide children the emotional and intellectual supports that help them balance the interaction between their visceral energy and their newfound insights. Just as traditional forms of teaching and childhood curricular arrangements are passé given the "new times," forms of discipline and control strategies are obsolete. Can kids who hold Kevin's knowledge of the world in general and the anxieties and tribulations of adulthood in particular be domesticated and controlled (not to mention the question of should they be) in the same ways as children of a different era of childhood were? Custodial schooling is no longer adequate for children; indeed, it was never adequate for children no matter what the era.

Education for domestication assumes that the information a child encounters can be regulated and sequentially ordered (Polakow 1992; Gaines 1990). Much schooling and child rearing is still based on such an archaic assumption, resulting in strategies that negate children's exploration, invention, and play. Indeed, the purpose of many of these strategies is to prevent the integration of acquired information from a variety of sources into the cognitive and emotional structures of an evolving personhood—growth itself. Thus child rearing insufficiently prepares children for adulthood or even postmodern childhood, as it ignores the world that surrounds children and shapes their lives. The lessons to be excavated from this quick analysis of the *Home Alone* movies are sobering in their urgency. The state of the contemporary family and the inability of the public conversation about it to transcend the most trivial forms of platitudes to the value of family in our "national character" are distressing. An effort to examine the nature of kinderculture and the forces that shape it simply does not exist in the surreal image-based politics of the present era. The ambivalent adult relationship with children is a suppressed feature of the cultural landscape, rarely, if ever, addressed in even the professional schooling of child welfare professionals, child psychologists, or elementary educators. These silences must end.

References

Aronowitz, S., and H. Giroux. 1991. *Post-Modern Education: Politics, Culture, and Social Criticism.* Minneapolis: University of Minnesota Press.

Best, S., and D. Kellner. 1991. *Postmodern Theory: Critical Interrogations.* New York: Guilford.

Coontz, S. 1992. *The Way We Never Were: American Families and the Nostalgia Trap.* New York: Basic.

Ferguson, S. 1994. "The Comfort of Being Sad." *Utne Reader,* July-August, 60–61.

Gaines, D. 1994. "Border Crossing in the USA." In A. Ross and T. Rose, eds., *Microphone Fiends: Youth Music, Youth Culture,* 227–234. New York: Routledge.

———. 1990. *Teenage Wasteland: Suburbia's Dead End Kids.* New York: Harper Perennial.

Galston, W. 1991. "Home Alone: What Our Policymakers Should Know About Our Children." *New Republic,* December 2, 40–44.

Griffin, C. 1993. *Representations of Youth: The Study of Youth and Adolescence in Britain and America.* Cambridge, Mass.: Polity.

Grossberg, L. 1994. "Is Anybody Listening? Does Anybody Care? On the State of Rock." In A. Ross and T. Rose, eds., *Microphone Fiends: Youth Music, Youth Culture,* 41–58. New York: Routledge.

James, C. 1990. "Scrooge Pens the Screenplay." *New York Times,* December 23.

Koch, J. 1990. "Home Alone Hits Home with a Powerful, Disturbing Pop-Culture Potion." *Boston Globe,* December 27.

Lewis, J. 1992. *The Road to Romance and Ruin: Teen Films and Youth Culture.* New York: Routledge.

Lipsky, D., and A. Abrams. 1994. *Late Bloomers, Coming of Age in Today's America: The Right Place at the Wrong Time.* New York: Times Books.

Morganthau, T., et al. 1994. "The Orphanage." *Newsweek,* December 12, 28–32.

Paul, W. 1994. *Laughing Screaming: Modern Hollywood Horror and Comedy.* New York: Columbia University Press.

Polakow, V. 1992. *The Erosion of Childhood.* Chicago: University of Chicago Press.

Postman, N. 1994. *The Disappearance of Childhood.* New York: Vintage.

Rapping, E. 1994. *Media-Tions: Forays into the Culture and Gender Wars.* Boston: South End.

Rodriguez, L. 1994. "Rekindling the Warrior." *Utne Reader,* July-August, 58–59.

Rubin, L. 1994. *Families on the Faultline: America's Working Class Speaks About the Family, the Economy, Race, and Ethnicity.* New York: Harper Collins.

Seiter, E. 1993. *Sold Separately: Parents and Children in Consumer Culture.* New Brunswick, N.J.: Rutgers University Press.

Seligman, K. 1993. "Poor Kids Often Home Alone." *San Francisco Examiner,* August 1.

Ventura, M. 1994. "The Age of Endarkenment." *Utne Reader,* July-August, 63–66.

ABOUT THE CONTRIBUTORS
AND EDITOR

Dennis Carlson is a professor in the Department of Educational Leadership and the Center for Education and Cultural Studies at Miami University in Oxford, Ohio. He is the author of books on democratic cultural politics in education, including *Leaving Safe Harbors: Toward a New Progressivism in American Education and Public Life* (2002). He has co-edited books in education, including *Keeping the Promise: Essays on Leadership, Democracy, and Education*, with C. P. Gause (Critics Choice Award, the American Educational Studies Association, 2007); and *Promises to Keep: Cultural Studies, Democratic Education, and Public Life*, with Greg Dimitriadis (Outstanding Book Award, Division B, American Educational Research Association, 2004). He is currently completing a Ford Foundation–sponsored study of the history of sexuality education, youth culture, and popular culture in the United States from the 1950s.

Daniel E. Chapman is a professor of curriculum studies at Georgia Southern University and a documentary filmmaker. His research interests include postcolonial studies, documentary studies, cultural studies, and critical pedagogy. He is the editor of *Examining Social Theory: Crossing Borders/Reflecting Back* (Peter Lang).

Greg Dimitriadis is a professor of sociology of education in the Graduate School of Education at the State University of New York, Buffalo. He is interested in urban education and the policies that serve urban youth. His most recent work has dealt with the contemporary complexities of qualitative inquiry, including its history and philosophical and theoretical underpinnings, as well as the ways "theory" generated outside the field of education can be brought to bear on the questions and concerns facing educational researchers and practitioners. He is author or editor of many articles and book chapters. His books include *Performing Identity/Performing Culture: Hip Hop as Text,*

Pedagogy, and Lived Practice; Friendship, Cliques, and Gangs: Young Black Men Coming of Age in Urban America; and *Studying Urban Youth Culture.*

Henry A. Giroux (www.henryagiroux.com) is an internationally known author of many books and articles on politics, popular culture, and education. He is the Global Television Network Chair in English and Cultural Studies at McMaster University. His most recent books are *Youth in a Suspect Society: Democracy or Disposability; Hearts of Darkness: Torturing Children in the War on Terror; America on the Edge: Henry Giroux on Politics, Culture, and Education; Take Back Higher Education: Race, Youth, and the Crisis of Democracy in the Post Civil Rights Era* (with Susan Searls Giroux); and the second edition, co-authored with Grace Pollock, of *The Mouse That Roared: Disney and the End of Innocence.* Giroux is a regular contributor to *Truthout* (www.truth-out.org/).

Sarah Hanks is an adjunct instructor in sociology at the City University of New York. She is involved in feminist/queer and vegan activism in Brooklyn and is a member of the Support New York and For the Birds collectives. Her research centers on how self-identified women and queer people negotiate physical, organizational, and social spaces and practices within the anarchist/radical left social movement.

Douglas Kellner (http://gseis.ucla.edu/faculty/kellner/kellner.html) is George Kneller Chair in the Philosophy of Education at UCLA and is the author of many books on social theory, politics, history, and culture, including *Camera Politica: The Politics and Ideology of Contemporary Hollywood Film*, co-authored with Michael Ryan. His other works include *Critical Theory, Marxism, and Modernity; Jean Baudrillard: From Marxism to Postmodernism and Beyond;* and *Media Culture and Media Spectacle*. Kellner recently edited *Media/Cultural Studies: Critical Approaches* with Rhonda Hammer (Peter Lang). His *Guys and Guns Amok: Domestic Terrorism and School Shootings from the Oklahoma City Bombings to the Virginia Tech Massacre* won the 2008 AESA award for best book on education. In 2010, he published *Cinema Wars: Hollywood Film and Politics in the Bush/Cheney Era.*

Joe L. Kincheloe (1950–2008) was the Canada Research Chair in Critical Pedagogy in the Department of Integrated Studies in Education at McGill University. He was the author of more than fifty-five books and hundreds of articles. Kincheloe's most recent books are *Knowledge and Critical Pedagogy* (Springer, 2008) and, with Shirley R. Steinberg, *Christotainment: The Selling of Jesus Through Popular Culture* (Westview, 2009). His research/teaching involved devising and engaging students in new, more intellectually rigorous, socially just ways of analyzing and researching education. He developed an evolving notion of criticality that constructed innovative ways to cultivate the intellect as it worked in anti-oppressive and affectively engaging ways. Joe founded the Paulo and Nita Freire International Project for Critical Pedagogy (http://freireproject.org), which aims to improve the contribution that education makes to social justice and the democratic quality of people's lives. Joe was engaged in both rigorous scholarship and the art of kinderculture. His intellectual gifts were punctuated by his love of the absurd and his claim that he would always retain the thirteen-year-old boy within him. He was the lead singer of Tony and the Hegemones, the father of four kids, and grandfather of seven.

Ruthann Mayes-Elma has a Ph.D. from Miami University in Oxford, Ohio. She has taught elementary school and classes at the undergraduate and graduate levels. Her passion and research interests include popular culture, media literacy, children's literature, and social justice. She has written two books on Harry Potter (*Females and Harry Potter: Not All That Empowering* and *Harry Potter: Feminist Friend or Foe?*) and various chapters in other books.

Claudia Mitchell is a James McGill Professor in the Faculty of Education at McGill University and co-founder and executive director of the Centre for Visual Methodologies for Social Change of the University of KwaZulu-Natal. Her research focuses on the use of such visual and other participatory methodologies as photo-voice, community video, and working with family photographs, particularly in addressing gender and HIV and AIDS, teacher identity, and the culture of girlhood within broader studies of children and popular culture and media studies. She is the co-author and co-editor of a number of books on girlhood, including *Seven Goes on Seventeen: Tween Studies in the Culture of Girlhood* (with J. Reid-Walsh), and *Girlhood Studies: An Interdisciplinary Journal.*

Grace Pollock recently completed her doctoral degree at McMaster University and a postdoctoral fellowship at the University of Western Ontario. Her ongoing research interests include cultural and media studies, historical formations of the public sphere, social policy, and community development. She is the co-author, with Henry Giroux, of the second edition of *The Mouse That Roared: Disney and the End of Innocence.*

Donyell L. Roseboro is an assistant professor in the Department of Instructional Technology, Foundations, and Secondary Education at the University of North Carolina, Wilmington. Her research and writing use critical race, feminist, and identity theories to explore the ways in which democratic education might create more equitable learning opportunities for students and more heterarchic governance processes for teachers. She is the author of *The Cyberspace Curriculum: Identity and Learning on the Internet* and *Jacques Lacan* *and Education: A Critical Introduction.* Her most recent book, co-edited with Dennis Carlson, is *The Sexuality Curriculum: Youth Culture, Popular Culture, and Democratic Sexuality Education.*

Ingvild Kvale Sørenssen is a doctoral candidate at the Norwegian Centre for Child Research at Trondheim University. Her main research interests are in the areas of children and media, children and consumer culture, and children and popular culture in general. Her doctoral thesis work looks at the construction of tweens through consumers and media goods, focusing in particular on the Disney Channels. This work is done by taking a cultural studies approach, looking at how the different stakeholders construct tweens as a category; analyzing the media output and spinoff products from Disney; taking Disney's perspective on tweens; and looking at how tweens relate to the media output and their own construction of tweens.

Shirley R. Steinberg (www.freireproject.org) is the co-founder and director of the Paulo and Nita Freire International Project for Critical Pedagogy. During the editing of this book, she served as research professor at the University of Barcelona, and she currently teaches at McGill University. She is the author and editor/co-editor of many books in critical pedagogy, urban and youth culture, and cultural studies. Her most recent books include *Teaching Against Islamophobia* (2010); *Encyclopedia of Boyhood Culture* (2010); *19 Urban Questions: Teaching in the City* (2010); *Christotainment: Selling Jesus Through Popular Culture* (2009); *Diversity and Multiculturalism: A Reader* (2009); *Media Literacy: A Reader* (2007); the award-winning *Contemporary Youth Culture: An International Encyclopedia; Kinderculture: The Corporate Construction of Childhood* (1997; 2004, with Joe L. Kincheloe); and *The Miseducation of the West: How Schools and Media Distort Our Understanding of the Islamic World* (2004).

John A. Weaver is professor of curriculum studies at Georgia Southern University. He is the author or editor of four books on popular culture issues, including *The Popular Culture Primer;* he is also the section editor of "Popular Culture Matters" in the *Journal of Curriculum Theorizing.* Although he has been a diehard college basketball and football fan since the 1970s, this is the first time he has written about sports. Weaver's most recent book is *Educating the Posthuman: The Biosciences, Fiction, and Curriculum Studies.*

NOTES

Chapter 2

1. For an introduction to and overview of the Buffy phenomenon, see *Fighting the Forces: What's at Stake in Buffy the Vampire Slayer,* edited by David Lavery and Rhonda Wilcox (2002); the website www.slayage.tv.; and the introductory book *Bite Me* by Sue Turnball and Vyvyan Stranieri (2003).

2. For my take on *The X-Files,* see Kellner, 2003; on the *Star Wars* cycle, which involves very different ideological problematics in different epochs during its long cinematic unfolding, see Kellner and Ryan, 1988; and Kellner, 2010.

3. Parenthetically, I'd argue, although this would require a separate paper, series creator and writer Joss Whedon and his gang have produced, on the one hand, a modernist text with a very specific vision and systemic structure while, on the other hand, engaging in postmodern pastiche, irony, metacommentary, and hipness. On different notions of modern and postmodern culture, see Best and Kellner, 1991, 1997, and 2001.

4. On the *Bildungsroman,* see Herbert Marcuse's study of the German artist novel (1978 [1922]) and the commentary in Kellner 1984.

5. At a 1998 seminar at the Museum of Broadcasting, Whedon and other cast members and producers stressed the importance of working with the then-new WB in terms of producing for a younger and hungrier network that needed to take chances to gain hits and was prepared to work more closely in largely supportive and unoppressive ways in comparison to traditional networks, which are often heavy-handed in their treatment of programs and do not allow more experimental and off-beat material. The marriage with the WB did not last, however, as the network refused in 2001 to meet the financial demands of the Mutant Enemy production company, and so the series went over to the rival UPN network, with Joss Whedon commenting: "I've been dumped by my fat old ex and Prince Charming has come and swept me off my feet. I'm mostly very excited because I now have a network that cares about my show as opposed to one that insults it."

6. Whedon is a third-generation TV creator. As David Lavery points out (2002): "[After working in radio,] Whedon's grandfather went on to contribute to *Donna Reed, Mayberry RFD, Dick Van Dyke Show, Room 222.* His father wrote for *Captain*

Kangaroo, The Dick Cavett Show, The Electric Company, Alice, Benson, Golden Girls, and *It's a Living.*"

7. Seasons One through Seven are available on DVD, making the series accessible for in-depth study. In referring to specific episodes, following recent *BtVS* scholarship, I will cite season and episode number with the year and episode as, for instance, 1007, for Season One, Episode Seven. I might also signal the growing connection between critical television research and DVDs and the Internet. When I began doing television research in the 1970s, you had to go to archives to find most classical TV material. But with video recorders and VHS tapes of popular series, and now DVDs, it is possible to do serious in-depth research on television programming. There are also incredibly rich resources online: in addition to www.slayage.tv and a profusion of Buffyverse websites, there are many other articles and resources online, including archives of scripts, laboriously typed out by fans. Kazaa has archives of *BtVS* episodes; there are chat rooms, media commentary, and much material on the series production and reception of a degree not available earlier.

8. On the war against youth in contemporary U.S. culture, see Giroux, 1996, 2002; Males, 1996; and Best and Kellner, 2003.

9. Interestingly, the Watcher and librarian Giles, a tweedy middle-aged and somewhat pedantic Englishman, is shown as technophobic and a firm believer that only books are a source of certifiable knowledge and wisdom. Willow, a sweet and lovable young science and technology buff, is presented as an Internet whiz who can quickly come up with important information, as is the computer lab teacher Jenny Calendar, who becomes Giles's love interest. Thus, ultimately the series overcomes sterile dichotomies between technophobia and technophilia, or arguments between bibliophiles and technophiles, and valorizes both books and the Internet as important sources of knowledge. Indeed, few television series have ever placed such importance on proper information and knowledge as the basis of action, valorized intellectual skills, and placed such emphasis on book and Internet research. On the dichotomies between technophobia and -philia that the series overcomes and on the battles within education over the relative importance of book and computer literacy, see Kellner, 2000.

10. In presenting interpretations of *Buffy* as allegory at a couple of Buffy conferences, I received skepticism from some prominent *Buffy* scholars who seemed to equate allegory as a theological type of Christian structure, or rigid type of literary structure. While it is true that allegory developed in biblical traditions and had a full-blown development with *The Pilgrim's Progress*, Dante and Milton's poetic epics, and other Christian allegorical texts, as Walter Benjamin noted in the early modern period (1977), another, more secular allegorical tradition emerged, and as I will argue something like a postmodern allegory is apparent in the contemporary era, ranging from forms of literature to media culture.

11. Meyer's four novels sold 25 million copies and the series generated more than 350 fan sites. Their popularity accelerated with the release of the film, which itself became a major pop culture phenomenon, grossing $35.7 million on its opening day and taking in $392,616,625 in worldwide box office receipts (see http://www.boxoffice

mojo.com/movies/?id=twilight08.htm; accessed September 5, 2010), and it was the most purchased DVD of 2009 (see http://en.wikipedia.org/wiki/Twilight; accessed September 5, 2010).

12. Meyer is a practicing Mormon and has made clear in interviews that her wildly popular *Twilight* novels advocate and are intended to inculcate abstinence, a point also visible in her website www.StephenieMeyer.com (accessed February 7, 2010). Hardwicke's film does not explicitly take this line, although implicitly the characters renounce sexual activity on account of its danger, given that the male character is a vampire. On how Meyer's website has nurtured her fan base, see Susan Carpenter, "Web gave 'Twilight' Fresh Blood," *Los Angeles Times*, November 29, 2008: E1, E6.

13. On the Harlequin novel genre and its attractions, see Radaway, 1991.

14. Hardwicke was reportedly expelled from the *Twilight* franchise for reasons unspecified. Bad reviews abound on *New Moon*'s Internet Movie Database site at http://www.imdb.com/title/tt1259571/ (accessed on December 25, 2009); see, in particular, the sharp critiques by Stephanie Zacharek, Roger Ebert, and Manohla Dargis.

Chapter 3

1. Press release on Multiplatform Video Report by Solutions Research Group, "Daily Hours Watching Video and TV to Match Sleep by 2013," Solutions Research Group, June 11, 2008, www.srgnet.com/pdf/TV%20Video%20Hours%20to%20Match%20Sleep%20Release%20(June%202008).pdf.

2. For a list of the Walt Disney Company's vast holdings, see *Columbia Journalism Review*, "Who Owns What," April 14, 2009, www.cjr.org/resources/?c=disney.

3. Allen D. Kanner and some of his colleagues raised the ethical issues with child psychologists helping marketers in a letter to the American Psychological Association. See Miriam H. Zoll, "Psychologists Challenge Ethics of Marketing to Children," *American News Service* (April 5, 2000), www.mediachannel.org/originals/kidsell.shtml. See also Allen D. Kanner, "The Corporatized Child," *California Psychologist* 39.1 (January/February 2006), 1–2; and Allen D. Kanner, "Globalization and the Commercialization of Childhood," *Tikkun* 20:5 (September/October, 2005), 49–51. Kanner's articles are online: www.commercialfreechildhood.org/articles/.

4. See also American Psychological Association news release, "Television Advertising Leads to Unhealthy Habits in Children, Says APA Task Force," APA Online, February 23, 2004, www.apa.org/releases/childrenads.html.

5. A transcript of this letter, dated August 13, 2007, is available online. See Meg Marco, "Walt Disney Demands Retraction from University of Washington over Baby Einstein Video Press Release," *The Consumerist*, August 13, 2007, http://consumerist.com/consumer/take-it-back/walt-disney-demands-retraction-from-university-of-washington-over-baby-einstein-video-press-release-289008.php.

6. This letter, dated August 16, 2007, is available online. See Joel Schwarz, "UW President Rejects Disney Complaints," *University of Washington News*, August 16, 2007, http://uwnews.org/article.asp?articleID=36148.

7. Additional factors affecting this loss of time include pressure on parents to produce "superachieving" children, which leads them to overschedule their kids' time in structured "enrichment" activities; and the restructuring of public schools to focus on academic study, which has led to decreased time for recess periods, physical education, and creative arts programming.

8. For an excellent critique of how parental fears are mobilized as part of a larger effort to professionalize parenting, see Frank Furedi, *Paranoid Parenting*, 2nd ed. (New York: Continuum, 2008).

9. "About Baby Einstein," Disney Baby Einstein website, www.babyeinstein.com/en/our_story/about_us.

10. Powered press release, "Disney Family.com and Sony Electronics Launch Virtual Classroom for Moms," RedOrbit, May 16, 2007, www.redorbit.com/news/entertainment/937334/disney_familycom_and_sony_electronics_launch_virtual_classroom_for_moms/index.html.

11. Disney news release, "Disney Creates One-Stop Online Resource for Parents," Walt Disney Interactive Media Group Newsroom, March 13, 2007, http://corporate.disney.go.com/wdig/press_releases/2007/2007_0313_familycom.html.

12. Powered press release, "Disney Family.com."

13. Disney news release, "The Walt Disney Company Acquires Club Penguin," Disney News Releases, August 1, 2007, http://corporate.disney.go.com/news/corporate/2007/2007_0801_clubpenguin.html.

14. Disney news release, "Disney Interactive Studios Announces Disney Fairies: Tinker Bell and the Lost Treasure for Nintendo DS," *Financial Post*, June 2, 2009, www.financialpost.com/markets/news-releases/story.html?id=1654467.

Chapter 6

1. In the initial years, DARPA focused on research and development related to defending against an attack from ballistic missiles. Richard Van Atta (n.d.) has an intriguing article that examines the history of DARPA located at www.arpa.mil/Docs/Intro_-_Van_Atta_2008071809205B1.pdf. He says that DARPA operates independently from the U.S. military and takes greater risks in its research and development programs because it seeks innovative technologies that produce significant results.

2. On September 3, 2010, 168 books appeared when I did a similar search.

3. See "Dave Chappelle for What It's Worth: Live at the Fillmore" (2005). Director Stan Lathan and Producers Mustafa Abuelhhija, Deborah Adamson, Dave Chappelle, Moses Edinborough, Justin Rodgers Hall, Jay Larkin, Stan Lathan, and Kimber Rickabaugh. San Francisco, CA.

INDEX